HENRY JAMES
The Later Novels

81█01105

HENRY JAMES

The Later Novels

BY

NICOLA BRADBURY

CLARENDON PRESS · OXFORD
1979

Oxford University Press, Walton Street, Oxford OX2 6DP

OXFORD LONDON GLASGOW
NEW YORK TORONTO MELBOURNE WELLINGTON
KUALA LUMPUR SINGAPORE JAKARTA HONG KONG TOKYO
DELHI BOMBAY CALCUTTA MADRAS KARACHI
NAIROBI DAR ES SALAAM CAPE TOWN

British Library Cataloguing in Publication Data

Bradbury, Nicola
    Henry James, the later novels.
      1. James, Henry — Criticism and interpretation
    I. Title
    813'.4   PS2124   79–40608

    ISBN 0–19–812096–6

*Printed in Great Britain by
Billing & Sons Limited, Guildford, London and Worcester*

Acknowledgements

I SHOULD like to thank Mr. A. O. J. Cockshut, Mrs. D. M. Bednarowska, and Professor Peter Buitenhuis for their interest and encouragement during the writing of the theses on which this book is based. Professor John Bayley offered generous and stimulating criticism, Paul Mallinson read patiently through some awkward drafts, and editorial staff at the Oxford University Press worked tirelessly with me in revision. Professor Richard Ellmann, amongst the unnumbered critics from whom I have learnt about James, kindly allowed me to adopt one of his ideas. I am grateful to them all—and to the Department of Education and Science, the Association of Commonwealth Universities in Canada, and the Fellows of St. Anne's College, Oxford, who arranged for me to be financed through a series of grants and scholarships.

AUTHOR'S NOTE

As this work is not intended as a systematic study of character and theme in James's novels, it seemed both difficult and misleading to compile an index. The works mainly discussed in each chapter are indicated in the Contents.

All page references to James's works are to the editions individually cited in the Select Bibliography, not, in the case of the novels, to the New York edition, although this has also been consulted.

Contents

I

Introduction:
The Process and the Effect

WHY DO we read James? And how?

Simple questions, for *The Portrait of a Lady*. We want to know how and why Isabel develops, and what is to become of her. We shall find the answers, if we read with imaginative attention, within the novel—though there will also be certain issues left open at the end.

But what if we ask the same things of *The Ambassadors, The Wings of the Dove,* or *The Golden Bowl*? It is not easy to know where to begin a reply. Yet the enquiry seems increasingly important. It is still true, of course, that we look to the novels for our answers, and that our imaginative sympathies and discriminating awareness are aroused by what we read. But the balance of the response, to what is actually within the works, and to the issues stretching beyond, has altered from the earlier James.

Character and plot still interest us in the late works as in *The Portrait of a Lady*; but with the development of an increasingly intricate novel style, the mysteries within the works merge with the complications of the novel process itself, to give a complex, yet intriguing, sense of difficulty. Questions 'within' *The Ambassadors*—What is going on in Paris? Will Strether find out? And what will he do then?—and even more, questions within *The Wings of the Dove* and *The Golden Bowl,* about the development and consequences of the protagonists' understanding, their growing awareness of the limitations of deceit and the power of knowledge —such questions, in their clusters and sequences, are connected not only in substance, but in their complex interrelations, with those that we as readers come to ask about our own relations with the novels, our own power of knowing, and what this entails.

This knot of questions, responses, and implications, which James presents not only through character and plot but through the surprising variety of style in his novels, in attracting and absorbing our attention, gradually diverts our curiosity from a search for answers towards an interest in the process by which questions arise. Through this means, our understanding (involving an awareness of both the extent of knowledge and its limitations: though we can 'read' appearances, we can never truly know what is going on in another person's mind) is linked with that of James's protagonists; but it is also bound up with the novelist's understanding: and it is the elasticity, variety, and expressive power, but also the ultimate limitations of the novel form itself (which must finally rely on suggesting what cannot be put into words), that represent in the reading process the reach and the inevitable boundaries of understanding.

It is in his preface to *The Golden Bowl*[1]—notoriously the most resistant to formulation of all his novels—that James himself links the how and why of author and reader, through 'the process and the effect of representation', his 'irrepressible ideal'. The phrase is little more than a point made by the way, for what interests James here is the quality, rather than the mechanics, of fascination in his work. Yet, as his words suggest, though the two may be distinguished, they cannot really be separated. Process and effect are bound up, for James, in reading a novel as in writing—precisely because these two activities are analogous. James has no hesitation, therefore, in asking his readers to respond as he suggests and queries. On the contrary, in the preface to *The Wings of the Dove,* he positively revels in the need for 'attention of perusal', as he stresses that

The enjoyment of a work of art . . . constituting . . . our highest experience of 'luxury', the luxury is not greatest . . . when the work asks for as little attention as possible. It is greater, it is delightfully, divinely great, when we feel the surface . . . bear without cracking the strongest pressure we throw on it.   (*The Art of the Novel,* pp. 304–5)

The 'novel language' (using the term in its widest sense) of the late James both tempts and requires us to pay attention to 'the surface' of his works. But the purpose and reward, the 'why' of our 'how', is the 'luxury' of the process, refined by its very difficulty into the essence of pleasure. What we enjoy in James is

<hr />

[1] Reprinted, together with James's other New York prefaces, in *The Art of the Novel: Critical Prefaces,* with an introduction by R. P. Blackmur (1934; rpt. 1962).

closely related to what James himself (writing at about the time of the New York prefaces) celebrated in the late Shakespeare:

> that . . . which seems to show us the artist consciously tasting of the first and rarest of his gifts, that of imaged creative Expression . . . to show him as unresistingly aware, in the depths of his genius, that nothing like it had ever been known, or probably would ever be again known, on earth, and as so given up, more than on other occasions, to the joy of sovereign *science*.[1]

A comparison of Shakespeare and James, or even of *The Tempest* and *The Golden Bowl,* would be perhaps a far-fetched conceit; but James's comment throws light on the critic as well as his subject, and focuses some important reflections. For what intrigued James in Shakespeare, and what seems curious to us in the novelist himself, is the mystery of an author apparently at the height of his powers, yet about to stop writing.

James did not suggest, any more than did Shakespeare, that his last great work was intended to be final. He began, indeed, two further novels,[2] as well as producing some of his most important short stories and autobiographical works.[3] There were external pressures also not to complete further novels: his own ill health,[4] the death of his brother William,[5] and the outbreak of the Great War, which was 'a nightmare from which there is no waking save by sleep'.[6] Nevertheless, there was a gap of good years left to James after *The Golden Bowl*; yet during this time his crowning literary achievement was no new undertaking, but the preparation of his collected New York edition.[7] Does this fact, together with our impressions of *The Golden Bowl* itself,

[1] 'The Tempest'; Introduction to Vol. XVI of the *Complete Works of William Shakespeare,* ed. Sidney Lee, 1907; rpt. in *Henry James: Selected Literary Criticism,* ed. Morris Shapira (1963; rpt. 1968), p. 345.

[2] *The Ivory Tower* (1917), and *The Sense of the Past* (1917).

[3] Including *The American Scene* (1907), *A Small Boy and Others* (1913), *Notes of a Son and Brother* (1913) and *The Middle Years* (1914).

[4] Leon Edel, *Henry James: The Master,* 1901–1916 (1972), pp. 438–48, reports James's conviction that he had a heart condition like that of his brother William; he took to his bed for a period with 'something of the nature of a "nervous breakdown" '.

[5] Edel (ibid. 452) quotes a letter from James to Edith Wharton in 1910: 'My beloved brother's death has cut into me, deep down, even as an absolute mutilation. . . .'

[6] Edel (ibid. 515) quoting a letter from James to Burgess Noakes.

[7] Published by Charles Scribner's Sons, 1907–9.

suggest that this became James's last novel because it completed his *œuvre*: that he had taken the novel form as far as he could, or even as far as it could then go?

This suggestion, impossible to 'prove' in any straightforward way through historical or biographical evidence, derives its interest from a mystery akin to the one James saw in the case of Shakespeare. The impenetrability of the personal, imaginative history of the author as a man is counterpointed by the lucidity of his 'public' achievement as an artist, not merely occupied with expression, but delighted with it: 'so generalized', as James writes of Shakespeare, 'so consummate and typical, so frankly amused with himself, that is with his art, with his power, with his theme, that it is as if he came to meet us more than his usual half-way' (*Selected Literary Criticism*, pp. 345–6). The author invites the reader, in effect, to join him in 'the surrender to the luxury of expertness' (ibid. 347). There is a recognition of distance on both sides, and of the unexplained nature and power of the 'Expression' through which they may communicate; but this is seen as a stimulating challenge. The very terminology of James's tribute to Shakespeare captures the balance of reverence and curiosity, in the poised ambiguity of his word *'science'*, which indicates both knowledge and discovery. Such a merging of past and future in a present at once still and moving is an achievement equalled at moments throughout James's career, but sustained, as I hope to show, only in *The Golden Bowl*, precarious even there, yet marking the limits for James of the novel form, through a 'style handed over to its last disciplined passion of curiosity' (*Selected Literary Criticism*, p. 351).

Though my linking of process and effect to 'science' implies an empirical ideal which we do indeed find in James, the 'un-resisting', accepting quality of 'joy' qualifies his spirit of enquiry. In the late novels, the word 'question', the search for knowledge, come up repeatedly. Yet we learn to approach them with circum-spection, mistrusting their implicit belief in an expressible answer. Recalling Strether's 'double consciousness . . . detachment in his zeal and curiosity in his indifference' (*The Ambassadors*, p. 4), we appreciate his response to Gloriani's look at the garden party in Paris: 'Was what it had told him or what it had asked him the greater of the mysteries?' (p. 146). For Fanny Assingham in *The Golden Bowl* the hidden paradox, the question-begging, is yet more clear: 'Asking is suggesting' (*The Golden Bowl*, I, 283). The ideal in this novel approaches what Keats described as 'Negative Capability, that is when a man is capable of being in uncertainties, mysteries, doubts, without any irritable reaching after fact and reason' (*Letters*, ed. Gittings, p. 43).

Taking *The Portrait of a Lady*, as the culmination of James's early career, *What Maisie Knew*, *The Awkward Age*, and *The Sacred Fount* as different experiments from his middle period, and then dealing at length with his three late novels, we can see how answer-seeking is traced back into the formulation of questions, changing the nature of the novel process in pursuit of 'the joy of sovereign *science*'. The poise between curiosity and restraint becomes an increasingly clearly recognized ideal, not only for the attitude of a protagonist to his experience, nor simply for the relationships between characters, but for that of character, author, and reader. Indeed, I have suggested that an understanding which knows its own limits is what distinguishes the novelist's attitude to his form, and through this, their dependent relations. A large claim—but one I hope to substantiate by showing in close readings how James's critical concepts are realized in his novels, and how the novels themselves tend increasingly towards a level of abstraction where our attention is directed towards 'the process and the effect' both through James's style and through the interest of the central characters in the same issue.

'Interest' was a preoccupation with James throughout his career. In his novels the word is often ambiguous, suggesting a selfish motivation; but in a critical context its connotations are usually positive: it is the business of the novel to take hold of our attention and imagination, though it is ours to be aware of this, 'unresistingly aware', perhaps. In 'The Art of Fiction'[1] James affirmed that 'The only obligation to which in advance we may hold a novel . . . is that it be interesting.' Twenty years or more later, in the New York prefaces, he discusses how 'the law of . . . kind' provides the conditions for things to become interesting (*The Art of the Novel*, p. 111), and writes of the narrative consciousness 'contributing . . . by some fine little law to intensification of interest' (p. 327).

This linking of interest to 'laws' might suggest that James was a didactic formalist. But the Prefaces *follow* the novels in order

[1] 1884; rpt. in *Selected Literary Criticism*, pp. 78–97.

of composition: it is in his fiction that James works out the 'poetics' he subsequently analysed with a kind of affectionate curiosity. And it is the *boundaries* of form that fascinated James: how they could be challenged, stretched, and the novel persuaded to do things it had not done before, surprising us into new awareness by adopting compositional laws (and hence the associated attitudes) from another form, such as the drama or visual arts, or by switching from mode to mode within the genre: now a detective story, now high romance. James's most intriguing, and exciting, analysis of the novel stresses its variety, elasticity, but its strength too, for 'the high price of the novel form' is a power not only 'to range through all the differences of the individual relation to its general subject-matter' but 'positively to appear more true to its character in proportion as it strains, or tends to burst, with a latent extravagance, its mould' (*The Art of the Novel*, pp. 45, 46). Again we notice a paradoxical restraint in exuberance itself: every new departure redefines the limits it has extended.

This riddle may focus, but not absorb, all our attention. When James wrote of 'the very obvious truth that the deepest quality of a work of art will always be the quality of mind of the producer' ('The Art of Fiction', p. 96), he included in that quality both 'the moral sense and the artistic sense'. 'Very near together', these senses are both involved in the process and the effect of representation, for, reviving a dead metaphor, James calls 'expression' a 'literal squeezing out of value'. The links between author, reader, and protagonist depend on the intimate connection of formality and morality, for it is through his use of the novel form that James conveys the 'cluster of gifts' constituting 'experience': not a matter confined to the past, but an imaginative potential: 'the power to guess the unseen from the seen, to trace the implication of things' ('The Art of Fiction', p. 85).

This early description seems uncannily to prefigure *The Ambassadors*: the first of James's late novels, and perhaps, with its fullness and assurance, the one most easy to relate to *The Portrait of a Lady*. Nevertheless, the experiments of James's middle years are implicit too in his account of 'experience': besides the 'solidity of specification' of the novel world—'the seen'—there is the uncertainty of the 'guess', the threat and potential richness of 'the unseen'; and there are also 'the power' and the sense of 'the implication of things' which mature in

James's later novels, *The Wings of the Dove* and *The Golden Bowl*.

Joseph Conrad's well-known description of Henry James deals with these aspects of the novelist in terms more 'scientific', though not less tied to morality:

Fiction is history—human history—or it is nothing. But it is also more than that; it stands on firmer ground, being based on the reality of forms and the observation of social phenomena . . . Mr. Henry James is the historian of fine consciences.[1]

By relating the 'signs' of the novel world to the very process of representation, exploiting and manipulating a variety of forms, James makes explicit the hidden reliance of the novel not only on convention but upon conventionality. A series of social and artistic codes—patterns of behaviour, signs conveying meaning—as well as recognizably literary devices, heighten our attention to the balance between matter and form in the novel, and this in turn corresponds to the wider pattern of consciousness brought to expression. Osmond's sitting while Madame Merle stands tells Isabel something about their relationship, and us something about his attitude to expression—an indication of his true character. Strether's misreading of an 'impressionist' Paris reveals the limitations of his experience (and hence of his 'power to guess the unseen from the seen'); but when, later, he sees Maria Gostrey in a setting reminiscent of a Dutch Interior, he can use his artistic awareness to place her—and this in turn helps place Strether for us. In *The Golden Bowl*, the highly formal situation of a game of cards, which images relationships for us, also provides an opportunity for Maggie to consider, not only these liaisons, but their formal (social and moral) contexts. This prepares both her and us for the shifting and complex exploitation of both social and literary form in the encounters with Charlotte which ensue: confrontations in which moral boundaries also seem protean, as truth depends on successful deception.

The briefest digression into examples from the novels illustrates James's own account of how 'relations stop nowhere, and the exquisite problem of the artist is eternally but to draw, by a geometry of his own, the circle within which they shall happily

[1] Joseph Conrad, 'Henry James: An Appreciation', *North American Review* clxxx (Jan. 1905), rpt. in F. W. Dupee, ed., *The Question of Henry James: A Collection of Critical Essays* (1945), p. 44.

appear to do so' (*The Art of the Novel*, p. 5). His ideal was not to abandon form, but to exploit it to the full, so that economy would support structural shape, while the boundaries of expression were extended by implication:

> Any real art of representation is . . . a controlled and guarded acceptance, in fact a perfect economic mastery, of that conflict: the general sense of the expansive, the explosive principle in one's material thoroughly noted . . . but with its appetites and treacheries, its characteristic space-hunger and space-cunning, kept down. (ibid. 278)

Recognizing 'the perfect dependence of the "moral" sense of a work of art on the amount of felt life concerned in producing it' (ibid. 45), James tried to combine fullness with compression through 'foreshortening'—an artistic term for the distortion of perspective which heightens the illusion of nearness; but for James, also, through a kind of pun: 'that particular economic device'—and through the 'operative irony' which 'implies and projects the other possible case, the case rich and edifying where the actuality is pretentious and vain' (ibid. 222).

The use of a narrative consciousness neither strictly limited to the awareness of the protagonist nor wholly independent and 'reliable' serves to contain this 'irony' as well as to focus the interaction of social and literary codes with the author's and reader's imaginative understanding. This is perhaps the most complex element of James's 'novel language', allowing fine discrimination between the approaches of author, reader, and protagonist to the experience of the novel. Though James tried several variations on this narrative method, from the 'dramatic technique' of *The Awkward Age* to the first person narration of *The Sacred Fount*, none could sustain the flexibility and imaginative authority of the last novels. In the preface to *The Golden Bowl*, James's acknowledgement of its difficulty begins diffidently, but grows into a statement of proud defiance:

> what perhaps most stands out for me is the still marked inveteracy of a certain indirect and oblique view of my presented action; unless indeed I make up my mind to call this treatment, on the contrary, any superficial appearance notwithstanding, the very straightest and closest possible.

In our first text, *The Portrait of a Lady*, Isabel Archer, the very type of the early Jamesian protagonist, sees herself—James revised the New York edition to describe her with a nice irony as having a 'conceit' of her own nature—as 'garden-like': 'She was always planning out her development, desiring her perfection, observing her progress' (I, 65). Her self-awareness acts as a foreshortening device (in both of James's senses: emphatic, yet economical), merging the exploratory and appreciative, or onward and present impulses in the novel. It also allows the reader an insight into Isabel's consciousness unforced by authorial omniscience yet without the 'terrible *fluidity* of self-revelation' (*The Art of the Novel*, p. 321) of a first-person narrative.

During his 'middle period' James refined this narrative subtlety derived from the economic device of the self-conscious protagonist, through experiments with multiple points of view and dramatic presentation of scene and dialogue. The late works, without abandoning 'showing' for 'telling', develop the consciousness of the characters beyond the demands of economic foreshortening almost to the point of distortion, in a reversion from the dramatic which draws attention to its own proceeding. Thus James brings to the explicit recognition of his style an approach to experience which remains implicit in his earlier works, and can only be revealed by ironic pointers such as the pun on 'conceit' in Isabel's fanciful pride: that is, as Dorothea Krook wonders, 'Given such a prodigious quantity of light what . . . will they *not* see?'[1]

Our analysis will not be concerned with the centre of consciousness alone, however. The problem of the 'blind spot' in the protagonist, though sometimes, as with Isabel's 'conceit', compounded by a trait of character, can be seen in a wider context. Beyond the quirks of personality, it appears analogous to the gap of 'absolute insulation' which Henry James's brother William saw as separating all individuals (*Principles of Psychology*, 1890, p. 226). Despite this 'irreducible pluralism', William James found a medium of communication in language, by analogy if not directly. He suggests a correspondence between linguistic relations and those of personal consciousness:

There is not a conjunction or a preposition, and hardly an adverbial phrase, syntactic form, or inflection of voice, in human speech, that

---

[1] Dorothea Krook, *The Ordeal of Consciousness in Henry James* (1963), p. 405.

does not actually express some shading or other of relation which we at some moment actually feel to exist between the larger objects of our thought. (ibid. 245)

In Henry James's novels, the form itself is such a language. But, like all languages (according to Ferdinand de Saussure, in his *Course of General Linguistics*), it works through a system of differences, preserving the possibility of meaning by maintaining distinctions. Thus James, in revising, called 'deviations and differences' his 'very terms of cognition' (*The Art of the Novel*, p. 337). Paradoxically, the gaps themselves are necessary. This is why, when words, literary and artistic references, modes of expression, kinds of character as well as what they do and say, seem to explore the process of communication as they perform it, this in turn leads us back towards the individual consciousness. In the novel, the relationship between perception and expression is realized in a way both literary and social, between author and reader, through characters and their relationships with each other, and through the representation of these things. There is an analogy between full perception and perfect communication, and the processes of 'seeing' and 'representation' provide related but not identical motive forces for the novel form, both arousing and satisfying our interest. Each combines the 'expansive principle' of 'seeing' with the constraint of understanding, involving coding or 'naming' experience.

Our reading should therefore ideally cover every aspect of expression and relate them all, through their process and effect, to their producer and their audience. The activities of author and reader are structurally analogous to those of the conscious protagonist within the novel, though they need not duplicate them: the ironic pattern of James's novels encourages us to anticipate the perceptions of the protagonist, and educates us through narrative patterns such as Isabel's involvements with various suitors, stylistic patterns such as the word-play of *The Awkward Age*, and the 'symbolic' understanding which Maisie achieves only with maturity. The 'explosive principle' of growth in such works is balanced by a containing understanding: the perceptions of the protagonist come to meet those of the narrator and reader. Nevertheless, the way beyond this 'closed' pattern is hinted even in James's middle works through the aspect of his novel 'language' I have chosen to discuss in Chapter Two: silence—which, interestingly, relates (though it does not confuse) both what cannot be put into words and what is deliberately concealed. These different kinds of silence are identified in James with opposite approaches to experience: one open, imaginative, and the other unscrupulously manipulative. When these traits are extended to personal relationships they are clearly moral: and I hope to show how James's 'heroes' (and heroines) are distinguished by their restraint from expression, while the villains manipulate both words and silence with equal ease.

In *The Ambassadors*, it is the implications of the 'unseen' that indicate the unspoken. Metaphors from the visual arts predominate, and I have taken 'perspective' as my own metaphor for the organizing principle of form here. 'Formality', or the code of laws governing artistic expression, develops in this novel from a condition of meaning into a potential metaphor for morality: the correct ordering of experience both permits and demonstrates the ideal of full consciousness. This establishes a close link between the author's process of expression, the protagonist's experience, and the reader's understanding. So fluent is the process by which the understanding that Strether comes to meet is inculcated in us, that even attentive critics have mistaken the degree to which we are directed by the narrative to rely on Strether's imperfect perceptions. They have failed to realize that this is not fixed, but constantly changing towards increased 'reliability', and have consequently misread the end of the novel as cruel, evasive, or unclear. We can see, however, that from the small units of expression—words, images, even points of grammar —to the 'discriminated occasions' of the novel structure, the reader is guided through James's combination of narrative irony and imaginative stimulation towards an understanding which Strether also acquires through his experience. When, eventually, Strether's insight equals that of reader and narrator alike, this gives him dignity and authority in the rejection of rewards he has seen through, and in acceptance of the 'open-ended' conclusion where only absolute standards, unlimited by time or place, apply. Perspective narrows towards, but paradoxically opens out into, the vanishing-point, which lies beyond the picture frame.

The movement through recognizable narrative patterns into an open state where we do not know quite what to expect is a recurrent one in James's later novels. The hierarchy of 'meaning', subject, and expression becomes increasingly difficult to determine, as our attention is both stimulated and baffled by shifts of style and approach. Categories of expression become fluid, whilst the rendering of experience grows increasingly meticulous, and it is no longer possible to suggest one organizing principle. We are not starved of entertainment, for the traditional elements of character, action, and plot are not abandoned by James. In the tension between local exuberance and overall shape, however, the novel form, paradoxically, grows more clearly defined in proportion as its boundaries are challenged. Far from the finality of *The Ambassadors*' concluding sentence, 'There we are', or the elegiac recognition of *The Wings of the Dove* that 'we shall never be again as we were', *The Golden Bowl* ends with a soundless embrace, at once accepting and challenging the limits of expression: 'Stillness . . . might be said to be not so much restored as created; so that whatever next took place in it was foredoomed to remarkable salience.'

In this progression from 'Words, words, words' to that peace where 'the rest is silence', we may find another Shakespearean parallel for James. But the ultimate luxury of understanding beyond expression is one that must be earned, by author and reader alike. What I hope to do is bring out how this works in James's late novels: to notice our reactions, look at the processes that lead to them, and the novel techniques that prompt those processes. I do not want to overstress the difficulty of late James, but to show how this difficulty itself gives rise to some of the pleasure of reading, because in it is distilled the author's delight in writing: that sense of luxury which gives us access to 'the quality of mind of the producer'.

II

The Unspeakable and the Unsayable:
The Development of Silence
as a Means of Expression

IN THE novelist's 'language', just as in the 'system of systems' examined by the linguist de Saussure, 'difference makes character, just as it makes value and the unit'.[1] The importance of silence is in its ability both to create and to bridge the gaps separating 'kinds', whether literary genres or other formal codes of expression available to the novelist. The simplest unit of expression, serving to divide up other units and make them comprehensible, silence is also a tribute to what lies beyond the bounds of form, and observes decorum with respect to the inexpressible.

Silence provides a medium for significant expression, and can be seen as necessary to communication. The recognition of a gap between minds, between objects, expression, and apprehension, the appreciation of a distinction between the surface and what lies 'behind', must come before the triumphs of perception, expression, and communication.

The shaping properties of silence, and its part in the exhilarating process of perception, are attributes as important in James's novels as its boundless extent, ambiguity, and its liability to mislead. This is true on many levels; yet even one example suggests how subtly it works. Isabel Archer becomes increasingly reticent after her marriage to Osmond, but her perceptiveness and understanding grow, while Osmond's constrictions of imagination appear more and more blatantly, in his dealings with Madame Merle, Rosier and Pansy, and finally with Isabel herself. Isabel's density and imaginative weight grow in proportion as Osmond's diminish, and the process is marked by the shifting balance of reticence between them. Though less susceptible to

---

[1] Ferdinand de Saussure, *Course in General Linguistics*, trans. Wade Buskin (1964), p. 121.

analysis, this is just as important in the imaginative structure of the novel as the localized silences in plot and action: the actual moment, for example, when Isabel comes upon Osmond and Madame Merle 'musing, face to face, with the freedom of old friends who sometimes exchange ideas without uttering them' (*The Portrait of a Lady*, III, 10).

In *The Portrait of a Lady* there is little exploitation of dramatic silences and their associated social conventions, from slang to speaking looks, which become so useful to James in support of the 'dialogue organic and dramatic' of *What Maisie Knew* and *The Awkward Age*. For this very reason, however, where these techniques of evasion are displayed, their power is distinctive. Madame Merle and Osmond, both individually and together, betray their unspeakable 'abysses' to the reader by their fluency in the forms of the unspoken. Madame Merle, in her silent Judas-kiss to the heiress, and Osmond in the tactful reticence of his courtship, know well how to exploit Isabel's quality of aloofness, her dread of vulgarity. It is in their joint silences that James demonstrates the relationship between these conspirators, their assumptions, and their social powers. Our first glimpse of their meeting is orchestrated with the silence of familiarity; when James repeats the word, silence begins to sound significant, and on his insistence it acquires an air of menace: 'The gentleman at the door, after dropping his exclamation, remained silent; in silence too the lady advanced. He gave no further audible greeting and offered her no hand, but stood aside to let her pass into the saloon' (II, 36). James makes much the same point at later encounters, not by complete silence, but by certain omissions, whether verbal or in movement, of social forms. Thus in a moment of low-voiced conversation at the Countess Gemini's, Osmond is able to remark, with a bald assumption of understanding amounting to rudeness both to the object and subject of his speech: 'She wants me to go to Rome with her' (II, 101): there is no need to voice the reference of the pronoun, because Isabel's name is part of a continuing unspoken dialogue between her manipulators. Later, in Rome, it is Isabel's glimpse of these two, sharing 'a sort of familiar silence' (III, 10), while Osmond remains seated before the lady, which betrays their former intimacy: 'the thing made an image . . .'

This almost melodramatic silence was to recur with equally

sinister effect in James's last novel, at the Judas-kiss of Maggie and Charlotte, and in Charlotte's attempt to involve the Prince in complicity with her through their secret expedition on the eve of his wedding. In *The Golden Bowl* too, James was to exploit the dual effect of beauty and pathos in the inviolable individuality of the person: the inner space of silence, which Ralph Touchett keeps free of trespass by the expedient of an entertaining public persona, an antechamber where a dance band protects his personal silence. Maggie Verver, shut out from the 'pagoda' at the centre of the garden of her existence, was to hear only an echo when she first knocked for admission. For Charlotte the prison of the self would be imaged as the gilded cage of the music-hall song; she would tap in a crescendo of urgency on the glass wall separating her from knowledge, from shared understanding.

There was to be an important development before *The Golden Bowl*, however, of another silence found in *The Portrait of a Lady*: the narrative silence of death. The audible hush which spreads through Gardencourt as Mr. Touchett lies dying is a device of emphasis, like the change in the weather, almost 'background music' in comparison with the more profound and subtle effect of James's narrative economy here: the omission of any actual description of the death, as the story turns to a new character and her impact on the scene. Not only is 'narrative silence', a felt absence, the clearest indication by negative definition of a presence less easy to state in positive terms, but the narrative opportunity provided by this turning-away from a Victorian deathbed scene mimes in terms of the novel the imaginative occasion which Madame Merle seizes for approaching Isabel. James's 'foreshortening' here is very effective: the music sounding through the silence of approaching death is played by Madame Merle, and her advent follows pat upon the exposure of Isabel to the exploitation of the fortune-hunters. The narrative tact with which James refrains from anticipating this disclosure adds to its imaginative power, for this is a perfect fusion of content and form.

In *The Portrait of a Lady*, silences of different qualities, and achieved by different technical means, help to 'orchestrate' character, action, and theme. The conspiratorial silence which unites Madame Merle and Osmond stands in contrast to the hush surrounding the death of Mr. Touchett, when Isabel is exposed to manipulation. This in turn is balanced by the silence of 'negative capability' at the death of Ralph, which provides an opportunity for Isabel to assert her moral integrity despite those who have used her. The narrative silences of death in this novel provide a model for the same technique, more fully exploited, in *The Wings of the Dove*; and this pattern of emphatic ellipsis can also be found in the work of James's admirer Conrad, who, in *Nostromo*, has Decoud suffer a similar isolation and betrayal, imaged by his being marooned on an island, but actually mimed by the deflected attention of the narrative.

In James's later novels there is a tendency towards articulating such different levels of expression as the conspiratorial silence and the narrative silence, so that reticence or explicitness in conversation and in action may be recognized as both shaping and shaped by the whole complex of moral, intellectual, and aesthetic impulses and circumstances which constitute 'felt life' for James: hence John Bayley's comment on *The Golden Bowl*: 'The nemesis of wrong-doing is the final stupidity of clarity and definition.'[1]

Silence can be the gap between thing and name, name and its place in a code of expression, which permits the triumph succinctly described in mechanical terms through Adam Verver: 'It wasn't only . . . that the word, with a click, so fitted the riddle, but that the riddle, in such perfection, fitted the word' (*The Golden Bowl*, I, 212). Yet the same phenomenon of silence, an absence of signs, may also mark the opposite effect: a lapse of expression. A further complication is that this inadequacy is not necessarily a failure of form, but may be rather a triumph of taste, perfect decorum in deference to what lies beyond speech: the opacity in which Isabel Archer feels the centre of her being, not susceptible to expression through the 'envelope of circumstances'. Silence in James may be the furtive disguise of treachery, as in Madame Merle's concealment of her relationship with Osmond, or the sublimity of generosity, as in Milly Theale's unostentatious gift of all her riches of life and love to Merton Densher. Between these extremes lies a range of cases less easy to determine: for example, silences of benevolent intent but pernicious effect, such as Ralph's secrecy to Isabel over the source of her fortune: a silence by no means counteracted by his decision to speak out against her marriage, which ends all possibility of confidences

---

[1] *The Characters of Love: A Study of the Literature of Personality* (1968), p. 239.

until his imminent death frees their relationship of normal social constraints and permits them an absolute truthfulness. Then how is the balance of decency between silence and speech to be decided for Maisie or for Nanda Brookenham, as they grow up in a society where children are to be seen and not heard, yet reticence lapses before them even while *'pas devant les domestiques'* remains a cardinal rule of social intercourse? Is Maisie to be blamed for adopting the subterfuge of silent stupidity, or Nanda for not doing so?

While the full complex of expressive values for silence is exploited most richly in James's last novels, the paradoxical effects are more accessible to criticism in a limited space in his earlier works. Through these 'transitional' novels, moving from a literary world not unlike that of George Eliot, with a firm moral structure, towards a turn-of-the-century world in which neither a moral structure nor the moral sense itself could be taken for granted,[1] James explores a situation in which the social and aesthetic codes are developed separately from the moral: where the unspeakable and the unsayable are not presumed to match. It is a dramatically effective example of narrative economy that *What Maisie Knew* and *The Awkward Age,* in which James developed 'really constructive dialogue, dialogue organic and dramatic, speaking for itself, representing and embodying substance and form' (*The Art of the Novel,* p. 106), should also be the novels most precisely located in worlds between two poles of silence: what must not, and what cannot be said.

There are no such large and powerful silences in *What Maisie Knew* as in the deathly hush of Gardencourt. Perhaps there scarcely could be, in a novel of manners, composed largely of dialogue. Silence has its value, however, both in tactical and moral terms, in opposition to the great range of 'social languages' of this novel. In showing us how Maisie learns to hold her tongue, and what she becomes through her discretion, James defines, very often through negatives, what this value may be. The sense of the languages, a 'system of systems', encoding through their interlocking patterns the claustrophobic world of this novel, is created with extraordinary economy. Maisie is the victim of unspeakable

[1] This trend is discussed by Sallie Sears, *The Negative Imagination: Form and Function in the Novels of Henry James* (1968).

parents, guardians, circumstances. What she learns is the expressive power of all the codes she must in self-defence master, but which she must refrain from using until this 'envelope of circumstances' could become 'an expression of self' for her. It is silence which protects the 'active, contributive, close-circling wonder . . . in which the child's identity is guarded and preserved' (*The Art of the Novel*, p. 158).

The key to this process is given in James's preface to the New York edition of *What Maisie Knew*: 'Small children have many more perceptions than they have terms to translate them; their vision is at any moment much richer, their appreciation even constantly stronger, than their . . . vocabulary' (*The Art of the Novel*, p. 145). The 'high firm logic' which James observed in making the innocent 'vessel of consciousness' the pivot of his narrative irony, is masterly. The reader's understanding of irony, which is necessary to his appreciation, condemns his interest at the outset as belonging to the adult world, and the marvel of Maisie's untainted growth is heightened by comparison. Although Maisie comes to know 'everything' eventually, her development is characterized by innocence from the first. While silence is debased in the ironic dimension by immediate 'translation' into the unvoiced 'subtext' of the unspeakable, Maisie's mind does not follow this slick manœuvre as a matter of course. When Sir Claude visits Mrs. Beale, Maisie provides a comic foil to their guilty understanding, since she finds their conversation impossible to follow. At one moment Sir Claude calls Mrs. Wix 'The old cat', (*What Maisie Knew*, p. 104) at another, 'the darling old dear' and Maisie is alternately appalled and appeased. She notices, but does not understand, when Sir Claude later uses the same phrase of Mrs. Beale; he is 'much diverted, and his loud, clear laugh was all his explanation' (p. 115). Maisie supplies a link where none exists, but cannot perceive it where one does. As full knowledge is matched by full understanding, however, Maisie's development foreshadows that of Maggie in *The Golden Bowl*, in that both heroines learn to understand and even to manipulate silence in a social context, without debasing their appreciation of the 'true silence' of the unsayable which is an image of the inviolate integrity of the individual.

In Maisie this is dramatized through the child's growing up, with an economy based on the fusion of action and symbolism.

The narrator occasionally inserts explanatory abstractions summarizing this process in a sophisticated vocabulary: 'The theory of her stupidity, eventually embraced by her parents, corresponded with a great date in her small, still life: the complete vision, private but final, of the strange office she filled' (p. 11). Yet an extraordinary amount is conveyed without such intervention, through the linking of images in the spare narrative, and the metaphorical force of narrative structures such as plot. Physical movement from house to house in Maisie's childhood enacts her exposure to different points of view, much as in *The Wings of the Dove* Densher and Kate will be concerned to find out 'where' they are, meeting for walks because they have no place together in society, and as in *The Golden Bowl* Maggie Verver and Fanny Assingham will use the periods of their cab journeys to come to some understanding of their place in the world. James resorts to a favourite 'late style' device, the exploitation of 'future hindsight', when he writes of Maisie: 'It was only for her later thought that the steps fell into their order, the steps through which, in a bewilderment not so much of sound as of silence, she had come to find herself, too soon for comprehension and too strangely for fear, at the door of the Exhibition with her Father' (p. 145).

In this progress through the stages of understanding, *What Maisie Knew* can be seen as a model of perceptual development presenting remarkably close analogies with that worked out later by the psychologist Jean Piaget.[1] In this reading, the physical manipulation by gentlemen who pinch her 'toothpick' legs, and by parents who push and pull her toward themselves or their partners, would appear as evidence of a 'sensori-motor' approach to experience indicative of the very earliest stages of development, when the subject is egocentric, and can only conceive of the world from his own point of view.

Maisie herself is not arrested at this stage, however, despite her environment. The images of her childish world, peculiar to her, begin to relate to the symbolic forms of language and the adult world, as James demonstrates with an immediacy and clarity reminiscent of Dickens, and the up-ending of Pip's world in the churchyard when Magwitch seizes him by the heels. From the infant's 'phantasmagoric' world of magic-lantern images,

[1] Summarized by Howard Gardner, *The Quest for Mind: Piaget, Levi-Strauss, and the Structuralist Movement* (1973).

impressions gradually become more familiar and solid. As a young child, Maisie 'found in her mind a collection of images and echoes to which meanings were attachable—images and echoes kept for her in the childish dusk, the dim closet, the high drawers, like games she wasn't big enough to play' (p. 8); but later, 'the stiff dolls on the dusky shelves began to move their arms and legs; old forms and phrases began to have a sense that frightened her' (p. 11). The imagistic pun on articulation is daring but effective: typical of James's spare style in this novel.

In developing social fluency amidst the unspeakable, Maisie learns to manipulate silence as her elders do. She recognizes the 'unmistakable language of a pair of eyes' (p. 13) as a substitute for speech, and she valiantly preserves the secret of Mrs. Wix's daughter, even when 'everyone, though Maisie had never betrayed her, knew even Clara Matilda' (p. 21). When Mrs. Farange snaps at Maisie, 'Learn to keep your thoughts to yourself', we find, 'This was exactly what Maisie had already learned, and the accomplishment was just the source of her mother's irritation' (p. 15). For the articulation of forms brings a sense of danger to the child, and understanding is met by 'a new remedy . . . the idea of an inner self, or, in other words, of concealment' (p. 11).

In Maisie's experience, ignorance is both ridiculous and dangerous, knowledge a power to play with: 'Everything had something behind it; life was like a long, long corridor with rows of closed doors. She had learned that at these doors it was wise not to knock—this seemed to produce, from within, such sounds of derision' (p. 28).

Maisie externalizes her perceptions safely by playing out with her doll the mysteries of her own experience, which Juliet Mitchell aptly calls 'the games people play'.[1] Maisie 'was enlightened by Lisette's questions, which reproduced the effect of her own upon those for whom she sat in the very darkness of Lisette' (p. 28). Yet the process of internalization through symbolic representation of experience necessarily involves the alienation of the perceiving self from the world around it; Maisie's consciousness itself isolates her as her dramatic experience of being tossed to and fro like a shuttlecock or football does: 'It gave her an odd air of being present at her history in as separate a manner

[1] Juliet Mitchell, '*What Maisie Knew*: Portrait of the Artist as a Young Girl' *The Air of Reality: New Essays on Henry James,* ed. John Goode (1972), pp. 168–89.

as if she could only get at her experience by flattening her nose against a pane of glass' (p. 88).

The concepts of language and silence grow together for Maisie, and silence is not merely an oblique, socially acceptable way of voicing the unspeakable, but it is a gap between experience and expression akin to the gap between self and world: the surrounding medium of the individual consciousness. While Maisie learns the social uses of silence, she also begins to apprehend what lies beyond the conception of her elders: the things that cannot be expressed. At the first parting from Mrs. Wix, Maisie remembers the 'thoroughly audible and voluble' scene six months earlier with Miss Overmore; now, 'It was dreadfully silent', and the only interruption comes not from Maisie but Mrs. Wix, with a 'spasm of stifled sympathy' (p. 24). Maisie's feeling for silence is shown by the way she converts the silence of the unspeakable to the quite different quality of the inexpressible, making Mrs. Beale's censorship an occasion for inward growth. After Mrs. Wix's letters are stopped, 'Her very silence became . . . one of the largest elements of Maisie's consciousness . . . a warm and habitable air' (p. 35).

While this inner growth continues, the playing with Lisette is followed in Maisie's 'operational' development by her attempts to 'bring people together', so as to bring order to her world. The most important operation of this sort is that uniting Mrs. Beale and Sir Claude; but the inadequacy of the approach is more starkly revealed in the encounter in Kensington Gardens which James in his preface labelled 'the type-passage . . . for the expression of its beauty.' In this episode, the physical manhandling of the child provides a brutal analogy to the assaults made upon her emotions and intelligence, with passivity in one relation corresponding to silence in the other, as the demonstrative qualities of both 'codes' are brought into play. To Mrs. Farange's indignant 'What are you doing with my daughter?' (p. 119), of which the narrator drily reports, 'Maisie had a greater sense than ever in her life before of not being personally noticed', Sir Claude can only retort in kind: 'Who the devil have you got hold of *now*?' Sir Claude's 'squeeze of the child's arm' is trumped by the mother's theatrical embrace: a gesture which is accurately registered, though not explicitly interpreted, as inhumanly violent. Maisie finds herself 'on her mother's breast, where, amid a wilderness of trinkets, she felt as if she had suddenly been thrust, with a smash of glass, into a jeweller's shop-front, but only to be as suddenly ejected with a push and the brisk injunction "Now go to the Captain!"' All these interchanges provide a dramatic contrast for that gentleman's effect. His brief occurrence in the novel is scarcely remarkable as a part of the pattern of Mrs. Farange's intrigues; but he achieves a certain distinction in his dealings with Maisie: 'He appeared to watch for a moment the effect on his companion of the emphasis; then he gave a small sigh that mourned the limits of the speakable.' Though it is social decorum which forbids the Captain to talk to his mistress's child of their relationship, this decency shades into a real desire to convey to her what cannot, rather than simply must not, be expressed. Who else demonstrates such concern, or such restraint? No wonder it is in this encounter that Maisie clutches at the possibility of breaking the pattern of inconstancy and attempts to establish an abstract moral good in the only way she knows how, by combating the vagaries of circumstance. She begs the Captain, who is never to be seen again: 'You *do* love her? . . . Do it always!'

Unlike the adults in their perpetual motion from partner to partner, the child finally outgrows this approach to experience. In the last part of the novel James shows Maisie achieving a maturity beyond that of any of her companions. It is significant that this takes place in France, for the geographical move, besides establishing appropriate social conditions in the novel world, with the removal from English codes of decorum, also suggests how the child's view of the world changes, becoming 'decentralized', with maturity. Maisie can now perform 'formal' operations, reshaping ideas and considering hypothetical developments entirely within her own mind.

Here, while Sir Claude wavers over making use of the child to 'legitimize' his relations with her stepmother, Mrs. Wix abandons any vestige of reticence with her charge, and actually begs her, 'Don't let me have been thrust for nothing into such horrors and such shames . . . I've had to keep up with you, haven't I?—and therefore what could I do less than look to you to keep up with *me*?' (p. 235). Maisie, a source of strength for the others as well as her own support, is the only one whose understanding is not confused by these moralistic but immoral compromises. When she contemplates Mrs. Wix's solution, that they should 'rescue' Sir Claude for themselves, 'What she [Maisie] had essentially done, these days, had been to read the unspoken into the spoken; so that, with accumulations, it had become more definite to her that the unspoken was, unspeakably, the completeness of the sacrifice of Mrs. Beale' (p. 223). On Sir Claude's alternative, 'they exchanged silences again—but only exchanged silences' (p. 289).

The paradoxical nature of perception, freed of egocentrism yet unalterably limited by what James's brother William described as the 'insulation'[1] of the self and the 'irreducible pluralism' of different minds, is shown in the way Maisie conceives the one question which demonstrates her own maturity in requiring an equivalent strength of Sir Claude. For in making him choose between moral responsibility with her and the abdication of integrity permitted by a submission to his mistress's domination, Maisie is aware that she is risking her companionship with Sir Claude. Yet her love is no 'abject' adoration: she will not compromise her integrity. In the event her 'integrity' is mirrored in narrative terms by her isolation, as she returns to England without Sir Claude, having only Mrs. Wix for company, and no surrogate parents.

The reader's reaction to Maisie's education in the ways of the world must often echo that of the 'good lady . . . distantly related to Mrs. Farange' who makes an early but abortive attempt to rescue the child from the awful alternation between the warring camps of her parents: 'The good lady, for a moment, made no reply: her silence was a grim judgment of the whole point of view. "Poor little monkey!" she at last exclaimed; and the words were an epitaph for the tomb of Maisie's childhood' (p. 3). As John P. O'Neill points out, 'Forced by James's technique into prolonged speculation . . . the reader may grope toward the safety of complete sympathy for the exposed innocent . . .'[2] Yet this satisfaction is withheld by James's unsentimental precision in revealing the perceptions and mistaken impulses of the child, in a narrative so taut that Barbara Hardy can suspect it of the opposite tendency, and find a lack of sympathy: '*What Maisie Knew* reduces appropriate feeling to a brilliant exercise in plotting. The response of

---

[1] *Principles of Psychology,* p. 226.
[2] John P. O'Neill, *Workable Design: Action and Situation in the Fiction of Henry James* (1973), p. 90.

the child is exploited rather than properly delineated, and the agility of form is achieved at the expense of feeling.'[1] This misses the muted pathos of undemonstrative feeling, which Maisie maintains against all odds in a heartless environment, but James rarely displays. When he does, the effect is exact, but not shallow: ' "Mamma doesn't like me," she said very simply. "Not really." Child as she was, her little long history was in these words; and it was as impossible to contradict her as if she had been venerable. Sir Claude's silence was an admission of this' (p. 69). The impossibility of withdrawal from her situation forces upon Maisie a development which moves from the perceptual to the moral sphere, and it is this development of consciousness in Maisie which James follows, showing her moral growth unstunted by her environment. She is protected by the very core of silence which makes the child's plight pathetic, but the grown child a strong moral agent, with an understanding of integrity.

Nanda Brookenham is taken at a later stage in her development, and shown more objectively than the young child, with a greater, though not a complete, reliance on dialogue 'speaking for itself' and a narrative based on many centres of consciousness. James presents a young lady deprived of the social asset of maidenly reticence, and develops a sophisticated technique of interplay amongst various social languages, in which the moments at the interstices of form reveal by indirection the inner silence which Mr. Longdon only finally sees when 'the form of expression [breaks] down' in Nanda's tears.

The hypocritical double standards of Nanda's world are revealed by 'doubletalk' which violates linguistic integrity much as the pushing and pulling in *What Maisie Knew* trespassed on personal decency. Here, as Van informs the shocked, old-fashioned Mr. Longdon, for whom decency and decorum are properly seen as inseparable, ' "It's impossible to say too much—it's impossible to say enough" ' (*The Awkward Age,* p. 21). Between the polar extremes of Mr. Longdon's 'suspended eloquence' and the social norm of hyperbolic extravagance, with all the resources of slang, heightened cliché, the joke, the negative, and the lie, there extends a field of discourse appropriate to a society which exists in and for its 'talk': talk which is good or bad as thinking makes it

[1] Barbara Hardy, *The Appropriate Form: An Essay on the Novel* (1964), p. 46.

so. Confronted with the restraints on freedom imposed by the society of an unmarried daughter, Mrs. Brook laments: ' "Good talk: you know— no one, dear Van, knows better—what part for one that plays. Therefore when one has deliberately to make one's talk bad—!" "Bad?" Vanderbank, in his amusement, fell back in his chair. "Dear Mrs. Brook, you're too delightful!" ' (p. 285).

It is the charmless Mr. Cashmore who exemplifies this society most clearly: 'He was an odd compound . . . and the air of personal health, the untarnished bloom which sometimes lent a monstrous serenity to his mention of the barely mentionable, was on occasion matched by his application of playful terms to matters of much less moment' (p. 122). This disregard for 'decorum', or appropriate expression, whether in speech or in other social codes, such as those governing the unchaperoned movement of unmarried girls in society, characterizes Mrs. Brook and her 'set', although a specious charm is acquired through their skill in manipulating the forms devoid of true expressive power. The Duchess has recourse to foreign phrases, always a danger-signal in James's work, and particularly suspect here, since the Duchess is foreign only by marriage. ' "There you are, with your eternal English false positions! *J'aime, moi, les situations nettes—je n'en comprends pas d'autres*" ' (p. 45). Yet at the culmination of a *tour de force* of unspoken bargaining between the Duchess and Mrs. Brookenham for the marrying of Mitchy, it is Mrs. Brook who dares to breach the pretended reticence with a demand skilfully poised between blatant commercialism and perfect propriety: ' "Speak to him, my dear—speak to him!" "Do you mean offer him my child?" ' (p. 47).

Mrs. Brook's assumed *naïveté* is flawless, and James uses repetition of praise, rather than direct condemnation, to suggest that her 'spontaneity' is really based on sophisticated calculation. As H. K. Girling explains, ' "Wonderful" first informs the reader that she is extraordinary; gradually that she is so extraordinary as to be outrageous, and finally, that she is so defiantly and persistently outrageous as to be loathsome.'[1] It is the Duchess in fact whose outrages are most flagrant, as when she depicts Nanda's feeling for Van as crudely bestial: ' "Nanda's fairly sick—sick as a little

[1] H. K. Girling, ' "Wonder" and "Beauty" in *The Awkward Age*', *Essays in Criticism* VIII (1958), p. 374.

cat—with her passion"'" (p. 190). The effect of this on Mr. Longdon is compounded of pity and disgust; but James conveys delicately how different is such distinction between content and form from mere confused ambivalence, for the reply turns on the ambiguity of one word: 'appeared'; 'It was with an intensity of silence that Mr. Longdon appeared to accept this.'

James uses degrees of silence and outspokenness as the first marks of personality in this highly articulate society; but it is the particular points of reticence which finally distinguish moral character. Van, who is too delicate to allow Mr. Longdon to mention the amount of Nanda's dowry, does not scruple to betray his confidence by speaking of it to Mrs. Brook, who immediately makes it public to Mitchy. Mrs. Brook and Van share a similar judgement of form: ' "Isn't it awful?" "That you should think of it?" "That I should talk this way"'' (p. 217). Mitchy, on the other hand, though as outspoken as Nanda herself in society, shares her fundamental delicacy. He complies in silence with her suggestion that he should marry little Aggie, and remains silent throughout his consequent sufferings. He also respects Nanda's reticence over her own sufferings, in a way no one else does: ' "Of course I know." "You know, you know!" Mitchy repeated. "Everything", she imperturbably went on, "but what you're talking about." He was silent a little, with his eyes on her. "May I kiss your hand?"'' (p. 398).

Only Mr. Longdon shows a greater sense of what cannot be said. Amidst the prevailing verbal inflation and moral disintegration, he 'maintained the full value of the word' (p. 15), and the possibility of integrity through a fusion of expression and substance. Yet even Mr. Longdon is brought to compromise this strict decorum in dealings with the modern world, when he attempts to make money a means of moral persuasion by offering to make it financially possible for Van to marry Nanda. This adaptability is shown in linguistic terms by Mr. Longdon's acquisition of something of the punning facility with which small-talk debases moral terms, but which may also reveal possibilities of significance in hackneyed expressions. As he says to Mitchy, with 'a head shake that was both sad and sharp. "It's all wrong. But *you*'re all right"'' (p. 371). The perception of potential meaning in the interstices of distorted form is a linguistic counterpart to the imaginative insight with which Mr. Longdon comes to recognize the moral stature of Mitchy and of Nanda herself despite their contravention of the form of decorum.

Formal rigidity breaks down at extremes of emotion and of insight, and Nanda's silent 'pride' is not obdurate: 'Oh, I don't know how to say it. . . . One must let the sense of all that I speak of—well, all come. One must rather like it' (p. 407). Though she has succeeded her mother as a mistress of the social codes, Nanda's most revealing moment comes when the social lie gives way to a truth of tears. Her attempted denial of real feeling is brave but vain:

Ah, but I don't—please believe me when I assure you I *don't*!' she broke out. It burst from her, flaring up, in a queer quiver that ended in something queerer still—in her abrupt collapse, on the spot, into the nearest chair, where she choked with a torrent of tears. . . . her old friend meantime keeping his place in the silence broken by her sound and distantly—across the room—closing his eyes to her helplessness and her shame.
(p. 410)

In James's mature work, silence, in narrative structures from the pattern of words and gestures to the larger shapes of character, action, and developing theme, is both a unit of specific expressive significance and an escape from the limitations of form. Coming at interstices of formal expression, silence may bear particular connotations in context, and it frequently has symbolic significance as an image of isolation, whether through death, betrayal, or simply as part of the construct of individual integrity. Yet silence is distinctive amongst units of expression in the flexibility of its form, or lack of form; it can function in different codes within the same novel, assisting the articulation of an 'organic' whole. Nanda's silence to Van over her love is very different from his to her, but the similarity of form permits a close comparison, and accentuates the pathos of their contrast. Silence is also unquantifiable, and much as the use of charged clichés enables James to articulate surface and depth in the novel by maintaining a colloquial fluency while preserving categories of judgement and the possibility of moral insight, so the resources of silence may function unobtrusively on the narrative or dramatic level, while reaching towards moral or even metaphysical significance.

The Sacred Fount, coming after the 'dramatic' and before the 'late' works, is a special case amongst James's novels, but its idiosyncrasies heighten several aspects of James's late style and its effect, and they provide a helpful contrast to the following novels. Two references to the 'little idea' for the work occur in James's *Notebooks*,[1] where the *'concetto'* appears likely to make a short story; and Leon Edel, in his edition of the novel,[2] quotes an unpublished letter from James to Mrs. Humphrey Ward about this 'small fantasticality' which makes it clear what James intended by it: 'the one thing it *could* be—a consistent joke. Alas, for a joke it appears to have been, round about me here, taken rather seriously. It's doubtless very disgraceful, but it's the last I shall ever make!'

Critical reaction has generally either dismissed *The Sacred Fount* as fantastical or taken the narrator at face value and proceeded to fault the novel for his excesses; but what this irritation reveals is how far short of appropriate such reactions are to other novels by James. F. R. Leavis's criticism of *The Portrait of a Lady*, for example, might with some justice be applied to *The Sacred Fount*; but this merely highlights its inadequacy to *The Portrait of a Lady*:

James's marvellous art is devoted to contenting us with very little in the way of inward realization . . . and to keeping us interested, instead, in a kind of psychological detective work—keeping us intently wondering from the outside, and constructing, on a strict economy of evidence, what is going on inside.[3]

This almost echoes Obert in *The Sacred Fount*, mentioning 'the *kind* of signs that the game takes account of when fairly played—resting on psychologic signs alone, it's a high application of intelligence. What's ignoble is the detective and the keyhole' (p. 57). The distinction is in the tone of James's 'detective story': the 'consistent' narrative law turns in baffling and teasing circles upon the first-person narrator, who may or may not be correct, but is certainly over-curious; the farcical extremes of interpretation undermine the narrative consistency and challenge our credulity. *The Sacred Fount* is important because its very excesses display James's recurrent preoccupations and techniques, not taking him to extremes, but taken by him for comic effect.

[1] *The Notebooks of Henry James,* ed. F. O. Matthiessen and Kenneth B. Murdock (1947; rpt. 1961), pp. 150–1, 275.
[2] Introduction, p. 14.
[3] F. R. Leavis, *The Great Tradition* (1948; rev. ed. 1962), p. 110.

D. W. Jefferson finds a nice balance between curiosity and detachment:

> On the first reading or readings of *The Sacred Fount* (1901), the desperate need to solve the riddle is liable to inhibit other kinds of interest. When the riddle has been abandoned as insoluble, the novel can be enjoyed as other novels are enjoyed. . . . The tortuosities, when they cease to torment, can be cherished for what they add to relationships between characters, dramatic effects and so forth. The success of the work can be seen quite simply as one of style, the prodigy of the heightening being in the language.[1]

The 'find out for yourself' theme which motivates Isabel Archer,[2] which Maisie echoes to her doll,[3] with which Maggie Verver is to challenge the Prince,[4] is flaunted in *The Sacred Fount* and undermined. The reader, led on to search for an answer which is not forthcoming, is prompted to question the whole process of investigation; but the questioning is external, detached from the novel, rather than comprehended in the consciousness of the narrator.

The 'silences' of integrity and understanding barely occur in *The Sacred Fount*; but it is pertinent to an investigation of silence in James, because the superficial silence which obstinately baffles the insistence of the narrator in his 'irritable reaching after fact and reason' exposes the whole process to ridicule: both fact and irritability are satirized. The 'detective story' works in the opposite direction from James's recurrent search for perception: starting with the external evidence of the effects of an intimate relationship, the narrator proceeds simply to construct a pattern for it, to allot the roles amongst his fellow guests, and to pursue a misplaced interest which subordinates the true mystery to a mere riddle. As Jefferson comments, 'transcendental verbiage mingles

---

[1] D. W. Jefferson, *Henry James and the Modern Reader* (1964), p. 176.

[2] In Chapter 15 of *The Portrait of a Lady* she tells Ralph: 'I do want to look about me. . . . I only want to see for myself.'

[3] *What Maisie Knew*, p. 29, reproduces with Lisette the 'darkness' of her own experience: 'There was an occasion when, on her being particularly indiscreet, Maisie replied to her . . . as she, Maisie, had once been replied to by Mrs. Farange: "Find out for yourself!" She mimicked her mother's sharpness, but she was rather ashamed afterwards, though as to whether of the sharpness or of the mimicry was not quite clear.'

[4] *The Golden Bowl*, II, 211, as the culmination of their confrontation over the broken bowl.

with the open zest of the scandalmonger'.[1] What saves the novel is not the trivialized emotional or moral drama, but that of the telling: 'the element of gesture, the open pleasure, sometimes almost irresponsible, of the raconteur in the game he is playing'.[2] The divorce between James as raconteur and the narrator as busybody is implied in the comic style; but the problem for the reader is to find his own stance apart from either.

The key to the comic style is its mingling of coy prevarication and explicitness, and one example of this is in the zest for names. The narrator is capable of noticing the obverse of this, of remarking 'some intimacy of unspeakable confidence' between May Server and Guy Brissenden: 'They hadn't to name it or to phrase it—possibly even couldn't had they tried . . .' (p. 104); but given the chance for 'an objective test', he cannot resist prying: 'if she understood the person I had not named to be nameable as Gilbert Long . . .' (p. 105). It has to be admitted that, 'Well, names are a convenience' (p. 206); but for one who can toy with the idea that he has fallen in love, and dismiss it with, 'That was as good a name as another for an interest springing up in an hour, and was moreover a good working hypothesis' (p. 75), names can be little more than a convenience: they are no solution to the mystery. Where the names are as interchangeably insignificant as they are here, teasing the reader with his attempts to follow or anticipate the plot, 'naming names' is clearly unprofitable: like the 'guess the ages' game, gossip-page journalese. Yet in James's later novels we see that it is the process itself which is suspect; the attempt to render the values of silence explicit. *The Sacred Fount* demonstrates the danger of all neat formulation: it is the notion of an expressible answer which is both facile and dangerous,[3] and other words, like names, may be used to fit the riddle

[1] Op. cit. 179.   [2] Ibid. 143.

[3] James's use of words as 'names' could be seen as one of the ways he 'unconsciously pragmatized' through fictional practice: it is illuminated by William James's *Pragmatism: A New Name for Some Old Ways of Thinking* (1909), p. 52: 'Solomon knew the names of all the spirits, and having their names, he held them subject to his will. So the universe has always appeared to the natural mind as a kind of enigma, of which the key must be sought in the shape of some illuminating or power-bringing word or name. . . . But if you follow the pragmatic method, you cannot look on any such word as closing your quest. You must bring out of each word its practical cash-value, set it at work within the stream of your experience. It appears less as a solution, then, than as a programme for more work, and particularly as an indication of the ways in which existing realities may be *changed.*'

with a click, as they do for Adam Verver when he decides to propose to Charlotte.

The claims on our 'interest' in *The Sacred Fount* are at least twofold; but these two scarcely support each other, and the effect of their conflict is to call the whole narrative process into question. On the one hand, there are various avowals of procedure in the Jamesian manner: the narrator, 'on the track of a law, a law that would fit, that would strike me as governing the delicate phenomena . . . that my imagination found itself playing with' (p. 30), and revelling in 'an analogy, and I declare I find it dazzling. I don't see the end of what may be done with it' (p. 56). The stress on pattern rather than evidence, like the 'psychologic signs' which supersede the clumsier keyhole (p. 57), are reminiscent of James's own comment on his 'consistent law' of narration. But their claims to intellectuality are belied by the nature of the clues actually followed: comically bathetic, in a farce which is pointed by the solemnity of James's phrasing. On the terrace, speculation is encouraged by nothing more 'psychologic' than 'a brown shoe, in a white gaiter, protruding from the other side of her dress?' (p. 68): the painstaking exactitude is purely physical. In the evening, indoors, it is 'poor Briss's back, now presented to me beside his wife's . . .' (p. 140); the full account is laboriously precise, ludicrously spattered with abstract terms, pedantic sententiousness, overweighting the simple observation so thoroughly that it almost convinces in the reading: the reader must laugh at himself for being momentarily taken in:

I watched, so long as I might, with intensity. I should in this connection describe my eyes as yet again engaging the less scrutable side of the human figure, were it not that poor Briss's back, now presented to me beside his wife's—for these were the elements of the combination—had hitherto seemed to me the most eloquent of his aspects. (p. 140)

Another moment of perception is related with heavy repetition as a series of 'winks': hardly the sublest of recognitions, between an artist and a Jamesian observer:

'It was just the fact that you did wink, that you *had* winked, at me that wound me up.'

'And what about the fact that you had winked at *me*? *Your* winks— come—' Obert laughed—'are portentous!' (p. 149)

Compared with Strether's reception of Gloriani's searching look in *The Ambassadors*,[1] this interchange is clumsy indeed: as the laugh on 'portentous' wryly points out.

The light of artistic perception is both lurid and inadequate for the narrator of *The Sacred Fount*: the scene in the gallery, anticipating the 'Bronzino scene' in *The Wings of the Dove*,[2] is here not mysterious, but simply incomprehensible, and the straight-faced solemnity of the narration points the comedy. The narrator's approach to the work of art is unscrupulously interested: he asks Long to repeat his interpretation, not out of any desire for understanding, but in order to prolong his opportunity to observe the relations between Gilbert Long and Mrs. Server. Though the painted figure holds 'an object that strikes the spectator at first simply as some obscure, some ambiguous work of art' (p. 50), the notion of deep insight within this ambiguity could not be more effectively dispelled than by the exchange that follows, where the considered tone of the cultivated spectators consorts ludicrously with the complete inconsistency of their views, and the heedless way they exchange them:

'Yes, what in the world does it mean?' Mrs. Server replied.

'One could call it—though that doesn't get one much further—the Mask of Death.'

'Why so?' I demanded while we all again looked at the picture.

'Isn't it much rather the Mask of Life? It's the man's own face that's Death. The other one, blooming and beautiful—'

'Ah, but with an awful grimace!' Mrs. Server broke in.

'The other one, blooming and beautiful,' I repeated, 'is Life, and he's going to put it on; unless indeed he has just taken it off.'

The false basis of this pretentiousness is starkly revealed in the narrator's last encounter with Mrs. Brissenden, his one-time fellow observer. So fixed are the narrator's ideas, so involved his approach to experience, that an appearance of innocence is taken

---

[1] At Gloriani's garden party, where Strether 'was to recall in especial, as the penetrating radiance, as the communication of the illustrious spirit itself, the manner in which, while they stood briefly, in welcome and response, face to face, he was held by the sculptor's eyes . . . the source of the deepest intellectual sounding to which he had ever been exposed' (p. 146).

[2] And possibly with reference to Oscar Wilde's *The Picture of Dorian Gray*, which had achieved notoriety on its publication in 1891. For Wilde's hero, 'This portrait would be . . . the most magical of mirrors. As it had revealed to him his own body, so it would reveal to him his own soul. . . . When the blood crept from its face, and left behind a pallid mask of chalk with leaden eyes, he would keep the glamour of boyhood' (1891, rpt. 1974), p. 106.

by now as the sign of its opposite. It is not the accuracy of this judgement here, but the assumptions behind it, which are brought into question for the reader:

I had needed the moment to take in the special shade of innocence she was by this time prepared to show me. It was an innocence, in particular, in respect to the relation of anyone, in all the vast impropriety of things, to anyone.

'I'm afraid I know nothing.'

I really wondered an instant how she could expect help from such extravagance. (p. 178)

Both Mrs. Brissenden and the narrator are exposed by this passage, and the reader's reaction must be detachment from this complex of outrageous surfaces and a penetration which is far from reliable. The pattern of hyperbolic disproportion between appearances, sentiment and expression, throughout the novel brings the 'process and the effect of representation' into question; the flaunting of narrative manner denies the reader a possibility of implicit assumptions shared with the author: there is no space of silent understanding. What *The Sacred Fount* offers is a display of virtuosity which teases the reader with his own search for answers, and denies him the sense of a community of interest leading to a shared understanding, a perception established as 'truth' between author, protagonist, and reader.

The first-person narrative, a form 'foredoomed to looseness'[1] in James's opinion, is not shapeless here; but neither does it allow for the 'interest' of the novel to be captured within the form. It is the disparity of process and effect, the way questions occur tangentially to the concentric circles of the narrative, that accounts for the disturbing quality of the novel. The narrator's hesitations are belied by his continuing researches, but reinforced by the disparity of process and effect for the reader. Compared with the intense seriousness of Conrad's Marlow, for whom 'the meaning of an episode was not inside like a kernel but outside, enveloping the tale which brought it out only as a glow brings out a haze',[2] who hates a lie, but will utter one rather than betray the mystery at the heart of darkness, the narrator of *The Sacred Fount* is a busy, shallow mind:

[1] Henry James, *The Art of the Novel*, p. 320.

[2] Joseph Conrad, *Youth, Heart of Darkness, The End of the Tether* (1902, collected ed. 1946; rpt. 1967), p. 48.

It was absurd to have consented to such immersion, intellectually speaking, in the affairs of other people. One had always affairs of one's own, and I was positively neglecting mine. . . . frankly, my affairs were by this time pretty well used to my neglect. There were connections enough in which it had never failed. A whole cluster of such connections, effectually displacing the centre of interest, now surrounded me, and I was—though always but intellectually—drawn into their circle.   (p. 72)

The paradox of *The Sacred Fount* is that of unsatisfied curiosity: the very zeal of the narrator in constructing 'explanations' for what he sees obscures the possibility of understanding. It is a salutary lesson; but only obliquely applicable to the later novels. There comic distancing carries the reader less far, and a subtler range of narrative techniques involves the reader in its own process. The implicit acknowledgement of the limitations of expression with respect to silence is the basis of a real understanding: not only the narrator's 'joy of the intellectual mastery of things unamenable' (p. 155), but the recognition that true understanding comes where 'the form of expression broke down'(p. 99).

Through James's career as a novelist, the possibilities for expression through silence develop not merely in number but in kind, so that his thematic and technical uses of silence offer one approach to the phases of his development, and in particular to his growing demands on the reader's awareness of the workings of the novel. In *The Portrait of a Lady* silence is largely a narrative resource, though it also carries weight as a symbol of moral isolation. During the 'dramatic' period when *What Maisie Knew* and *The Awkward Age* were written, James extended the scope of silence as a means of specifically 'not saying' things; yet this linguistic use of silence as a kind of lie is in pointed contrast with the developing recognition of an 'inner silence' of truth which may remain inviolate. It may seem a perversity in keeping with *The Sacred Fount,* yet it is one required both by the comic distancing of tone and the closed circles of narrative method, to recognize in this novel a demonstration by default of the values of silence. Through the fruitless curiosity of the narrator, and more immediately through the teasing experience of the book's dazzling yet unilluminating style, James obliquely tells and directly demonstrates to the reader that understanding may elude explicit statement, or 'naming'. Shortly after this, in *The Ambassadors,* James was to turn the heightened stylistic consciousness of *The Sacred Fount,* and the comic distancing, to good effect, not by simplifying but by advancing his 'narrative law', to increase the complexity of the novel process and thus to create a function for the reader in appreciating this complexity: an experience analogous to that of Strether within the novel itself. This appreciation of process, the heightened awareness of the gaps in formal expression which must be crossed by the perceiver, is to become a source of 'interest' and of 'joy' in the last novels.

III

'The Still Point':
Perspective in The Ambassadors

'FRANKLY, QUITE the best, "all round", of my productions' (*The Art of the Novel*, p. 309), was James's estimate of *The Ambassadors*. The rounded 'medallions' of the twelve books (*Notebooks*, p. 415) chime with this judgement. *The Ambassadors* is James's most finished work. Yet it is the true precursor of the last novels in being open-ended. Duality, rather than roundness, is the characteristic of *The Ambassadors,* and the 'detachment in his zeal and curiosity in his indifference' (*The Ambassadors,* p. 4) which James attributes to Strether are encouraged in the reader too, through the author's own poise. Through this novel we can learn how to read late James.

The germ of *The Ambassadors,* Strether's 'Live all you can' speech to little Bilham at Gloriani's garden party, has frequently been read as the author's own expression of faith. But the *Notebook* entries and later New York Preface to *The Ambassadors* reveal the Master analysing a latent ambivalence in the cry, and creating for it the context in which it could be 'led up to' with 'seemingly inevitable' complexity. James immediately recognized in the 'beautiful outbreak' the 'ironic' accent of a 'false position'. His approach to the narrative fuses process and effect as, avoiding 'the mere muffled majesty of irresponsible authorship', he aims at an 'ambiguity of appearance that is not by the same stroke, and all helplessly, an ambiguity of sense'.

The minutiae of stylistic technique in *The Ambassadors* are, therefore, both decorative and functional, stimulating imaginative identification and detached discrimination too. As the Preface points out, 'Art deals with what we see . . . But it has no sooner done this than it has to take account of a *process.*' James had already written: 'The business of my tale, and the moral of my action, not to say the precious moral of everything, is just my demonstration of this process of vision.'

James's terminology reflects an interest in the visual arts which persisted throughout his career. In 'The Art of Fiction' (*Selected Literary Criticism,* p. 80), he had written, 'The analogy between the art of the painter and the art of the novelist is, so far as I am able to see, complete.' To him 'A psychological reason is . . . an object adorably pictorial; to catch the tint of its complexion—I feel as if that idea might inspire one to Titianesque efforts' (ibid. 94). Yet the picture, like the novel, has its compositional laws. The artist is confronted with a radical duality of substance and form, which may sometimes be related and sometimes distinguished, in order to combine economy and clarity of perspective:

> To give the image and the sense of certain things while still keeping them subordinate to his plan . . . to give all the sense, in a word, without all the substance or all the surface, and so to summarise and foreshorten, so to make values both rich and sharp, that the mere procession of items and profiles is not only, for the occasion, superseded, but is, for essential quality, almost 'compromised'—such a case of delicacy proposes itself at every turn to the painter of life . . .
>
> (*The Art of the Novel,* p. 14)

In this context, 'formality', or the code of laws governing artistic expression, becomes more than a condition of expression: it offers a potential metaphor for the subject itself.

The discriminating appreciation required from the reader in this process mirrors that developing in James's protagonist within the novel. As Dorothy Van Ghent recognizes, since 'in James's world the highest affirmation of life is the development of the subtlest and most various consciousness', therefore, 'James was able to use the bafflements and illusions of ignorance for his "complications", as he was able to use, more consistently than any other novelist, "recognitions" for his crises' (*The English Novel: Form and Function,* p. 216). In *The Ambassadors,* as in a late Shakespeare romance, the 'recognition scene' crisis is a turning-point: a stage in the action at which the intellectual and the moral consciousness of the observer come together in imaginative understanding.

The aesthetic of this fusion of discrimination and synthesizing imagination is formulated by the art critic and psychologist Rudolph Arnheim, in the notion that 'all perceiving is also thinking, all reasoning is also intuition, all observation is also invention' (*Art and Visual Perception: A Psychology of the Creative Eye*, p. viii). Such a complex situation does not lead to confusion because 'The situations we face have their own characteristics, which demand to be perceived "correctly". . . . This objective element in experience justifies attempts to distinguish between adequate and inadequate conceptions of reality.' Thus, in *The Ambassadors*, the growth of consciousness in Strether enables him to achieve a more 'adequate' conception of 'reality', as he understands what is behind the forms of social behaviour which he sees. Yet Strether's understanding is not limited to the placing of his experience. Pursuing the art metaphor further, the end of *The Ambassadors* can be likened to the 'vanishing-point' of a picture composed according to central perspective. Instead of a rigid two-dimensional structure of meaning, the ambiguity of simple irony, the drama is a three-dimensional development, leading towards a pointed but not limiting conclusion, which transcends the imagination that conceives it. In Arnheim's terms:

In central perspective, infinity paradoxically assumes a precise location within finite space itself . . . It is within reach and unreachable at the same time. . . . Finally it should be observed that central perspective locates infinity in a specific direction. This makes space appear as a pointed flow, entering the picture from the nearsides and converging towards a mouth at the distance. The result is a transformation of the simultaneity of space into a happening in time—that is, an irreversible sequence of events. The traditional world of being is redefined as a process of happening. (op. cit. 207)

The stress on the temporal links the pictorial metaphor with James's other major analogy: the drama. Although the drama is distinguished from the picture by its dynamism, it is similar to it in being governed by rules of composition which prevent 'confusion' and the 'stultification of values'. This linking thread runs through the alternating sequence of picture and scene in *The Ambassadors*, just as Strether's development of consciousness does; for it is in his appreciation of the structures of meaning, whether in fine art, the drama, or the social code, that Strether's understanding is demonstrated or ironically qualified. Through 'double consciousness', the reader is allowed an ironic apprehension of the fact which Strether does not at first see. 'Form', whether artistic, dramatic, or social, is used in the setting up of a situation which appears different to the reader who knows, and to Strether who does not know, 'the rules'; but form is later seen as a mere location for something beyond these conflicting views. After measuring and 'going behind' appearances, in the Jamesian phrase, there is the going beyond.

James's formal devices may be followed one after another as they appear in *The Ambassadors,* through the analysis of stylistic idiom, location, and action. Strether apprehends experience in this way, through time; and every reading of a novel is sequential. Yet there is also a 'spatial' or synchronic apprehension, essential to irony. The pattern built up by comparison and contrast (for example between the 'case' of Chad and that of Strether) is revealed, as we shall see, not only through the 'formal device', but the 'scene', or dramatic unit of composition.

The dynamic tension of dualism is encapsulated in the scenic method. James saw this in terms of its links with both picture and drama. He notes 'the odd inveteracy with which picture, at almost any turn, is jealous of drama, and drama . . . suspicious of picture'. But this conflict helps define the subject: 'Between them, no doubt, they do much for the theme; yet each baffles insidiously the other's ideal' (*The Art of the Novel*, p. 298). Out of this contention is created 'the discriminated occasion—that aspect of the subject which we have our choice of treating either as a picture or scenically . . . Beautiful exceedingly, for that matter, those occasions . . . when the boundary line between picture and scene bears a little the weight of the double pressure' (ibid. 300).

Recognizing the 'discriminated occasion' as a basic structural unit in *The Ambassadors* emphasizes the solidity of the various formal devices which James uses both to create and to resolve ambiguity. The verbal metaphor exemplifies only one extreme of a series of devices functioning 'metaphorically', or sometimes with the full weight of symbols. Whole scenes may do this, as well as single figures of speech, and deeds as well as words may carry symbolic significance. The action of *The Ambassadors* is 'framed' by Strether's voyage to Europe and his prospective return, and on a different level the novel is punctuated by figures of speech concerned with water and boats. The theme builds to a superbly economical climax when the 'figure' is realized dramatically as Strether watches two people in the boat of his Lambinet scene, and perceives the true nature of the relationship between them.

The precise context of a perception is all-important. In Arnheim's pictorial terms: 'The frame of a painting creates . . . an enclosure. It is a fence that to some extent protects the play of forces in the picture from the fettering influence of the environment', yet 'a visual pattern cannot be considered without regard to the structure of its spatial surroundings . . . ambiguity can result from a contradiction between form pattern and location pattern'.[1] In *The Ambassadors*, Strether's misunderstandings arise from his attempt to 'place' the Parisian situation in a New England framework of moral judgement, and to interpret the behaviour of those in Paris according to the patterns of New England custom and prejudice. On his first evening at the theatre with Maria Gostrey, Strether fails to appreciate the framing effect of the proscenium arch, and in his cultural *naïveté* thinks, 'It was an evening, it was a world of types, and this was a connection, above all, in which the figures and faces in the stalls were interchangeable with those on the stage' (p. 40). In the Lambinet episode he commits the opposite fault, in drawing a fanciful frame around a dramatic scene, and thus mistaking the 'formal context' of the phenomena he witnesses. It is a recognition which marks Strether's full consciousness: not new experience, but the placing of his perceptions in perspective, within the right frame.

The frame, implied through the details of style, is accessible to the reader before Strether becomes aware of it. On every level of expressive diction, from that of sound to the syntactic, the imagistic to the scenic, two kinds of stimulus are offered: one encouraging a 'substantiating' imaginative identification, the other developing detached discrimination, or 'placing'. Before noticing these techniques in context, as a reader does, it may be helpful to group them critically, according to their effect. 'Substantiating' devices include James's use of clichés, his play upon recurring thematic words, the literalization of figurative expressions, and the concrete rendering of abstracts. Larger structural devices, such as thematic imagery on the interlocking verbal and scenic levels, also enhance the 'solidity of specification' of the novel world. In contrast to these devices, a group of 'dissociative'

---

[1] Arnheim, op. cit. 9. That James approved of fences, both real and metaphorical, is suggested by his flourish, in *The American Scene*, on 'this especial decency of the definite, the palpable affirmation and belated delimitation of College Yard' at Harvard (p. 62).

techniques encourage intellectual, rather than imaginative, attention. 'Poetic' effects such as alliteration, inversion, and incremental
repetition are formal and exaggerated in the novel; and excess also
characterizes James's comic hyperbole, and, in a different way,
the heavily stressed formalism of the recurring art and drama
metaphors. Somewhere between the 'substantiating' and 'dissociative' groups come certain idiosyncratic Jamesian techniques
which both require imaginative involvement and encourage
detachment. The quasi-surrealistic technique of focusing attention on parts of the body, which endows seemingly independent
'eyes' or 'elbows' with intense life, has this dual effect: one T. S.
Eliot was to exploit as a satirical device in his early poetry. James
also uses a series of 'paired' words,[1] which effectively draw together the sympathetic and discriminatory visions at the same time
as pointing the contrast between them.

'Paired' words are used to present the contrasted Woollett and
Paris versions of Strether's experience; but that they may do more
is hinted at the outset. The paradox of his 'double consciousness'
places Strether outside the rigour of the mutually exclusive
categories of Woollett and Paris alike: the first glimpse of a
transcendent consciousness which will free him from both
worlds.

The simple opposition of terms early in the novel—'failure/
successes' (p. 33), 'wicked/charming' (p. 41), 'divine/impossible'
(p. 45), 'brutalized/refined' (p. 52)—becomes less and less straightforward. Amidst the hesitations of 'advance and retreat . . . his
impulse to plunge and . . . his impulse to wait' (p. 64), Strether
considers an opposition which is one of concepts, but not of
balanced vocabulary: here the contrasted terms are two forms of
the same verb: 'These were instants at which he could ask whether,
since there had been fundamentally so little question of his keeping anything, the fate after all decreed for him hadn't been only
to *be* kept' [James's italics] (p. 64).

Another complication is suggested when Strether is over-
whelmed by Paris. Though his confusion is unequivocally stated,
and 'what seemed all surface one moment seemed all depth the
next' (p. 67), the two terms used for the city, 'the vast bright
Babylon' and a 'glittering jewel', are scarcely paired opposites.

[1] Professor R. Ellmann first drew my attention to these 'pairs' in a lecture at
Oxford, 1973.

The variation on a pattern indicates how Strether's judgement is swayed under the impression of Paris.

A different variation is the nice play on words in the comical interchange between Strether and Waymarsh after Strether has seen Chad's apartment:

'I saw, in fine; and—I don't know what to call it—I sniffed. It's a detail, but it's as if there were something—something very good—*to* sniff.'
. . . 'Do you mean a smell? What of?'
'A charming scent. But I don't know.'
Waymarsh gave an inferential grunt. 'Does he live there with a woman?'
. . . 'I don't know.'

(p. 79)

One is reminded of Lear's Fool: 'All that follow their noses are led by their eyes but blind men.' Waymarsh, with his almost animal 'grunt', indeed sees the implications Strether misses here; yet Strether's 'charmed' sense is nearer the truth which he ultimately accepts, of the value of the relationship he comes out to destroy but stays, unsuccessfully, to preserve.

The technical figure of paired contrasting words is the basis for the most important riddling phrase of *The Ambassadors*: the 'virtuous attachment'. Little Bilham's quibble salves his conscience without *quite* misleading the reader. Like the description of Madame de Vionnet as 'dressed in black, but in black that struck him [Strether] as light and transparent; she was exceedingly fair' (p. 156), or the paradox, 'if she were worse she would be better for our purpose' (p. 172), the phrase becomes more than a pun. These riddles are not simply ambiguous and ironic: they rise beyond the constrictions of an 'either—or' meaning, just as Strether's understanding is to do. The 'bliss and bale' (p. 429) are inextricable, and, as Marie de Vionnet despairingly asserts, success is only in failure: 'It's never, a happiness . . . to *take*. The only safe thing is to give. It's what plays you least false' (p. 427). Her restatement of the ancient Christian paradox is noticeably opportunist, in keeping with her Parisian morality; but Strether himself demonstrates that 'to give', though far from safe, is his 'only logic. Not, out of the whole affair, to have got anything for myself' (p. 457).

The comparison and contrast of two points of view is more

economical in James's use of cliché. In a novel which links the development of consciousness with that of *savoir-faire*, the cliché, at once a meaningless social token of communication and a potentially valuable unit of expression, is an important stylistic device. Through a kind of double bluff, the mere pattern of words can become a daringly overt statement of the 'subtext'. Yet colloquialism also provides a 'bridge' between dialogue and the thoughts of Strether, and thus furnishes a flexible medium of narration.

The significant clichés of *The Ambassadors* are numerous, and have been noticed by many critics. The central moral concern, for example, is pointed by the repetition of such clusters as 'a good woman', 'excellent', 'better', and in the catch phrases 'all right', 'awfully good' and 'too good to be true'. The group is extended through the more complex quips: 'Well . . . it *is* at the worst rather good', and 'If she were worse she would be better for our purpose' (p. 172). At the other extreme is Maria Gostrey's deliberately oversimplified phrase, 'the wicked woman', and her 'bad for him' (p. 41).

The theme of 'knowledge', Strether's quest in two senses, also recurs frequently. Maria 'knew her theatre, she knew her play, as she had known triumphantly, for three days, everything' (p. 37). Strether laughs, 'I *don't* really want to know!' (p. 45). In conversation with Waymarsh in Paris, the words are insistent in their repetition:

'I don't know. . . .'
'Then what the devil *do* you know?'
'Well,' said Strether almost gaily. 'I guess I don't know anything!'
(p. 79)

Later, with Waymarsh,

'Doesn't he know what *she* is?' he went on.
'I don't know. I didn't ask him. I couldn't. . . . Besides I didn't want to . . . You can't make out over here what people do know.'
. . . . . .
'Oh,' Strether laughed, 'You're not one of *them*! I do know what *you* know!'
(p. 81)

'Knowledge' acquires almost biblical overtones, or perhaps half-echoes of *Paradise Lost*: the clichés of 'the feeling . . . had borne fruit almost faster than he could taste it', and 'the fruit of experience' extend the image of European 'corruption', 'the trail of the serpent' (p. 94). The Old Testament flavour of Woollett righteousness is hinted too in the cliché of 'sacrifice' (p. 216). Strether's uneasy conscience is vividly exaggerated: 'I want . . . to have been . . . expiatory. I've been sacrificing so to strange gods . . . I feel as if my hands were embrued with the blood of monstrous alien altars' (p. 337). The 'sacrifice' theme intersects disturbingly with the materialist ethic as the phrase 'sacrifice mothers and sisters' (p. 362) links with 'give people away' (p. 117), 'give . . . up' (p. 245), or 'give over to' (p. 279). Miss Barrace's comment that Marie de Vionnet 'has too much at stake' (p. 343) hovers uneasily between the primitive motif of sacrifice and the sophisticated decadence of the gambling theme.

This last is worded in two ways. One set of phrases, based on 'play', makes a verbal connection with the acting theme, while another, centred on the dead metaphor 'plunge', obliquely reflects the water imagery of *The Ambassadors*. Thus the phrases 'playing . . . any game' (p. 131), 'play fair' (p. 246) and the 'play of innuendo' (p. 276) may be linked with the social 'trick' (p. 159) and 'on the cards', besides the sense of 'plunging' and 'Strether took the plunge' (p. 358).

The social game is largely pretence, 'acting . . . on instructions' (p. 99), or having 'acted his part'. Madame de Vionnet creates a 'drama' not far removed from the London theatre or the Comédie Française; Strether feels the lack of 'the power of any act of his own' (p. 278) when Madame de Vionnet is 'a part of the situation'.

Strether, however, learns to distinguish acting from action. 'I see', 'see for myself', 'he saw now', relate sight and understanding. Miss Barrace's 'see about' and Maria Gostrey's 'see you through', on the other hand, betray an opportunist ethic, common to both Woollett and Paris, which Strether eventually leaves behind.

The conditions of perception arise from the scene. 'In the light of Paris one sees what things resemble' (p. 153), but not necessarily what they *are*. Strether is 'in the dark' (p. 248); and even when it seems 'at present . . . there was light' (p. 93), it is liable to be the delusory 'light of Paris', the social glitter, like that of Marie de Vionnet, whose very blackness strikes Strether as 'light and transparent', or Chad's, who 'was excellently free and light about their encounter' (p. 156).

It is at these points that Strether must 'judge' on the 'evidence', the 'facts', not be misled by the 'charming' or by 'glamour'. The approach of the strict enquirer conflicts with that of the romancer again and again, and whenever they occur, these words act as warning signs that Strether is liable to be mistaken.

The 'realization' of images through setting also promotes a dual awareness in the reader. Strether's situation lends itself to James's extended puns: he 'pays' for his experience in cash as he does in suffering, and the social gambles of Marie de Vionnet and Maria Gostrey too are equally concretely rewarded. Strether comes to Europe by boat, literally, finds himself 'in the same boat' as Madame de Vionnet and Chad, metaphorically, and finally sees them literally sharing one boat in the 'midstream' of the Lambinet scene. Strether is 'launched' (p. 281) and 'at sea' (p. 86); little Bilham has suffered 'shipwreck' (p. 94); Strether decides to 'burn his ships' (p. 90), but hopes 'it may be plain sailing yet'.

This sort of punning invites 'substantiating' imaginative involvement, but also draws attention to its own artifice, and promotes an intellectual, detached response: a surrealistic awareness. Strether's view had 'taken a bound' (p. 84); he had 'taken hold' (p. 93), 'got his job . . . in hand' (p. 93). Maria Gostrey proves adept in 'bustling traffic' in 'the exchange of such values as were not for him to handle' (p. 96). Madame de Vionnet 'by a turn of the hand' makes an encounter into a relation. Chad is expert in manipulation: 'One doesn't know quite what you mean by being in women's "hands". It's all so vague. One is when one isn't. One isn't when one is. And then one can't quite give people away' (p. 117).

The jaded sensibilities of those familiar with social form are roused, or thrown into relief, by means of a slightly distorted view, and James's technique hovers between comedy and the grotesque. Strether is happy to find himself 'face to face' (p. 37) with Maria Gostrey, but disturbed to find he must 'look his behaviour in the face' (p. 253). He admires the ease with which Chad (p. 112) and Madame de Vionnet (p. 224) sit, 'elbows on the table', but winces with the Pococks at 'a play of innuendo as vague as a nursery rhyme, yet as aggressive as an elbow in his side' (p. 276). Encounters 'face to face' and 'meeting his eyes' are commonplace; but the repetition heightens our apprehension of the parts of the body so that an ordinary phrase becomes charged with meaning, and there is a poetic intensity about Strether's having 'by this time struck himself as living almost disgracefully from hand to mouth' (p. 215), while Sarah Pocock's plight is positively grotesque as 'she felt the fixed eyes of their admirable absent mother fairly screw themselves into the flat of her back' (p. 333).

Not only the 'visual' devices for emphasis, but the verbal 'poetic effects' which James uses in *The Ambassadors* are generally dissociative rather than sympathetic. At the outset, both the richness and confusion of Strether's imagination are revealed in his mixed metaphors, as he relishes 'such a deep taste of change' and hopes 'to colour his adventure with cool success' (p. 4). Strether's romantic tendencies have a certain literary quality, which is rendered rather than stated. There is a conscious poeticism about the inversion: 'deep and beautiful, on this, her smile came back' (p. 185), or, 'strange and beautiful to him was her quiet, soft acuteness' (p. 229). The editor of the green review formulates his experience in such terms; but Strether comes to recognize artificialities of diction, and to be conscious of his form of expression.

As Strether is initiated into the deceptions of Parisian *savoir-faire,* a double negative further negated betrays his confusion as well as his inexpert duplicity: '*He* knew, more or less, what she meant, but the fact was not a reason for her not pretending to Waymarsh that he didn't' (p. 98). An over-used comparative provides another syntactic signal of confusion. In Gloriani's garden, there is a nice irony in Strether's relishing 'what was presently clear . . . what was clearer still . . . what was clearest of all' (p. 163). On the same occasion, a similar point is made through Strether's string of adjectives (unpunctuated in the New York edition): 'bright, gentle, shy, happy, wonderful'; and the irony is completed with the alliterative claim, 'All vagueness vanished', and the Woollett security of the declaration: 'He saw the truth' (p. 163).

Stylistic devices make a dual appeal to the reader's fancy and judgement, and we enter into Strether's experience while preserving sufficient detachment to avoid his mistake; syntactic ambiguity is perhaps more stringent. Strether learns, however, that it is 'the proportions', the very 'conditions of perception', the 'terms of thought' (p. 250) that must be adjusted according to situation, and this is what we too are required to attempt, in order to read irony correctly. Ambiguity is particularly evident in conversation, and often turns on the use of pronouns. In an early interchange with Maria, Strether's talk of his career is mistaken for a more personal confession: a revealing error:

'I *never* made a good thing!' he at once returned.
She just waited. 'Don't you call it a good thing to be loved?'
'Oh we're not loved. We're not even hated. We're only just sweetly ignored.'
(pp. 49–50)

The 'we' transposes the subject from Strether's relations with Mrs. Newsome to his relations with the world through the green review which Mrs. Newsome finances. Maria, comically and tellingly, assumes that this is a brilliant sidestepping of the personal issue:

She had another pause. 'You don't trust me!' she once more repeated.

This interchange provides a clue to Maria's interest in Strether, and a warning as to her motivation in Paris. Whilst she appears to be helping Strether arrive at the truth, her efforts are qualified by the need to protect him both from a shock which would precipitate him into the arms of Mrs. Newsome, and from a suspicion of his confidante which might turn him towards Marie de Vionnet.

When Madame de Vionnet meets Strether, her first impulse is an outspoken honesty appropriate to her own estimation of her feelings for Chad and of the evident good she has done him. In Paris, she might be regarded with respect. But to Woollett prejudice, such openness could only be grounded on conscious innocence: a purely Platonic relationship. Seeing this, Madame de Vionnet is forced to abandon her first brave honesty, and to adopt the very subterfuge which Woollett would expect of a 'fallen woman'. Thus, when to her 'Tell her [Mrs Newsome], fully and clearly, about *us*' (p. 186), Strether stares: 'You and your daughter?' Madame de Vionnet climbs down, to accept the assumption he has made about the antecedents of her pronoun: not Chad, but, 'Yes—little Jeanne and me.'

Miss Barrace is less adept at following or anticipating the changes of subject made over unspoken assumptions than the main characters, who are all remarkably quick to catch an allusion.

The very clumsiness of her interchange with Strether at Chad's dinner draws the reader's attention to the way in which this kind of formal ambiguity works:

> 'At all events' he roundly brought out, 'the attachment's an innocent one.'
> 'Mine and his? Ah,' she laughed, 'don't rob it of *all* romance!'
> 'I mean our friend's here—to the lady we've been speaking of.'
>   (p. 196)

Strether, Waymarsh, Miss Barrace, Chad, and Madame de Vionnet are in turn referred to, either through pronouns or through nouns of general applicability: 'our friend', 'the lady'. Miss Barrace does not understand; and her hesitation engenders a comical excess of speculation in Strether:

> Mystified by his abrupt declaration, she had glanced over at Gloriani as the unnamed subject of his allusion, but the next moment she had understood; though indeed not before Strether had noticed her momentary mistake and wondered what might possibly be behind that too. He already knew that the sculptor admired Madame de Vionnet; but did this admiration also represent an attachment of which the innocence was discussable? He was moving verily in a strange air and on ground not of the firmest.

One final example is in a sense the development of our first: an interchange between Strether and Maria Gostrey whose unspoken subtext is a concern for the relationship between them. Strether has now grown beyond the mere aptitude with guessed meanings; his curiosity for the truth is tempered with an understanding of what is better not expressed, since silence is less hurtful that denial. Maria can only ruefully concur, retiring with a good grace:

> 'No. Tell her [Madame de Vionnet] nothing.'
> 'Very well then.' To which, in the next breath, Miss Gostrey added 'Poor dear thing!'
> Her friend [Strether] wondered; then with raised eyebrows: 'Me?'
> 'Oh no. Marie.'
> He accepted the correction, but he wondered still.
> 'Are you so sorry for her as that?'
> It made her think a moment—made her even speak with a smile. But she didn't really retract.
> 'I'm sorry for us all!'   (p. 441)

The *Ambassadors* is a dense, though not a heavy book. James's style exacts the kind of attention we cannot here afford; nor is there room to trace 'the process and the effect' of each 'discriminated occasion' in relation to the whole. We shall have to concentrate on a few scenes and sequences. It is important, however, to remember and acknowledge that any selective appreciation omits details James considered necessary, for 'everything in [*The Ambassadors*] that is not scene . . . is discriminated preparation, is the fusion and synthesis of picture' (*The Art of the Novel*, p. 323). Close reading shows not only how we are led and Strether misled, but also how preparations are made for an eventual reversal of this misapprehension.

Strether's first meeting with Chad exemplifies this clearly. The whole of the third book of *The Ambassadors* is used to delay their confrontation in narrative terms, as Chad does through his social manœuvres. When the encounter finally takes place, it is in contrast with the kinetic tension of the preparatory movement, with its series of other, less important, interviews, that this, with its curiously static quality, stands out. The theatrical setting recalls Strether's evening with Maria in England, and in turn prepares for the drama of the Lambinet scene. Standing out against the 'framed' quality of 'the waxed and gilded vista' in the Louvre, this episode at the Française also trains the reader, while it marks a stage in the development of Strether, in distinguishing picture and drama.

Within the 'discriminated occasion' itself, James uses various 'formal codes' to reveal exactly what is happening. On a social level, Chad's late entrance demonstrates his expertise: Strether knows he could not have managed this so easily. Strether's New England unsophistication is obliquely reinforced in literary terms through a series of verbal echoes of Henry Thoreau, famous for his straightforward and markedly 'unsocial' thinking. The textual parallel with Thoreau's *Walden* ironically implies a similar renunciation by Strether of social artifice and temporizing: activities which flourish in Paris. And, of course, in the novel: James's manipulation of the New Englander's ideas plays masterfully with this threat to his own complex and devious form, subordinating it to his design whilst extracting from it both aspects of an interest distinctly ambiguous. Thus, Strether echoes Thoreau in wanting to keep 'the sky of life' clear of 'clouds of explanation', and to preserve instead 'a grand idea of the lucid'. What begins as a faint literary echo turns into full pastiche. Yet, while teasing, James's account of bluff New England honesty provides a startling challenge to Parisian intrigue—

A personal relation was a relation only so long as people either perfectly understood or, better still, didn't care if they didn't. From the moment they cared if they didn't it was living by the sweat of one's brow; and the sweat of one's brow was just what one might buy one's self off from by keeping the ground free of the wild weed of delusion. It easily grew too fast, and the Atlantic cable now alone could race with it.

(The Ambassadors, p. 105)

recalling *Walden*:

What sort of space is that which separates a man from his fellows and makes him solitary? I have found that no exertion of the legs can bring two minds much nearer to one another.

It is not necessary that a man should earn his living by the sweat of his brow, unless he sweats easier than I do.

and Thoreau's warning:

We are eager to tunnel under the Atlantic and bring the Old World some weeks nearer the New; but perchance the first news that will leak through into the broad flapping American ear will be that Princess Adelaide has the whooping cough.[1]

Postponed by such digressive, but ironically apt, considerations, the interview between Chad and Strether really begins some ten pages after Chad's entrance: although Strether attacks immediately, the edge has already been taken off what he has to say, and Chad's is the managing hand. As Stephen Spender explains, James

revolutionizes the method of presentation in the novel; altering the emphasis from the scene to that intellectual and imaginative activity which leads to the scene, so that his scenes are always symptoms, not causes; always anti-climaxes, not climaxes, in the sense that any explosion, any break-down of nervously accumulating forces is anti-climactic.[2] *The Destructive Element* (1938), p. 16.

When Strether speaks, verbal ambiguity is brought into play,

---

[1] Henry David Thoreau, *Walden: or Life in the Woods* (1854, rpt. 1889), pp. 208, 123, 84–5.
[2] *The Destructive Element* (1938), p. 16.

as his announcement has the double force of the charged cliché. 'I've come, you know, to . . . take you straight home' (*The Ambassadors*, p. 109), could mean 'home immediately' or 'honourably'. The note is ironically taken up again with Strether's 'If you'll promise me—here on the spot and giving me your word of honour—to break straight off, you'll make the future the real right thing for all of us alike' (p. 113). Only later does Strether come to realize that the two meanings are in conflict with each other, and the 'straight' thing is for Chad to stay.

Although the encounter appears to be seen through Strether's eyes, social 'language' as well as the diction of the narrative helps us understand more than he does. When Chad leans forward with his elbows on the table, Strether perceives how 'at bottom, and in spite of the shade of shyness that really cost him nothing, he had from the first been easy about everything.' The cliché is significant in this materialist world; but equally so is the gesture of ease.

Strether finds a formula for Chad's appearance: 'that of a man of the world'; he sees that the younger man is 'brown and thick and strong'. This is reported directly, but from the oblique diction of the ensuing description the reader cannot tell how much Strether himself sees, and how far his perceptions are refined by the narrator. The effect is unobtrusively to improve on Strether's understanding: starting with Strether's impressions, we have a deeper apprehension of what they imply. To us, it is clear that Chad's good appearance is essentially of the surface: it is described in artistic terms, which indirectly recall Titian's 'overwhelming' 'young man with a glove' in the Louvre. Chad's development has 'retouched his features, drawn them with a cleaner line . . . cleared his eyes and settled his colour and polished his fine square teeth—the main ornament of his face; and at the same time it had given him a form and a surface, almost a design'. We are alerted by the ambiguous force of the word 'design', and the 'improvement' is suspect. Chad's shining teeth, in particular, seem a feature of ambivalent significance. Maria Gostrey warned Strether in England that two things might have happened to Chad: 'One is that he may have got brutalized. The other is that he may have got refined.' These teeth, curiously and confusingly, strike both notes, and the prepared categories of judgement are thrown into disarray.

Strether himself is lost in wonder at Chad's changed appearance, so that he fails to read the signs correctly. His acceptance—'What were such marked matters all but the notes of his freedom?'—smacks to us of licence here as well as liberty. It is not until Strether meets Maria again that what he has missed is spelt out. We, if not Strether, must be alerted by her exclamation: 'I've known nothing but what I've seen, and I wonder . . . that you didn't see as much. It was enough to be with him there' (pp. 124–5). For Maria, it is enough to see that 'the fact itself *is* the woman' to guess the nature of their relationship. But Strether, bringing the moral standards of Woollett to judge a lady, does not understand her 'good' or 'excellent' qualities in the way that Paris does. Despite Maria's hint that 'You must forgive him if it isn't quite outspoken. In Paris such debts are tacit' (p. 126), the narrator continues, in complicity with the reader, 'Strether could imagine; —but still——!'

It is at Gloriani's garden party that Strether first meets Marie de Vionnet and has an opportunity to see her with Chad; and the occasion necessarily obscures the intimacy of their relationship with the formality of normal social decorum. The episode reveals more about the Parisian *monde* than about the 'attachment' itself; but it introduces Strether, and us, to the Parisian 'conditions of perception' in a way which marks a deepening of his involvement in the situation, while allowing us a certain detachment.

The scene is remarkable for the balance of economy and an impression of fullness. 'The expectation of something special' (p. 143) is rapidly built up; yet there is in the very diction a warning that the reader is not to be wholly caught up in Strether's excitement. Critical tension is established between hyperbolical excess, which demands reduction, and an insistent repetition of words and phrases recurring throughout the scene, and importantly used elsewhere in the book. We are likely to ignore the warning in a phrase which seems obliquely to express Strether's own hyperbole: 'He had by this time . . . let himself recklessly go' (p. 143); but the same sentence carries a threat in its developed insistence: 'cherishing the sense that whatever the young man showed him, he was showing at least himself.' The 'show' is converted in the ironic dimension of meaning from a revelation to a spectacle, which entertains by artifice and illusion; Chad becomes a 'cicerone', Strether is 'smothered in flowers', and the 'panem et circenses' smack of decadence and corruption, so that Strether's conscious hyperbole becomes for the reader an accurate indication of the ironic truth.

The ambiguous extremes of appearance and reality are clearly marked for us, though Strether himself is unable to recognize the significance of Chad's 'game, his plan, his deep diplomacy' as long as he persists in the 'almost angry inference that this was only because of his [Strether's] odious inbred suspicion of any form of beauty' (p. 143). We recall a whole body of 'play' images, connecting 'acting' with 'gambling', and indicating the undercurrents of social intercourse within which Chad is able to manipulate the 'ambassador' through a 'deep diplomacy' which the older man will only recognize in 'touching bottom'. Meanwhile, Gloriani's garden, like Paris on Strether's first impression, 'twinkled and trembled and melted together, and what seemed all surface one moment seemed all depth the next'.

The unwittingly ironical diction of Strether's thoughts maintains an equilibrium for the reader, who is not required to condemn Strether's blindness, but merely to perceive more than Strether yet does. While Strether sees 'reluctance to pry' as 'consecrated', we are warned by the phrase 'judged in the light of that talk' that vigilance must be maintained. The 'silence' 'offered . . . as a reserve' by Chad may be a gift, like the 'panem et circenses' and the smothering flowers, designed only to distract the observer.

Such hesitations are abandoned by Strether, but not by us, once the observer is 'launched' into the mood induced by the powerful but vague and confusing influence of the place. The 'medium of the scene' retains an element of deliberately illusionary artifice, which overwhelms only the culturally unsophisticated New Englander. For him, 'the place itself was a great impression . . . sweeping away, as by a last brave brush, his usual landmarks and terms' (p. 144). Strether is not only launched, but adrift.

Syntax as well as thematic vocabulary conveys the effect of this scene upon Strether. Parallel phrases are juxtaposed without conjunctions, like the brush-strokes of the impressionist painting, which conveys the perception of the observer with sensory immediacy, without the disciplined interpretative 'perspective' of formal, classical rules of line and outline. Strether 'had the sense of names in the air, of ghosts at the windows, of signs and tokens, a whole range of expression all about him, too thick for prompt discrimination' (p. 145). There is a clear distinction between the impressionist rendering of experience which Strether enjoys here, and James's own concern with 'Expression, the literal squeezing out, of value.'

The precise nature of Strether's inability to appreciate the 'assault of images' is further defined when he meets Gloriani the sculptor. It is not art itself that is illusionist and deceptive, but the confusion of forms in imprecise apprehension. Strether finds Gloriani 'almost formidable', and invests the artist with 'the light, the romance, of glory'. He realizes his own *naïveté*, 'quite aware he couldn't have spoken without appearing to talk nonsense' (p. 146). Yet he is sufficiently conscious to realize that he has 'positively been on trial', and although he describes Gloriani's smile, with a vague romanticism, as 'charming', Strether sees the 'terrible life behind it', and sees too that it 'was flashed upon him as a test of his stuff'. Both judgement and depth of vision are evidently within Strether's capabilities, even if they are not exercised upon this occasion.

When little Bilham approaches, Strether gives way to the impression, rather than exercising the faculties, of visionary inspiration: the romantic 'fit was on him'. Though the encounter with 'reality' dramatized in the meeting of eyes with Gloriani is analytically conveyed in this conversation, Bilham warns Strether that he is 'not a person to whom it is easy to tell things you don't want to know'. The young man does not insist; 'What more than a vain appearance does the wisest of us know? You'll see for yourself. One does see.' Whatever their specific context, such reverberating phrases are read in relation to the moral drama in which Strether is only partly aware of his involvement. They have more than the simple irony of a double meaning: the one Strether sees and the one he does not. The paradox of the 'vain appearance' remains, like that of the 'virtuous attachment', which both is and is not virtuous, to the extent that it remains an attachment, and which at the same time can be either the link of a real affection or a constricting bond.

The next 'relation' within the scene, Strether's meeting with Miss Barrace, lightens the pressure of moral significance, yet does not wholly relax the ironic tension which has been built up. 'Seeing', the abstract perception, becomes in this context a pragmatic 'seeing about'; Miss Barrace has 'given it up', and merely admires those who 'face' 'these things'. Although her words find a place in the structure of recurrent phrases, their moral weight is barely stressed here. While Miss Barrace, unlike Strether, can see 'in the light of Paris . . . what things resemble', her appreciation of appearances does not penetrate what lies beyond. Strether is right to reflect, 'You've all of you here so much visual sense that you've somehow all "run" to it. There are moments when it strikes one that you haven't any other.' 'Any moral', as little Bilham explains. Miss Barrace's 'resemblance' foreshadows Madame de Vionnet's ambiguous remark upon the *'invraisemblance'* of the occasion in the country, Strether's Lambinet scene. The gallicism of both ladies' expressions 'places' them in the context of a society which uses appearances; but this may also make the point for the discriminating reader 'that every like is not the same'.

Meanwhile the impressionist scene in the garden develops dramatically: Chad is 'again at hand', and the reader, like Strether, is swept into the supreme 'connexion' with Madame de Vionnet. The interplay of narrative voice and reported speech and thought allows for a simultaneous apprehension of Strether's feelings on the occasion and his subsequent analysis; and this creates an impression of growing awareness which is a development rather than a mere sequence. Though Strether is sufficiently aware to feel 'estimated . . . handed over and delivered; absolutely, as he would have said, made a present of, given away' (p. 155), Chad controls the scene. Yet half-recognized or unattached apprehensions gather for Strether: 'There were precautions, he seemed indeed to see, only when there were really dangers' (p. 156). There is an advance towards his reading of the 'evidence', and 'the thing really unmistakable was that it rolled over him as a wave that he had been, in conditions incalculable and unknowable, a subject of discussion' (p. 157). The impressionist figures give way to judicial and analytical terms, as the 'motives behind' (p. 158) are sensed. The encounter is interrupted, however, by 'a trick played with a social art of which Strether . . . felt himself no master' (p. 159): again, deception is linked with gambling in the 'play' motif, and Chad's hand is discovered for the reader behind apparent accident.

The recognition of this manipulation does not come yet, however. Strether's central 'Live all you can' speech to little

Bilham is the first outcome of his supposition that 'if at the worst he had been overturned at all, he had been overturned into the upper air, the sublimer element with which he had an affinity and in which he might be trusted awhile to float' (p. 160). James is again invoking the echo of Thoreau, for whom Heaven was 'under our feet as well as over our heads' in Walden pond (*Walden,* p. 438). But the transcendentalist paradox goes beyond ironic ambiguity, and rises above Strether's limitations as a judge of appearances. It is impossible to say precisely how far the undermining effect of a knowledge of Strether's delusion at the garden party destroys his statement of faith to little Bilham. Comic ambiguity in the social drama of manners gives way to near-tragic irony in a different perspective:

'I see it now. . . . and now I'm too old . . . for what I see. . . . One lives in fine as one can. Still, one has the illusion of freedom; therefore don't be, like me, without the memory of that illusion.'   (p. 161)

This address, which might be taken as a concluding statement, has a dual force which is established and maintained by the ambiguous quality of the scene in which it occurs. The 'false note' is sounded particularly in the phrase 'the illusion of freedom'. Yet far from ending the illusion, Strether's speech suggests recognition of the unreality only to give way to the fancy again, and this is heightened rather than undermined.

The resumed pattern of encounters re-echoes that of the 'first half' of the scene, but with Jeanne de Vionnet now being introduced to Strether. Strether's 'full picture' is ironically shown to exceed both logical and artistic decorum, as it has 'another impression . . . superimposed' (p. 163); and the contradiction of reality in Strether's interpretation of appearances is embodied in the disjunction of form and content in the expression of his thoughts.

Chad sweeps little Jeanne off to rejoin her mother, with a proprietorial air that Strether mistakes for that of the accepted suitor: 'There was the whole of a story in his tone to his companion, and he spoke indeed as if already of the family' (p. 165). Strether's romantic fancy creates the 'story': 'It made Strether guess the more quickly . . .'. But little Bilham has gone: there is no one to tell his thoughts to, and no one to point out his mistake.

When Miss Gostrey joins Strether, the reader is enlightened

more than Strether himself as to Madame de Vionnet's position. Labouring under the delusion of an attachment between Chad and little Jeanne, Strether is not prepared to read between the lines of what Maria Gostrey says. Both of them consider the truth so obvious as to be understood without being plainly stated, but they have different ideas of what it is. The non-communication between them is so gross that the only thing plain to the reader is the fact of a misunderstanding. When Strether exclaims, 'It's the child!'—a statement hardly so explicit as to stand without further elaboration—Miss Gostrey's response is seen from Strether's point of view: 'And though her direct response was for some time delayed he could feel in her meanwhile the working of this truth.' There is no indication here that this interpretation is wrong: that this is the speechlessness of incomprehension, rather than assent. Not until the metaphors in the next sentence recall Strether's fanciful impressions earlier in the scene is there any hint, building on that cumulative irony, that his extravagance is wrong again. The indirect diction used for Strether's thoughts and for the objective narrative alike blurs distinctions even here between supposition and reality. It is left for the imagery of flood, the gallicism of 'ces dames', and the sheer difficulty of the syntactic and logical sequence of the sentence to reveal to the reader that nothing exists but confusion worse confounded by the illusion of clarity. It is a situation not reported or analysed, but rendered through the very diction of the narrative:

It might have been simply, as she waited, that they were now in presence, altogether, of truth spreading like a flood and not, for the moment, to be offered in the mere cupful . . .

The 'simply' is quietly ironic; the sentence grows increasingly involved:

inasmuch as who should *ces dames* prove to be but persons about whom—once thus face to face with them—she found she might from the first have told him almost everything? (p. 166)

There is a subtle shift in the middle of this sentence from 'the narrator-taking-Strether's-point-of-view' to 'the narrator-reporting-Maria's-thoughts'. The voice of the narrator is a constant factor; but this glosses over the confrontation of two misdirected presuppositions of an 'understanding' which does not exist.

The irony of misunderstanding, which all but the most alert reader will have failed quite to grasp, as it is mimed in the sentence with the shifting point of view, is made increasingly plain throughout the interchange between Miss Gostrey and Strether. There is both direct and oblique warning in the text itself:

There could be no better example—and she appeared to note it with high amusement—than the way, making things out already so much for himself, he was at last throwing precautions to the winds.

There is also simple irony:

It was a relief, Miss Gostrey hinted, to feel herself no longer groping . . .
(p. 166)

Amidst such clear short sentences of spoken or reported speech, Strether's continuing misapprehension is obliquely revealed, not in the sense, but in the 'poetic style' of his thoughts. There is alliteration, grandiose diction, limitless imagery, in this conception, entirely at variance with the true state of affairs:

The waste of wonder might be proscribed; but Strether, characteristically, was even by this time quite in the air.   (p. 167)

The vision of the soaring intelligence of the observer is nicely put between two precise locations: Miss Gostrey's clarity—'She's coming to see me—that's for *you* . . . but I don't require it to know where I am'—and Strether's security of ignorance: 'By which you mean that you know where *she* is?'

The word-games are set aside, however, once Maria Gostrey translates these theoretical, even metaphysical, abstractions into the terms of social intercourse. In social language, her sentence is unequivocal: 'I mean that if she comes to see me I shall . . . not be at home'.

The mounting delusion of the garden scene 'explains' Strether's stance here, while on the other hand the blatant irony here 'reads back' to confirm the ironic distance of truth from appearance throughout the preceding scene. Miss Gostrey's admonitions and repeated rephrasing of her stance would be excessive in this context, were they not also setting right in retrospect the fantastical romanticism of the preceding scene. 'I shall . . . not be at home. . . . Don't be so literal. I wash my hands of her. . . . *I'm* impossible. It's impossible. Everything's impossible' (p. 167).

For Strether to respond to this with a sublimely unaware, 'I see where you're coming out. Everything's possible', is a stroke of irony made possible only in the context of a delusion stretching both before and after this. Thus it is that Maria's outburst can warn the reader almost directly of the secret hitherto revealed indirectly through the use of ambiguous formalities in the garden scene, yet Strether can remain unaware of the truth so plainly put, without appearing stupid in his blindness. It is a question of process as much as of effect, for reading the novel is more than a series of discrete perceptions.

The conversation with Maria Gostrey 'concludes' this 'occasion' by confirming the delusion which Chad has artfully created, and the romantic Strether elaborated for himself. The interchange also acts, however, as a transition to the next move and further confirmation of the mistaken view of Chad and Madame de Vionnet. There is no perceptible break between the scene at Gloriani's house and the sequence of further meetings, first with Chad, then with Madame de Vionnet, and finally at Chad's dinner party, where the two of them are present, acting as host and hostess.

The visit to Madame de Vionnet's house illustrates James's conception of the 'organic form' of the novel, in which everything is 'all one and continuous'. The scene is economical yet densely allusive, full of the 'solidity of specification' which realizes setting, and rich in ambiguous dialogue; it is an education in imaginative appreciation. Both description and conversation form part of a developing sequence. Besides the series of interviews beginning at Gloriani's garden party and leading towards Chad's dinner, this meeting contributes to the pattern formed by Strether's encounters with Marie de Vionnet alone. This carries the reference back to the garden party, and forward to the encounter at Notre Dame and the intimate luncheon by the Seine. Most importantly, the visit provides a pattern of 'the habit of privacy, the peace of intervals, the dignity of distances and approaches' (p. 179), which will stand in contrast to the climactic last meeting between Strether and Marie, set amidst the same surroundings, but quite different in tone.

The visit is formally set in a social context, even the time, 'quite by half-past five', establishing the situation. Besides the referential value of the hour it has various social connotations: the time after tea and before dinner, when only acquaintances of a certain degree of intimacy are received. There is also a *trompe l'œil* narrative effect, fitting this scene between the garden party and the dinner without apparent interruption: in this telescoped sequence, the pace of events meets the imaginative pressure of Strether's experience.

It is through the setting that Madame de Vionnet's 'credentials' are given. Far more than any explanatory apologies from Chad or Maria Gostrey, this scene 'justifies' Strether's misplaced confidence in Marie's tone. The 'hereditary, cherished, charming' furnishings, described in one long leisurely sentence, represent a sense of age, value, and an assured taste. The contrast with Chad's house and Maria's 'little museum of bargains' is felt; but Strether is clearly not yet able to evaluate its significance. In the later interview with Marie in these rooms, he will be able to perceive her as distinct from her setting, to appreciate how much she gains from it, and correspondingly, what her personal stature is. At this first interview, however, Strether is represented as artistically perceptive but culturally naïve, unable to communicate on equal terms with a woman for whom he has an imaginative, but untutored, sympathy. We see the limitations of Strether's understanding without losing sympathy for his attempts at clearer perception, while we ourselves are being prepared to make the finer distinctions of the concluding scene.

The greater the charm of Madame de Vionnet, the better we can understand Strether's reaction to her 'very presence, look, voice, the mere contemporaneous *fact* of whom, from the moment it was at all presented, made a relation of mere recognition'. This is the beginning of a development which imaginatively justifies Strether's turning away from both Mrs. Newsome and Maria Gostrey. That he does not, in the end, turn from them to Marie de Vionnet will be gradually and substantially accounted for as her relation with Chad is revealed; but, for the moment, 'at the back of his head, behind everything, was the sense that she was—there before him, close to him, in vivid imperative form—one of the rare women he had so often heard of, read of, thought of, but never met . . .' (p. 185). There is a direct, unequivocal comparison: 'That was not the kind of woman he had ever found Mrs. Newsome, a contemporaneous fact who had been distinctly slow to establish herself; and at present confronted with Madame de Vionnet, he felt the simplicity of his original impressions of

Miss Gostrey. She certainly had been a fact of rapid growth; but the world was wide, each day was more and more a new lesson.' 'Fact', as applied to Mrs. Newsome and Maria Gostrey has a bathetic vulgarity which is quite absent in connection with Marie de Vionnet. Here it has an almost existential weight, enhanced by the positioning of the verb 'was' before the syntactic break of the parenthesis. Like Cleopatra, Madame de Vionnet is a 'rare' being.

Through the sequence of 'discriminated occasions' representing Strether's encounter with Chad, Madame de Vionnet, and the Parisian *monde*, James interrelates the minutiae of style and tone within each scene and between the various occasions. Ironic ambiguity points Strether's misapprehensions for the reader; but we, like Strether, are carried along by the pace and flow of the narrative, sharing his experience. James uses the social situations and draws on pictorial dramatic, and literary allusions too, not only to 'place' Strether, the New Englander in Paris, but to prepare for the eventual movement through this perspective towards an 'infinity' paradoxically located but not contained by it. We may smile at Strether's *naïveté* now, but we shall be ready to respect his judgement and his feelings in the end.

The temptation to pursue an analysis of 'the process and the effect of representation' through the discriminated occasions of *The Ambassadors* is increased both by their individual power and by the 'architectural' strength with which they support each other. To take less than the whole is to do the novel an injury. But in our limited space for close reading, I shall concentrate not on the Lambinet scene, which has been extensively and sensitively explicated,[1] but on the sequence of encounters at the conclusion of the novel: in a sense, these scenes balance those we have already noticed.

The closing movement cannot be utterly divorced from its context. The comicality of the Pocock embassage is as important in preparing for the end as the earlier 'romance' of the garden party, the encounter at Notre Dame, the luncheon *à deux* by the Seine. When fresh ambassadors arrive from New England and Strether's alignment with the Parisians is confirmed, there is an opportunity to count the cost to him of the abandonment of his

---

[1] Notably by David Lodge in 'Strether by the River', *Language of Fiction* (1966).

old protectress. He will not have to stoop to such considerations at the end.

The Lambinet episode too clarifies the position. Before the end, Strether's disillusionment, the disgust at 'the quantity of make-believe involved, and so vividly exemplified, that most disagreed with his spiritual stomach' (p. 413) has already been digested. Within a page of that nadir, Strether has 'found himself supposing everything'—emended in the New York text to 'innumerable and wonderful things (p. 413).

The last book of *The Ambassadors* comes after both illusion and disillusionment. Neither condemnatory nor condoning moral failing, it shows Strether, now 'seeing' clearly, coming to terms with human beings as they are, but not accepting their condition as the best conceivable.

The isolation of the perceiver, confronted with experience but not one with it, is now reflected both in themes and style. The familiar motifs of fantasy and artifice recur, but there is a greater explicitness in the interpretation of symbols and the statement of conclusions. The protagonist's vision has come to equal that of the narrator, and although he remains a romancer, Strether is distanced enough to recognize the extent of his fancies. In the *Postes et Télégraphes* office, Strether sees with comic clarity what his position now is, amidst 'the influence of the types, the performers concocting their messages; the little prompt Paris women, arranging, pretexting, goodness knew what . . . He was mixed up in the typical tale of Paris, and so were they, poor things . . .'. This is Strether looking over his own shoulder, and acknowledging with colloquial forthrightness: 'They were no worse than he, in short, and he no worse than they—if, queerly enough, no better; and at all events he had settled his hash.'

When the final interview begins, Strether still sees Madame de Vionnet in artistic terms, but these are explicitly voiced: 'the picture that, each time, squared itself, large and high and clear, around her: every occasion of seeing it was a pleasure of a different shade' (p. 419). Strether is critically discriminating: an interesting adjective qualifies the noun in his reiterative image: 'He was moving in these days, as in a gallery, from clever canvas to clever canvas'. While he accepts the conditions of perception, he does so consciously, and with an appreciation that has no hint of delusion: 'The light in her beautiful, formal room was dim, though it would do, as everything would always do'. Strether's vision of Madame de Vionnet as a tragic heroine, an aristocratic victim of the Revolution, is fanciful, but not inappropriate. It is warranted both by its intensity and because it elucidate. the situation. The 'historic sense' befits the Parisian drama, and Madame de Vionnet has a 'tragic rôle' in that context, whatever the limitations of her stature seen in a different perspective.

Strether is not impervious to the old impressions which he has learnt to appreciate, but he knows that 'whatever he should find he had come for, it wouldn't be for an impression that had previously failed him'. He is aware both of the local value of all that Marie de Vionnet embodies, and of how far this value is localized, rather than infinite. The knowledge that 'he should soon be going to where such things were not' (p. 422) progresses beyond his recognition in the Lambinet scene that 'in *these* places such things were' (p. 403). When there is repetition in Strether's account, its effect is not to alert the reader to excess, but to suggest how Strether himself recognizes the movements of his imagination: 'He knew in advance he should look back on the perception actually sharpest with him as on the view of something old, old, old, the oldest thing he had ever personally touched' (p. 422). He distinguishes between the 'facts' of place and setting, and the temporary expedients of artifice, recognizing the value of each:

She might intend whatever she would, but this was beyond anything she could intend, with things from far back— tyrannies of history, facts of type, values, as the painters said, of expression—all working for her, and giving her the supreme chance, the chance of the happy, the really luxurious few, the chance, on a great occasion, to be natural and simple. (p. 422)

There is an ironic contrast between this and the thrice-repeated, hollow, 'charming chance' of the recent Lambinet scene.

The sense of proportion and appreciation is insistent throughout the interview, even while Marie becomes increasingly emotional. Strether responds to her oblique, coquettish appeal—'He was not to mind if she bored him a little: she had behaved, after all,—hadn't she?—so awfully, awfully, well'—with an impatience, not at the delivery, but at the appeal itself: he could be relied on now to take such preliminaries for granted. He is 'the more prepared of the two' and knows it. Though Marie runs through every pose from self-abasement—'Selfish and vulgar—that's what I must seem to you'—to proud appeal—'How can I be indifferent . . . to how I appear to you?'—her self-interest is as clear to Strether as it is to the reader. Even Marie's recognition of Strether's 'dislocation' is bound up for her with the selfish desire to have him stay in Paris to 'consecrate' her liaison with Chad. Her insight is not wholly vitiated by her interest, however. Her words place Strether at least negatively—as infinity, though it cannot be pinned down, can be indicated by the lines of perspective in a picture. This is the positive implication of her question:

> 'Where *is* your "home", moreover, now—what has become of it? I've made a change in your life, I know I have; I've upset everything in your mind as well; in your sense of—what shall I call it?—all the decencies and possibilities.'   (p. 426)

Marie's declaration of the need to 'give' is equally pertinent to Strether's vision, and equally inverted. Against the selfishness of her recognition that 'it's not, that it's never, a happiness, any happiness at all, to *take*. The only safe thing is to give. It's what plays you least false' (p. 427), Strether's true generosity will eventually stand out in his disinterested avowal that 'not, out of the whole affair, to have got anything for myself' is the only way 'to be right' (p. 457).

Madame de Vionnet does not recognize the privileges of Strether's 'displaced' position. He can see, as she cannot, Chad's limitations, and the limitations of her work on him, which, despite the 'consecration' of Strether's interest, remains 'of the strict human order'. Unlike Strether, 'she had but made Chad what he was—so why could she think she had made him infinite?'. As the lady weeps, Cleopatra-like, descending to the level of that maidservant, 'vulgarly troubled', that Jeanne de Vionnet never became (pp. 429, 192), there is a certain theatricality in her collapse: ' "It's how you see me, it's how you see me"—she caught her breath with it—"and it's as I *am*" '. Strether remains outside the storm of emotion, detached, though not unsympathetic. Though 'serving her to the end', he is quite conscious of 'some vague inward irony in the presence of such a fine free range of bliss and bale.' So far has his understanding risen above the half-truths and histrionics of Paris that though he pities Marie de

Vionnet, he does not find his moral categories compromised by this response. While she is pathetic, Strether attains to the dignity of tragic understanding, unflawed by self-pity. He is a little remote: 'It was actually, moreover, as if he didn't think of her at all, as if he could think of nothing but the passion, mature, abysmal, pitiful, she represented, and the possibilities she betrayed'. There is a quiet irony in Strether's ambiguous parting words, of which the most certain thing is the finality of the past tense: 'Ah, but you've *had* me'. He has loved Marie, and she has used him; but he will not be used again.

After the finality of this parting, Strether's isolation grows, with an inevitability compounded of collusion amongst his erstwhile 'friends' and the distancing within himself of clearer perception. This isolation is not in space only, though at the end of the book it will be imaged in geographical terms, but in time as well: when Strether thinks of Waymarsh, it is, 'Waymarsh who already, somehow, seemed long ago'.

Though Strether at first waits to be summoned by Madame de Vionnet and by Chad, his passivity is based on patient understanding: he remains in control of his own conduct.

Strether assumed, he became aware, on this reasoning, that the interesting parties to the arrangement [Chad and Madame de Vionnet] would have met betimes, and that the more interesting of the two—as she was after all—would have communicated to the other the issue of her appeal. (p. 432)

The fact that Strether is able to pause in the midst of this formulation for a parenthetical appreciation of Madame de Vionnet shows how far he is from the blindness of close involvement with the situation he is shortly to leave behind; but it demonstrates also that Strether's detachment does not decrease his imaginative appreciation of the qualities which his experience during the course of the novel has taught him to value.

The pause between the interview with Marie de Vionnet and that with Chad is taken up with a quieter interlude with Maria Gostrey. Though she is another woman whose as yet unvoiced claims will eventually have to be made explicit and met, there is no real doubt as to the settlement of the account; and Strether's 'using' Maria to fill this time rests on generous confidence in her understanding rather than a blind or cruel misleading of the confidante. James makes it clear in the New York Preface that he supposed the 'redundancy' of Maria at the conclusion of the novel self-evident, and was mainly concerned that it should not be too obtrusive. The inevitability of the final parting is shown obliquely in the penultimate encounter and more directly in the last scene. Strether's taking Maria shopping, his showing her the penny steamboats and the *bateaux mouches*, are more than indulgence in the romantic delights of 'Kubla Khan', destined to end at the dreadful 'reckoning'. These activities, while the reckoning is postponed, are calculated to demonstrate how far Strether has come through the novel, since the time when Maria guided him around the shops and he watched Chad and Marie de Vionnet in a boat on a river. Strether has now no practical need of Marie or Maria: he can indeed, as Maria once prematurely put it, 'toddle alone'.

The necessity of separation is not solely based upon redundancy, however. It is not simply that Maria has outlived her usefulness, but that she, like all the other women in Strether's experience (except the young ladies: Jeanne suffering in silence, and Mamie, 'disinterestedly tender'), has betrayed his trust, putting her own desire for him above his need for the truth. This realization has been gradual for Strether, and on a careless reading we too may miss the signs of the confidante's betrayal. Yet the recognition lurks near the surface before it is made explicit; Strether 'knew, that is, in a manner—knew roughly and resignedly—what he himself was hatching; whereas he had to take the chance of what he called to himself Maria's calculations' (p. 434). His indifference to Maria's motives here is not callous, but shows a proper regard for the rightness first of all of his own actions. Strether's moral fineness is exhibited in a 'supreme scruple' which can have reference only to his own motives, and not to those of the people surrounding him:

> He wished not to do anything because he had missed something else, because he was sore or sorry or impoverished, because he was mal-treated or desperate; he wished to do everything because he was lucid and quiet, just the same for himself on all essential points as he had ever been.   (p. 435)

The 'sameness' of Strether's need 'to be right' is not stasis, but 'infinity': an affirmation that certain values transcend the limitations of time and space. In the 'vanishing-point' of the novel, Strether is not transformed, in the sense that he becomes super-human or inhuman; but his humanity moves into the freedom of absolute imaginative morality, away from the constrictions of formal decorum inevitable in social intercourse. When Maria Gostrey tells Strether 'You're magnificent' (p. 439), he replies, 'You're too much struck with everything' (in the New York edition, James revised the terms to 'You're complete' and 'You're always too personal').

The movement beyond Paris is one Strether must make alone. Marie de Vionnet, who was once 'his youth', is left behind: 'She was older for him tonight, visibly less exempt from the touch of time'. Maria Gostrey has long since been outdistanced, though it is only now that Strether realizes why. He becomes 'even sure that she was in possession of things he himself couldn't have told; for the consciousness of them was now all in her face and accom-panied there with a shade of sadness that marked in her the close of all uncertainties' (p. 436). Maria has been biding her time; but having 'played strictly fair' is not enough. She would still be willing to take what the situation 'might furnish forth to her advantage'. With the close of all uncertainties, it becomes clear that for Strether to bind himself to Maria would be to sell the freedom of his imaginative experience, to exchange 'infinity' for a fixed location.

The settlement of accounts with Chad is different in tone from that with the two women, although the thematic pattern is similar. Strether has already grown away from Chad, recognizing that he has 'other qualities. But no imagination, don't you see? at all', and that Marie de Vionnet, the more interesting of the couple, 'had but made Chad what he was—so why could she think she had made him infinite? . . . he was none the less only Chad'. The situation now is simple for Strether: 'he must see Chad, but he must go. The more he thought of the former of these duties the more he felt himself making a subject of insistence of the latter'.

This interview, like those with Marie and Maria, is in a familiar setting: a fact which has imaginative force as well as narrative shapeliness; for there is a sense of foreknowledge of the end, rather than any uncertainty. Strether himself recognizes the 'completed' quality of this experience, as he approaches Chad's rooms:

Present enough always was the small circumstance that had originally pressed for him the spring of so big a difference—the accident of little Bilham's appearance on the balcony . . . at the moment of his first visit, and the effect of it on his curiosity. He recalled his watch, his wait, and the recognition on the young stranger's part that . . . had brought him up—things that had so smoothed the way for his first step.   (p. 442)

There is a brief concession to be made to the present situation before Strether can be freed of Chad, and of all local ties. This is expressed in Strether's acknowledgement that Chad's presence on the balcony represents 'clearly a conscious surrender', whilst his own concern demonstrates that he is 'still practically committed —he had perhaps never yet so much known it'. In fulfilling the undertaking he made to Marie de Vionnet—the counterpart to his original mission for Mrs. Newsome—Strether will finally free himself of all obligations; though he will also renounce his 'youth':

If he had just thought of himself as old, Chad, at sight of him, was thinking of him as older; he wanted to put him up for the night just because he was ancient and weary.   (p. 444)

Chad, like Marie, would be prepared to keep Strether 'indefinitely'; but there is hardly any wavering over this. The interview is not to settle Strether's fate, but Chad's and Marie's. 'He had come to say goodbye—yet that was only a part; so that from the moment Chad accepted his farewell the question of a more ideal affirmation gave way to something else' (pp. 444–5). It is the way Chad treats the question of his relations with Madame de Vionnet as being of interest to Strether rather than absolute in themselves, that betrays him. Just as Chad would once have returned to Woollett at his mother's summons, so now he treats his faithfulness as a tribute to Strether: a gesture. Strether understands 'that he would abound for him, to the end [the ironic ambiguity of this phrase is nicely unstressed], in conscientious assurances'. The 'conscientious' is the restrictive note of Woollett; but Strether is moving amidst the greater truths of absolute right and wrong: the morality which distinguishes humanity rather than society. He warns Chad, 'You'll be a brute, you know—you'll be guilty of the last infamy—if you ever forsake her'. Restated, this becomes even more clearly a question of right, not of reputation or appearances: ' "It's not a question of advising you not to go," Strether said, "but of absolutely preventing you, if possible, from so much as thinking of it. Let me accordingly appeal to you by all you hold sacred".' In the New York edition there is a third admonition, after the appeal of humanity and of the sacred, sinking to the terms of mere legality: 'You'd not only be, as I say, a brute; you'd be . . . a criminal of the deepest dye.' It is to this warning that Chad responds, with a 'sharper look', and the disturbing protest, 'I don't know what should make you think I'm tired of her.'

The fusion of Strether's understanding with the omniscience of the narrator, the guiding intelligence of the author himself, is nowhere clearer than here, where no colloquialism is needed to indicate that the implications of the situation are perceived by Strether, though apparently presented through the narrator. Abstraction, the use of the verb 'to be', neologism, an unusual word-order, and the use of imagery, all mark Strether's intelligence, though the attribution of his thought-processes is oblique: 'there was none the less for him [Strether], in the very manner of his host's allusion to satiety as a thinkable motive, a slight breath of the ominous'.

By comparison with Strether's insight and feeling, Chad's words sound vulgar and unimaginative. He is the colloquial speaker—'An awful ass, wasn't I?'—the crassly commercial—'If one *should* wish to live on one's accumulations?'—the complacent egotist—'And he scrupulously went further. "She has never been anything whatever that I could call a burden." ' The inadequacy of Chad's imagination is epitomized, in 'Jamesian shorthand', when he calls advertising, a commercial manipulation of the aesthetic, 'an art like another, and infinite like all the arts': an allegation to which Strether responds with dry precision: 'Advertising *is* clearly, at this time of day, the secret of trade. It's quite possible it would be open to you—giving the whole of your mind to it—to make the whole place hum with you'.

The isolation of Strether in this scene is clearly a positive move, though negatively revealed through the exposure of Chad's baseness. To be free of such relations, the 'relations involved in staying', is shown to be a good thing; and the presentation of this fact throws stress on what Strether escapes rather than on what he is now to do: a difficult question, but not one which the conclusion allows us to dwell on.

The final scene with Maria comes as a sort of coda after the series of three interviews. It is introduced as 'another separation to face', and the issue is never in doubt. But James uses the facts of setting to substantiate this certainty. The 'little Dutch-looking dining room' of Maria's apartment, the 'retreat' he could find with her, is scarcely inviting: 'at the back of the house, with a view of a scrap of old garden that had been saved from modern ravage'. The ironic imagery of setting is meticulously detailed and pointed: 'To sit there was, as he had told her before, to see life reflected for the time in ideally kept pewter.' The shift of tenses here into the pluperfect, and the suggestion of a short-lived future too, perfectly exemplifies James's minute narrative tact. Details such as this acquit the scene of any charge of raw sarcasm, and contribute to an extended ironical appreciation of true and of transient values.

Strether is now 'out, in truth, as far as it was possible to be', and although there is a question of 'getting in again', the movement must be unencumbered by gain. Maria's offer of a haven 'might well have tempted. It built him softly round, it roofed him warmly over, it rested, all so firm, on selection. And what ruled selection was beauty and knowledge'. Yet even these things, which Strether's experience has taught him to appreciate, are now an unnecessary constriction. Beauty and truth, in this sense, are ways and means for vision, not a goal. Strether recognizes that they are not of the order of the eternal: 'so far as they made his opportunity, they made it only for a moment'.

The final movement for Strether must be onwards and alone, not because he has been deserted, nor because he has abandoned his fellows, but because in his near-tragic stature, he has no fellows: there is no one else in the novel who 'can't do anything else' but acknowledge and be ruled by what is 'dreadfully right'. In his final words, there is no uncertainty, but a reassurance to Maria, an approval, an almost existential acceptance of the order of things: 'Then there we are.'

Coming out of the development of the novel, comprehensible only within the terms set up there, and in return, lending direction to the flow of the whole, Strether's last words carry the two qualities of stillness and movement, that characterize the vanishing-point. The 'negative capability' lacking in *The Sacred Fount* is achieved here: an end without finality. As Eliot puts it:

Except for the point, the still point,
There would be no dance, and there is only the dance.

IV

'World Enough and Time':
The Expansive Principle in
The Wings of the Dove

LIKE THE opening of a Shakespearian tragedy, the first book of
The Wings of the Dove does not lead us to the heroine, but into the
world of her chief antagonist, Kate Croy. Nor is this a superficial
introduction, playing on the reader's impatience to add piquancy
to the entrance of Milly Theale. Rather, like Milton's Satan, or
like Iago, Kate is given a setting, potential, and constrictions
enough to excite our sympathy. Indeed, some critics have taken
this so far as to consider Kate, with her well-founded grievances
and her demonstrable spirit in the face of them, James's unrecognized heroine. Milly would, as James recorded in his Preface to
The Wings of the Dove, '*herself* be the opposition—to the catastrophe
announced by the associated Fates' (*The Art of the Novel*, p. 290);
but the first step was to 'create the predicament promptly and
build it up solidly, so that it should have for us as much as possible
its ominous air of awaiting her' (ibid. 294).

From its opening *The Wings of the Dove* is clearly of a different
kind from the preceding novel: not more complex, in that
complexity involves variety subordinated to a single pattern;
but compounded of distinct elements. The imaginative force is
outward, straining towards a meaning not to be found within the
work, but beyond it, escaping the constrictions of Kate's mean
world and of Milly's death-bound 'box': a meaning Densher will
come to recognize only in its absence, as an opportunity passed:
the state to which those who can never again be 'as we were'
might have aspired.

This obstreperous, disjunctive tendency involves many of the
formalities of *The Ambassadors,* but uses them differently, setting
them against each other, without subordination to a single guiding
rule like that of 'perspective'. Reading the book is difficult, and

we are tempted to simplify in retrospect, although the abrupt shifts of mode, of time and place, of mood, prevent this as we read on. The recurrent motif of the journey, the 'way', Kate and Densher's search for a place, and Milly's for a time to live, is not like Strether's movement towards 'placing' experience. The movement of *The Wings of the Dove* is more erratic; the centres of consciousness and locations are more varied; though the novel ends where it began, everything is changed. Neither Milly nor the lovers find 'world enough and time'; the dominant tone is the elegiac recognition of a lost future: 'We shall never be again as we were.'

The strenuous relation of parts to the whole of *The Wings of the Dove* precludes either of the simple approaches which *The Ambassadors*, with its balanced structure, invites. Neither a straightforward reading through the work, nor the critical paradigm which regulates the whole and can clarify each part, is adequate for the later novel. *The Wings of the Dove* is not without pattern, repeated motifs of imagery and diction; but due weight must be given in analysis to the reading experience of disproportion, shifts of mode and texture, which the unifying structural devices counterbalance. Where *The Ambassadors* uses duality, *The Wings of the Dove* has multiplicity, contraries which are not reconciled, but challenge and supersede each other; different approaches are tried and abandoned, both in the narrative, for the reader, and in the characters' understanding of their own story. Hypothesis and extravagance characterize *The Wings of the Dove,* and resolution comes not from a reconciliation, but from the rejection of excess. The process and effect of the novel are much less poised than in *The Ambassadors*.

The Wings of the Dove works with 'sufficiently solid *blocks* of wrought material' (*The Art of the Novel*, p. 296), and we must do the same, although this crude approach is modified on reflection. *The Ambassadors* is a novel where change is anticipated through the ironic narrative method, and part of the modulation in pace is due to the fact that Strether's greater consciousness brings him level with both narrator and reader, so that the progression slows to one of experience and reaction, rather than the 'foreshortened' pace of irony. *The Wings of the Dove* rarely looks forward to resolution: ahead is death, for Milly, an arranged marriage for Kate; for Densher, 'up to his neck' in Milly's 'general . . . kind of

beatific mildness' (p. 424), there is no future from the moment
Kate sleeps with him: 'Wasn't it perhaps even rather the value
that possessed *him*, kept him thinking of it and waiting on it,
turning round and round it and making sure of it again from this
side and from that?' (p. 442) Like Shakespeare's account of lust,
'Mad in pursuit and in possession so,/Had, having, and in quest
to have, extreme' (Sonnet 129), or like Macbeth, the tragic hero,
caught between tenses and losing both present and eternity,
Densher, knowing 'that he might on any other system go straight
to destruction' (p. 455), is reduced for a significant, though short,
part of the novel, to the trap of a false position, and a riddling
defence: 'he best kept everything in place by not hesitating or
fearing, as it were, to let himself go—go in the direction, that is
to say, of staying' (p.456). At the end, the wandering Milly is
freed from the 'box, their great common anxiety . . . in this grim
breathing-space . . . the practical question of life' (p. 207), and
endowed with an infinity of space and time, while Kate and Densher find like Dante's unlawful lovers that they are just beyond
limbo, with the post-tragic recognition of irrevocable loss.

The structure of *The Wings of the Dove* has a complex relation to
this elegiac effect. James was not happy about the imperfect
realization of his narrative idea, and bewails in his Preface the
'makeshift middle' and 'latter half, that is the false and deformed
half,' of *The Wings of the Dove* (*The Art of the Novel*, p. 302). For us,
however, the distortions of form convey the constrictions of
existence for the characters, whose circumstances cramp their
development.

The first 'block' of material is characterized by 'not only no
deformities but . . . a positively close and felicitous application of
method . . .' (*The Art of the Novel*, p. 302). Its control, density and
multiplicity of aspects challenge each stance we take up, demonstrating the need for continued alertness in avoiding clichés of
response.

The opening scene invites this kind of 'recognized' approach,
through the 'solidity of specification' of Kate's world, and through
a narrative mode which owes a great deal to Dickens and Thackeray
and the realistic tradition of the early Victorian novel. The
reader assumes a role in relation to the material presented, which
he is later to be brought through different narrative techniques
to abandon. This shift of attitudes will alter not only his sympa-

thies and opinion of Kate, but the very readiness to adopt any fixed stance. It is a Jamesian version of the Shandean technique for stimulating the attention of the reader: a narrative irony which brings the operation of the novel itself into question.

Of this there is no hint at the outset. The air is one of control: the slight extravagance of style seems to offer an assurance of the author's reliance on the intelligence and experience of the novel reader. Thus in the very first sentence, a simple inversion in the opening clause, the use of a pronoun followed by its reference in apposition, mimes Kate's impatience and the check of self-control; but it also, apparently incidentally, invites the reader to enter a bond of superior knowledge with the author, offering a compliment on his understanding: 'She waited, Kate Croy, for her father to come in . . .' There is no portentousness to suggest that this is a hint of the tone and action of the whole novel, with its restrained impatience, and preoccupied attention to the coming event. On the contrary, James plays on the attitude invoked in his first sophisticated nod to the reader. Kate's father kept her 'unconscionably': the word, we suppose, is her own, though it also seems to be the narrator's, invoking Austenian echoes of an age of decorum and predictable sentiment for the novel reader. Though it may hint Mr. Croy's lack of scruples, the main force of the adverb is in its pedantic, archaic tone. From this note, the irritable precision of diction increases, gradually converting the 'complimentary' authorial reliance on the reader's intelligence into a functional trust, necessary to the rendering of Kate's mood. The syntactic sequence is broken by parenthesis, weighted with a change of tense; and it is not certain whether the implied viewpoint is that of Kate herself or of a putative observer in the room:

She waited, Kate Croy, for her father to come in, but he kept her unconscionably, and there were moments at which she showed herself, in the glass over the mantel, a face positively pale with the irritation that had brought her to the point of going away without sight of him.

(p. 3)

The shift from the decorum of 'unconscionably', through the alliterative intensity of 'positively pale', to the phrase 'to the point', which will be picked up in the next sentence's 'It was at this point', is no decorative play, but a manipulation of the reader's reactions between various different modes. Between the waiting for her father to come in, and the point of going away, Kate changes from the first female subject, the one who can appear unnamed, who must surely be the heroine, to a self-willed young lady whose qualities we hesitate to approve without further assurance.

The first section pursues this line, somewhere between the traditional realistic novel and a strenuous refusal, in the style of Meredith, to follow the expectations set up, from diction to syntax as well as in character. Kate's world seems to 'bristle', rather as Milly's did in prospect for James, with meanings, relations, and forms. There is the rhetoric of a Dickensian vision, with its use of repetition: 'The vulgar little street, in this view, offered scant relief from the vulgar little room.' That this is Kate's own view, and that it is to some extent an artificial one, a patterned response deployed to contain the horror of her circumstances, is also obliquely suggested by the diction, which can reach a non-Dickensian level of abstraction:

The vulgar little street, in this view, offered scant relief from the vulgar little room; its main office was to suggest to her that the narrow black house-fronts, adjusted to a standard that would have been low even for backs, constituted quite the publicity implied by such privacies.

(p. 3)

Yet the same devices, repetition, balance and rhythmic alliterative patterning, can be used to create a view encompassing Kate herself in a Hamlet-like heaviness of despair:

Each time she turned in again, each time, in her impatience, she gave him up, it was to sound to a deeper depth, while she tasted the faint, flat emanation of things, the failure of fortune and of honour. (p. 3)

This passage has a resonance of expression which comes of the fusion of narrative imagination with that implied for Kate herself; but it does not abandon the 'distance' established earlier. Nor, though it uses that consciousness, does it wholly subsume it in imaginative energy. There is a measure of vigour about the almost punning synaesthesia of 'sound', taste and touch, all applied to abstract qualities, which transcends its context. The implication is that Kate herself is aware of this, and is better able to cope with the situation than the rhetoric of despair would imply:

To feel the street, to feel the room, to feel the table-cloth and the centre-piece and the lamp, gave her a small, salutary sense, at least, of neither shirking nor lying. This whole vision was the worst thing yet . . . and for what had she come but for the worst? (p. 4)

The rhetoric of this opening manipulates the reader's reactions; and such overt confessions do not annul the effect. They add a further awareness, which qualifies the inclination to credit our structures of context, stylistic placing, for each reaction. Though we may create such patterns, prompted by the experience as readers which the narrator has already established we enjoy, we can do so only in the expectation of having them disrupted.

The temptation to try out formal patterns develops a dual function. It becomes a method of characterization as well as a technique of representation. Mediating between the powers of the novelist and those of the character, this challenges both our comprehension and our tacit assumptions about narrative control. We find this first with Kate. Tracing the impressions of her surroundings back to their source, we take it that this is in her mind. But there is no clear line dividing her musings from the author's exposition. The blurring of this boundary, counterpoising the operations of consciousness itself, creates a mood of hypothesis, yet suggests authority. Expression involves simultaneously breaking down and building up narrative structure: a complex, shifting process. The nearest thing to an acknowledgement of this comes obliquely, through an odd metaphor, switching from verbal to musical terms:

Her father's life, her sister's, her own, that of her two lost brothers— the whole history of their house had the effect of some fine florid, voluminous phrase, say even a musical, that dropped first into words, into notes, without sense, and then, hanging unfinished, into no words, no notes at all. (p. 4)

The musical metaphor prefigures later characterizations of *The Wings of the Dove* in terms operatic, besides the 'tune' of the mental cash-registers which begin to sound before this scene is over, in Kate's offer to choose her father before her aunt, for a consideration: 'I'll wash my hands of her for you to just that tune.' Meanwhile, however, it is merely one of a series of expressions which endow Kate herself, either explicitly or by implication, with the imagination of a novelist. The distance between

her awareness and her conception of herself, her situation, noted
above as an aspect of style, acquires an extra force here. Kate's
view unlike the romantic Isabel Archer's, unlike that of a Susan
Stringham with her fairytale princess, is poised, distinct. She
sees the situation as a matter of elements and forms, and of the
relation between them: character and motive, plot and theme;
though she also shows something of the novelist's delight in
expression, a wry turn of phrase:

Why should a set of people have been put in motion, on such a scale,
and with such an air of being equipped for a profitable journey, only to
break down without an accident, to stretch themselves in the wayside
dust without a reason?   (p. 4)

The transition from this view of the novel to an even more
formal one is easy: a matter of animating abstractions and
granting them a role in the drama of consciousness:

The answer to these questions was not in Chirk Street, but the questions
themselves bristled there, and the girl's repeated pause before the mirror
and the chimney-place might have represented her nearest approach to
an escape from them.   (p. 4)

James himself made a similar transition from experience to
analysis, in the episode which biographical critics such as Leon
Edel have seen as the core of *The Wings of the Dove*. Matthiessen
quotes a letter from James to Grace Norton on the death of
Minny Temple:

Her life was a strenuous, almost passionate question, which my mind,
at least, lacked the energy to offer the elements of any answer for.[1]

Kate's analysis is prolonged with an abstraction akin to the
modern structuralist view of character and its function: 'She
might have seen that, after all, she was not herself a fact in the
collapse.' Like the structuralists, she uses the metaphor of language
to convey this form: 'She hadn't given up yet, and the broken
sentence, if she was the last word, *would* end with a sort of meaning.'
The sense of character as a force, rather than simply an element
of plot, which is created by having Kate devise impressions of
herself and her environment, is an animating principle of a world
whose 'solidity of specification' extends beyond surfaces and

[1] F. O. Matthiessen, *Henry James: The Major Phase* (1944, rpt. 1963), p. 48.

forms. The vigour which gives imaginative being to Kate's environment remains as a reserve of power, The 'novelist's imagination' with which Kate will essay a plot for herself and Densher, subordinating Milly's life to her scheme, has a destructive power which is seen also in Aunt Maud, and even in Susan Stringham: it is a perverse attribute of the society where 'The worker in one connection was the worked in another' (p. 148).

Kate's presentation, as well as her character, offers her as the first of several, perhaps the most richly developed save Milly, of those 'formed at once for being and for seeing'. There is a peculiar irony in her father's figuration of her 'case':

> 'You can describe yourself—*to* yourself—as, in a fine flight, giving up your aunt for me; but what good, I should like to know, would your fine flight do me?'
>
> (p. 13)

The imagery of flight, the 'weighted' words, 'fine', 'good', the theme of giving up, the wrought emphasis of the verb 'do': all these are fully recoverable only in retrospect. Looking back, Kate's case reflects Milly's before it works upon it. Densher too will have some symbolic apprehension of their common 'box': his upbringing, like Kate's, marks him; like Milly he is formed as a cosmopolitan:

> But brave enough though his descent to English earth, he had passed, by the way, through zones of air that had left their ruffle on his wings, had been exposed to initiations ineffaceable. Something had happened to him that could never be undone.
>
> (p. 79)

Imaginative links such as these give resonance to the structure made verbally explicit and effected through style, in which the pervading consciousness of the novelist informs the characters themselves: in imaginative terms, as well as those of motive and plot, the workers in one connection are the worked in another; the interested and the interesting are two sides of James's 'medal'. Kate's consciousness promotes a particular level of awareness, and a reflexive sense of attention from the reader:

> It wouldn't be the first time she had seen herself obliged to accept with smothered irony other people's interpretation of her conduct. She often ended by giving up to them—it seemed really the way to live—the version that met their convenience.
>
> (p. 21)

Kate exercises intellectual control through the process of making images: an approach whose sophisticated indirection is conveyed through the terms used to describe it:

> It was not in truth, however, that the forces with which, as Kate felt, she would have to deal were those most suggested by an image simple and broad; she was learning, after all, each day, to know her companion, and what she had already most perceived was the mistake of trusting to easy analogies. (p. 26)

Kate has, however, a vivid imagination: she sees the nature of relations in the cannibalistic terms which will recur throughout *The Wings of the Dove*. The exaggeration of her diction provides a cover for the introduction of ideas which will survive the discounting of excess, while the image in turn colours the artifice of intellect and makes it acceptable: 'There were always people to snatch at one, and it would never occur to *them* that they were eating one up. They did that without tasting.' (p. 28)

The awareness revealed in Kate is less highly developed at this stage in Densher: 'You would have got fairly near him by making out in his eyes the potential recognition of ideas; but you would have quite fallen away on the question of the ideas themselves'. Where Kate's intelligence ranges over 'facts', Densher's approach is a less abstract apprehension of experience. What is realized through word play for Kate is frequently shown in setting, the 'facts' of existence, for the young man. The novelist's imagination gives place, point, to the moral through the imagined world; there is a series of puns relating the two: building up the structure of the novel as a 'realistic' document, and breaking down naturalism through its intellectual manipulation: creating the conditions of meaning: 'It was a medium, a setting, and to that extent, after all, a dreadful sign of life; so that it fairly put a point into her answer.'

F. O. Matthiessen warned of the dangers of excessive stress on imagery in James criticism, that a novel cannot depend on this element of expression to the same extent as a poem or play. Yet Vernon Lee, before this, advocated careful attention to words, as the material of 'Expression and Impression', or the relation of writer and reader. 'Words', she points out with comprehensive simplicity, 'will be efficacious for various reasons: chiefly their familiarity on the one hand, and their unfamiliarity on the other'.[1]

[1] *The Handling of Words* (1923), p. 45.

A modern critic, Kenneth Graham, notes another reason for scrupulous attention: 'All of this novel's exhaustive and cunning methods—so analysable and so admirable for their own sake—have for their end not self-display or a purely formal beauty but dramatic exploration.'[1]

The 'key vocabulary' of *The Wings of the Dove*, irreducible to Maria Gostrey's 'cases or categories' in *The Ambassadors,* derives from a multiplicity of minds proposing with conscious art a variety of artistic paradigms. The imaginative power of these words is as subject to variation as their semantic function, and they contribute to the texture of the novel as well as its thematic development. The senses of space and of direction are both strong, but do not always support each other: besides 'position' we have 'point' (ambiguously directional and static), the 'spot', 'place', 'space' itself; there are 'the way', 'line', 'direction', 'journey', 'flight'; but there are also the 'abyss', the 'labyrinth', the 'maze', and the 'clue'. Amongst verbs, 'go' and 'do' are significant. The encompassing view is that of 'the world', and the ironic pointer, the clichés, 'man of the world' and 'woman of the world'. For the world is both a limitation and an opportunity for existence. The relationships of exploitation and reciprocity conveyed not only in the 'do', but 'give' and 'take', 'possess' and 'work' paradigms, permeate society because they govern life itself; the 'hand of Fate' is amongst those hands which are lent, given, taken, or washed; then there are the hands that are tied, the underhand, the handling. Amidst this structure of words, Kate, in her Hamletian prison, can manipulate a *double entendre*; but it is Milly who triumphs with Mercutian irony over the solemnity of those who feel 'that what you had most to do, under the discipline of life, or of death, was really to feel your situation as grave' (p. 89). She makes a riddle of her situation:

Since I've lived all these years as if I were dead, I shall die, no doubt, as if I were alive . . . You'll never really know where I am. Except, indeed, when I'm gone; and then you'll only know where I'm not.

(p. 165)

Mrs. Stringham 'would have felt . . . that she joked about it . . . had not her scale from grave to gay been a thing of such un-nameable shades that her contrasts were never sharp'. The intelli-

[1] *Henry James: The Drama of Fulfilment* (1975), pp. 160–1.

gence, like money in James's remarks on Balzac (1902), may perhaps be seen as a resource to be subordinated to the imagination.

The verbal density of the opening of *The Wings of the Dove* is complemented by a range of devices in action and theme which build up a cumulative effect, and reverberate in retrospect, or in a reading which is not the first. Kate's meetings with her father and sister compound the sense of inexorability in being 'beastly poor'. Lionel Croy's scheming prefigures Aunt Maud's and Kate's; Kate's waiting, at the outset, sets a pattern for the whole novel. Above all there is the manipulation and jockeying for social position. The world of which Milly is not a woman is squarely seen, though it is neither delightful nor stable. The hints of loss begin before Milly appears, when Kate looks out and sees that 'the world was different—whether for worse or for better—from her rudimentary readings, and it gave her the feeling of a wasted past' (p. 23). Amidst the flux, the only unchanging characteristic is that of exclusion. Like an amalgam of the Mad Hatter's tea table and the later Jacob's room, it is a place where there is no room, a setting neither defining nor defined by Milly, despite the wordly power of her wealth.

After Kate's entry, the introduction of Merton Densher is not auspicious. First characterized by Lionel Croy as 'some blackguard without a penny', and first named by Marion, he appears as a displaced and apparently aimless person, wandering in Kensington Gardens during the day, when most men are at work. The continual difficulty for Densher, a cruel *double entendre* in Venice, 'that he had nowhere to "take" his love' (p. 254), contrasts pointedly with Kate's assurance to her father: 'I shall go my way —as I see my way' (p. 19). Densher's relation to Kate is a kind of bond, which she characterizes with unwitting irony, in her declaration: 'I engage myself to you for ever' (p. 80).

The ambivalence of their relationship is revealed to the reader from the first, in a brave recognition of their differences which is compounded by the recurrence of words carrying financial connotations. Remembering 'the tune' of Kate's family, the reader finds the clichés of romance invested with a hard material value, which the lovers will be unable to ignore:

Any deep harmony that might eventually govern them would not be the result of their having much in common—having anything, in fact, but their affection; and would really find its explanation in some sense, on the part of each, of being poor where the other was rich.

(pp. 43-4)

The metaphor is robbed of poetic force, and language itself makes plain their state of affairs: it is a small triumph of common sense over sensibility: a pun with no spark of delight.

Kate shows ominous signs of accepting this 'precious unlikeness', and of establishing through her attitude the distance between her and Densher. The degeneration from appreciation to possessiveness, and thence to manipulation, is appallingly easy: it is encompassed in two sentences, between 'He gave her a long look' and 'she . . . took it intensely home':

He gave her a long look, and whatever else people who wouldn't let her alone might have wished, for her advancement, his long looks were the thing in the world she could never have enough of. What she felt was that, whatever might happen, she must keep them, must make them most completely her possession; and it was already strange enough that she reasoned, or at all events began to act, as if she might work them in with other and alien things, privately cherish them and yet, as regards the rigour of it, pay no price. She measured it 'every which' way, took it intensely home, that they were lovers; she rejoiced to herself, and frankly to him, in this wearing of the name; but, distinguished creature that she was, she took a view of this character that scarce squared with the conventional.

(p. 25)

Through an alternating integration and disjunction of the effect of syntax and that of vocabulary, this passage achieves a sense of precarious imbalance between statement and development: the inexorability of the process is as it were unwillingly revealed. Densher is the subject of the first clause, and the verb 'gave' picks up the 'give and take' theme already established as one basis of relationships; form and substance are one. But the next part of the sentence, with Kate's mind as the implied medium, disintegrates into a complexity of clauses and sub-clauses, double negatives and subjunctives, finishing with an emphatic statement ugly in its concluding particle and uneasy in the complementary use of a plural and a singular noun: 'his long looks were the thing in the world she could never have enough of'. The next sentence begins clearly from Kate's standpoint, with another

declaration, a cleft sentence with a deictic pronoun;[1] but the
rhetorical control counterpoises feeling with form, and the repetition, 'what . . . whatever . . . she must keep them, must make
them . . .' creates a sense of too much protestation. A semicolon,
a stronger point than the comma of the preceding sentence, marks
a turn, not a continuation in sense. The next deictic construction
points a transition from Kate's stance to a judgemental one, for
we now see what Kate could not yet admit freely to herself. The
hesitation, 'or at all events' seems to qualify, but actually changes
the direction of the sentence; and its prevarication is picked up
in the subtle shift from the assurance of particularity, 'the thing
in the world', to the compromise of multiplicity, 'with other and
alien things'. The ironic overtones of the verb 'work', and the
damning materialism of 'pay no price' show the verbal effects
once again fusing with the syntactic, in a vision more complex
and more compromising than seemed possible at the outset.
Densher is left behind, protesting at the security of simple cliché,
but with the unspoken sexual drama focused in the ambiguity of
his resentment:

Densher, though he agreed with her, found himself moved to wonder
at her simplifications, her values. Life might prove difficult—was
evidently going to; but meanwhile they had each other, and that was
everything. This was her reasoning, but meanwhile, for *him*, each
other was what they didn't have, and it was just the point.

On this level of syntactic and semantic subtlety James 'works'
the reader to an appreciation of the small, significant shifts of
stance which may appear in the alteration of subject, mood, or
form of a verb, but translate on the scale of action to a substantial
change of direction. This is the groundwork for James's broader
verbal effects: the ones of which the characters themselves seem
aware, yet which, lacking the fundamental understanding supplied
to the reader, they cannot always 'place' securely. Thus Densher
and Kate cover the anomalies of their position by adopting just
that balance of interest and amusement 'colloquially and con-
veniently classed by both of them as funny' (p. 54); but this is a
poise easily upset. The gross examples of Lionel Croy and Marion
in the first book, with their debasing of 'duty', their slang, show

---

[1] Seymour Chatman offers an extended analysis of the use of this construction in
The Later Style of Henry James (1972) Chs. 9, 10.

the extremes to which hyperbole can go when 'the family sentiment, in our vulgarised, brutalised life, has gone utterly to pot'
(p. 15). There is a danger in the lovers having 'settled, for intercourse, on the short cut of the fantastic and the happy language
of exaggeration' (p. 56). Though Kate, 'lucid and ironic . . . knew
no merciful muddle' Densher simply cannot produce 'twaddle'.
To him, 'We're a caution'; to Kate, ' "Yes", she took it straight
up; "We're hideously intelligent" ' (p. 62).

This distinction of sensibility is revealed in other ways, through
non-verbal signs. Kate's materialism is projected from a time
before the opening of the novel, and given substance through a
series of adjectives and heavy, repetitive phrasing, which converts
a 'figure' into solid fact: 'The tall, rich, heavy house at Lancaster
Gate, on the other side of the Park and the long South Kensington
stretches, had figured to her, through childhood, through
girlhood, as the remotest limit of her vague young world' (p.
22). She sees Aunt Maud's personality in terms of stature: 'prodigious, and the great mass of it loomed' (p. 25): this is just; but
we wonder about a similar attitude to Densher: 'He represented
what her life had never given her . . . all the high, dim things she
lumped together as of the mind' (p. 44). There is a crudity about
the descent from a Keatsian 'high, dim' view to the solid 'lump'
which may indicate Kate's own awareness of the bathos; but it
does not cancel out the effect for the reader. It is harsher than
the irony of disparity between 'weakness' and 'strength', cliché
and logical thought, the abstract and material, in Densher's
aspirations: 'The fact of his weakness, as he called it, for life—his
strength merely for thought—life, he logically opined, was what
he must somehow arrange to annexe and possess' (p. 44).

Densher is not blind to the material, but alien to it, in a way
that Kate, with her 'dire accessibility to pleasure from such sources'
is not. Densher can figure himself and Kate, from Mrs. Lowder's
point of view, in terms of visible assets and market forces. Mrs.
Stringham will later do the same for Milly, who 'couldn't get
away from her wealth'. Her image of Milly as a princess weighs
like a physical burden: 'a perfectly palpable quality . . . the weight
under which she fancied her companion's admirable head occasionally, and ever so submissively, bowed' (p. 101). The fact that
such formulations are not restricted to Milly, but extended to
Kate, indicates that they express a quality of their world rather

than a peculiarity of Milly herself. The myth-making process is part of the manipulative categorization of other people, and an assertion of the self through its environment: expression, rather than communication. Densher finds this at its most crudely effective in Aunt Maud's house: 'the message of her massive, florid furniture, the immense expression of her signs and symbols ... so almost abnormally affirmative, so aggressively erect, were the awful ornaments that syllabled his hostess's story. . . . It was the language of the house itself that spoke to him . . .' (pp. 65–6). It is the *difference* in languages that is revealing: 'These things finally represented for him a portentous negation of his own world of thought—of which, for that matter, in the presence of them, he became for the first time hopelessly aware.' Though Densher appreciates Aunt Maud, and perceives the need to 'keep setting up "codes" ' with 'the great public mind', the two worlds of thought and things are beyond communication: his compromise cannot defeat her domination.

The incompatibility of these worlds is dramatized through Milly. 'Superficially so absent' in the first two books, her appearance now, apparently inconsequent, actually follows directly on Densher's admission to Kate of 'why we [men] 've such an abysmal need of you [women]' (p. 84). The imaginative introduction is ironically apt; and the process of deflecting the reader's expectations, which marked presentation of Kate, continues with Milly.

It is 'the two ladies', 'lone women', travellers whose bravery consists in defying warnings about the weather, who appear in Switzerland, 'reinforced by a travelling-library of instructive volumes'. A less portentous introduction could scarcely be conceived. A paragraph of such small claims barely allows expression to 'the impatience', the 'bolder dreams' of the younger amidst the cosy pomposities of indirect statement. The obliquities of diction cloud the point of view, but we come to realize that our approach to Milly is manipulated through Mrs. Stringham, who

moved, the admirable Mrs. Stringham, in a fine cloud of observation and suspicion; she was in the position, as she believed, of knowing much more about Milly Theale than Milly herself knew, and yet of having to darken her knowledge as well as make it active.　　(p. 88)

The 'duplicities and labyrinths' of the narrative, subtle and modest here, are a variation on the method of the opening book of *The Wings of the Dove*. Mrs. Stringham creates narrative structures, devoting 'personal subtlety' to 'a new personal relation', not with Kate's authoritative direction, but with a passivity explicable psychologically as a reaction to Milly, but conveyed imaginatively in the very manipulation of the author himself. James's mastery is demonstrated in this shift of tone, from Kate's authority to Susan Stringham's apparent helplessness, which makes the same technique serve a different imaginative function, even while both duplicities support the author's refusal to set the narrative stance firmly enough for it to become a limitation on developing understanding. Mrs. Stringham's 'subtlety' is no nearer Kate's than the 'design' of the two ladies is to Lionel Croy's 'design', or their 'flights of fancy' to the 'fine flight' he attributes to Kate. Nor is it further away. Susan Stringham has a novelist's imagination, different in power and in kind from Kate's; so, to some extent, has Milly. 'Experience', for James, was 'the very atmosphere of the mind', and the 'solidity of specification' of the novel world goes beyond the material furniture, the geography of houses, countries, weather conditions, to the forms of feeling and of thought. There is a refined relation in *The Wings of the Dove* between the operations of society and those of the narrative structure: the workers in one connection are the worked in another, and the whole alternates between overt display and duplicity, conscious manipulation and exposure to unseen forces. The process of reading conveys the effects of the world, but the correspondence is marked by the 'fine cloud' of shifting authority and stance in relation to the material on which the imagination works.

The obliquity of the narrative does not extend to concealing this variation: on the contrary, the overt literary, dramatic, and pictorial references frequently draw attention to an element of artifice which is effective less obtrusively on the level of syntax itself. Yet not all Susan Stringham's modest literary pretensions, nor the complacency of her 'personal subtlety', have sufficiently alerted many critics to the fallibility of her imagination. Though Milly is first presented, with a subtlety so consistent that it must be deliberate, through her companion's eyes, such are the reader's desire for certainty and the habit of stereotyping character that Mrs. Stringham's version is often accepted, even on a second or later reading, as substantially accurate, and the myth of the fragile princess is sustained more readily than the robust and extraordinary character James actually creates.

That this is less the result of a flaw in the narrative than the outcome of deliberate vagueness may be concluded from the degree to which the author supports the 'princess' vision. Though it is qualified so that the complexities of Milly's personality and of her position in relation to others are not constricted by the 'heroine formula', she is never robbed of the status originally attributed to her by Mrs. Stringham. She gains other qualities without losing the potential for the first.

This is a helpful perspective on the much-discussed Alpine scene. It is not usually noted that the viewpoint throughout this episode is that of the romantic Mrs. Stringham. All we know of Milly's actions is that she goes for a walk alone, abandons her *Tauchnitz*, sits 'at her ease' on the edge of a precipice where the view is magnificent, and reappears 'late in the afternoon' with a wish to alter her plans and set off again in the morning. The interpretation of these events comes from Mrs. Stringham, and the view of Milly's 'liability to slip, to slide, to leap, to be precipitated' which has led critics to 'slip, slide, perish/ Decay with imprecision', is hers rather than the author's.

Our trust in Mrs. Stringham's interpretation can partly be accounted for by her indirect literary authority in this scene. The episode derives its special status from the biblical flavour of the imagery; this has a force which seems to imply the author's warrant. F. O. Matthiessen dismisses this as 'carelessness and obliviousness on James's part' (*The Major Phase*, p. 65), finding, 'One thing notably absent from such a compelling image [as the 'temptation'] is any apparent awareness by James of its full religious implications' (ibid. 64). Oscar Cargill, however, sees this scene as part of a larger pattern: 'a thickening of Christian imagery in the book which is irrelevant until the second apotheosis [of Milly's appearance at her party in Venice]' (*The Novels of Henry James*, p. 345). We cannot suppose either that James was oblivious of the religious implications of his imagery or that he abandoned his usual authorial consciousness in deploying this imagery here. Setting the images in the context James provides qualifies their effect, however.

Mrs. Stringham's lack of experience and abundance of romance have already appeared. In this scene her reactions range through several clichés. There is the detective story, with its simplicity and repetitive phrasing: 'She struck herself as hovering like a spy, applying tests, laying traps, concealing signs' (p. 98). Susan's account of Milly's 'expressive, irregular, exquisite' features for 'the stupid' is novelettish: 'When Milly smiled it was a public event—when she didn't it was a chapter of history' (p. 99). The tendency to categorize experience is suggested by the 'well-thumbed case' of Mrs. Stringham's past. Her 'pilgrimage' is a strange compound of the biblical and the Romantic, with 'the taste of honey and the luxury of milk' mingling with the 'sound of cattle-bells and the rush of streams, the fragrance of trodden balms and the dizziness of deep gorges'.

The vision of the 'princess in a conventional tragedy' (p. 101) is well placed in this mountainous setting; and Susan sustains the picture with her view of 'a bewildered old woman, a very fearful person to behold', who might equally have come from the Brothers Grimm or from Wordsworth, but who is certainly larger than life. The narrator's distance from Mrs. Stringham's interpretation is clear at this point in the gentle comedy of the 'very fearful' yet 'bewildered' old lady, the mockery of 'our unappeased enquirer', and the display of his greater knowledge: 'What on earth had become of her? Mrs. Stringham, I hasten to add, was within a few minutes to see.' The mountainous scenery is fitted to Mrs. Stringham's 'abysmal' imagination rather than to Milly, 'at her ease'; and the half-echo of Othello's 'steep-down gulfs' in Susie's 'gulfs of air' is a small ironic pointer to this fact.

The cluster of clichés at this crisis of 'good fortune, if not . . . the worst', marks a descent into pure melodrama, with the absolute simplicity of 'a mere maiden', the vague horror of 'whatever was beneath', and the reaction: 'Mrs. Stringham stifled a cry'. Any aspirations to literary analogy, perhaps with Milton's Lady in *Comus* and her 'thousand fantasies/ . . . of calling shapes and beckoning shadows dire', are satirized through the literal view: 'A thousand thoughts, for the minute, roared in the first lady's ears, but without reaching, as it happened, Milly's. The Miltonic 'syllable men's names' becomes Mrs. Stringham's patterned response, expressed with the archaic verb form of the Gothic novel: 'as if a sound, a syllable, must have produced the start that would be fatal'. The 'horrible, hidden obsession' is more likely, in this account, to be Susan's than the girl's. So, equally, is the perhaps exaggerated recoil: 'that if the girl was deeply and recklessly meditating there, she was not meditating a jump . . . She was looking down on the kingdoms of the earth . . .' (p. 104).

The qualification, once noticed, is great. The disparity between the biblical phrase and the idea 'that of itself might well go to the brain' neutralizes the exalted tone of the image. There is a hint of denial in the account of what Mrs. Stringham 'saw, or believed she did'; and the strategic retreat: 'It would probably be safe enough to withdraw as she had come'. Mrs. Stringham has no further doubts: on the contrary, the certainty arises that 'the future was not to consist for her princess in the form of any sharp or simple release from the human predicament'. The whole episode thus serves to 'feed Mrs. Stringham's flame', and to provide a vision for us of Milly's great worth, without requiring, or indeed permitting, extended exegesis. It works, in fact, tangentially to the narrative: a separate little process, contributing to the effect of the whole incidentally.

After this quasi-operatic 'Wagner overture', Milly herself slips into the novel unobtrusively: 'The girl said nothing, when they met . . .'. The texture of the novel changes with their conversation. Yet the artful control of the narrative is not abandoned. The emotion generated during Mrs. Stringham's imaginings and undercut by the narrative method, is here taken up again. The 'logic' of this is poetic rather than analytic: it is an effect which works in reading but does not yield to critical analysis.

The existence of a level of meaning just beyond the surface of the narrative, and accessible only through such tangential paths, is attested in *The Wings of the Dove* through devices ranging from the fanciful to the absurd. This threatens form rather than elaborating upon it, and acknowledges what Susan Stringham terms 'some deeper depth than she had touched . . . the suspected presence of something behind [Milly's state]' (p. 97).

The 'open' conversation, 'where more is meant than meets the ear', is peculiarly able to modulate between these levels of controlled farce and comic grotesque. The manipulation of flagrant rudeness with no more than a veneer of pleasantry is the first note of conversation in *The Wings of the Dove*, when Lionel Croy and his daughter manœuvre through a negotiation of family ties

and duties in which blatancy replaces tact and the unspeakable is
not avoided. Their outbursts and pauses, repartee and tangential
progression, capture exactly the rhythm of a conversation which
has none of the social manner of Mrs. Brookenham's 'set' in *The
Awkward Age*:

> 'Well then,' said Kate . . . 'Here I am.'
> He showed with a gesture how thoroughly he had taken it in; after
> which, within a few seconds, he had, quite congruously, turned the
> situation about.
> 'Do you really suppose me in a position to justify your throwing
> yourself upon me?'
> She waited a little, but when she spoke it was clear. 'Yes.'
> 'Well then, you're a bigger fool than I should have ventured to
> suppose you.'
> 'Why so? You live. You flourish. You bloom.'
> 'Ah, how you've always hated me!' he murmured with a pensive
> gaze at the window.
> 'No one could be less of a mere cherished memory,' she declared
> as if she had not heard him.   (p. 12)

The rhythmic change from his insult to her staccato challenge;
his murmurous response, with its sequence of slow open vowels,
capped by her reply, whose logic is only superficially disconti-
nuous, tart at first, and slowing to a sweet sarcasm: this is a
match of equals, and tells the reader as much about Kate as it
does about Lionel Croy.

With Marion, blundering into clumsy explicitness, the pace is
quite different, and Kate is clearly in control:

> 'I don't know what makes you talk of Mr. Densher,' she observed.
> 'I talk of him just because you don't. . . . If I name that person
> I suppose it's because I'm so afraid of him. If you want really to know,
> he fills me with terror. If you want really to know, in fact, I dislike him
> as much as I dread him.'   (p. 32)

Marion's insistence is graceless as well as slightly hysterical, and
Kate, 'civil, but perfunctory', is unscathed.

The third conversation in the sequence again involves Kate,
this time with Densher. He is perhaps as intelligent as Lionel Croy,
but like Marion, lacks something of Kate's assured control. The

rhythm of the lovers' speech is swift, broken, yet balanced: quite unlike the lengthy, complex sentences surrounding it, in which their independent appreciations and shifts of position are reached. Though their minds work separately and differently, they take in not only each other's 'short cuts', but also 'periods of silence, side by side, perhaps even more, when "A long engagement!" would have been the final reading of the signs on the part of a passer...' (p. 51). In their first interchange, the sequence of Kate's idea, that Aunt Maud means to write, Aunt Maud's idea, voiced by Densher, that he is 'at the best, not good enough for you?' and Kate's capping, 'Not good enough for *her*', runs swiftly. Densher's reaction is quick, but not certain: an understanding of Kate's stance, rather than an acceptance: ' "Oh, I see. And that's necessary." He put it as a truth rather more than as a question ...'. Already there are signs of their trifling with the absolute, trusting their understanding above the conditions of meaning itself: 'He had put it as a truth rather more than as a question; but there had been plenty of truths between them that each had contradicted. Kate, however, let this one sufficiently pass ...'. In Kate and Densher's conversation from the outset there is an element of dangerous incomprehension, much as later between Kate and Milly, where expression itself becomes concealment: 'the broken talk, brief and sparingly allusive, seems more to cover than to free their sense' (p. 364). The charm of the unspoken is too easily converted into confusion, and lack of communication provides an opportunity for the evasion of responsibility.

Milly's first conversation in *The Wings of the Dove* exhibits something of Kate's range and flexibility, without the 'measurement' provided by Kate's foils: she seems to escape being fully expressed or defined through her own speech. 'With no discussion at all', 'abruptly, with a transition that was like a jump of four thousand miles' (p. 107), Milly conjectures beyond the logic of question and answer. Her stance is clear only to the extent that it is beyond the comprehension of her companion. This lady's eagerness, her start, enthusiasm, wonder, seriousness, stares, anxiety and tenderness, her perplexity and urgent incomprehension all function reflexively to contrast with Milly's implied natural ease. The residue of concern generated by Mrs. Stringham's melodramatic imaginings lends force to Milly's half-expressed questions, without the limitation of specific meaning, so that it seems imaginatively plausible, if scarcely open to explanation, that the white-faced girl, who has just climbed a mountain, should be speculating on how long she will ' "have" everything': particularly as her attitude is almost laconic in comparison with the nervous excitement of her friend.

A further dimension of unstated meaning is hinted in the text through the equivocation over a shifting subject. There is no overt mention of any cause of distress other than illness: but this does not account for Milly's sudden desire to move, nor for the mystery and embarrassment surrounding it. Milly's 'dim show of joy' has a double irony. Besides the tragic dimension: Othello's 'If it were now to die, 'Twere now to be most happy', reverberating with the dark hints of struggle and illness, there is the less portentous mystery of the young man Milly is too shy to name.

The name itself cuts through her evasive gaiety. We already know it. Our slight shock of recognition diverts our attention from the sort of coincidence in plot which would be intractable to logical explanation. A connection is formed, a background of unknown complications suggested, in such a way as to lend the irregularity and surprise of life to the artifice of the eternal triangle. The shock as one structure of expectations is broken down, with the recognition that Milly wants to meet her gentleman friend, turns into the surprise of recognizing his identity. The similarity of the independent reactions of Kate and Milly to the naming of Densher heightens the balance which characterizes their triangle; and the pattern of concealment followed by revelation is an economical device, suggesting further similarities and the inevitability of conflicting interests.

After the caginess of Milly's ambiguity and the challenge of Susan's naming Densher, the narrative slips into an easy reported speech which 'contains' stray significances and emotions and re-establishes the proprieties, before the introduction of the two ladies to London society. The pace of revelation increases here, with the links between Milly and Densher and those between Susie and Aunt Maud revealed, and this acceleration in the shaping of the narrative is transposed by the reader from the intellectual to the imaginative. The opening of the fourth book seems almost a response to this sense, as it directs excitement towards an appreciation of Milly's development:

It had all gone so fast after this that Milly uttered but the truth nearest to hand in saying . . . that she scarce even then knew where she was: the words marking her first full sense of a situation really romantic.

(p. 121)

It is the sensation of speed and relish which characterizes Milly's introduction to London society: the 'world' which she has come down from her mountain to enjoy. Her 'fairy godmother' image of Susie, the vision of Kate as a 'wonderful creature', the bishop, 'with a complicated costume, a voice like an old-fashioned wind instrument, and a face all the portrait of a prelate', all testify to Milly's exhilaration, and to 'how she was justified of her plea for people and her love of life'. She senses the air of the place and pitch of the occasion, but more than this, recognizes the intractability of its elements, beyond formulation: 'Mrs. Lowder and her niece . . . had at least in common that each was a great reality.' Unlike Lord Mark, Milly cannot label 'their hostess's "set" '. Yet she is not simply naïve; what we see is not impressionability, but her awareness of it: 'observation', 'alertness', 'sensibility' are the subject of her reflections.

The narrative distance in this scene is set through the use of reported speech. Lord Mark's comments and Milly's speculations alike are overheard: the impressionism, like that of Emma's ball at the Crown, commentated by Miss Bates's flow of words, is modulated through authorial selection. But Milly's is the point of view, and everything contributes to the reader's sense of her lively intelligence. D. W. Jefferson's appreciation of Milly Theale as 'intelligent, ironical, self-reliant' (*Henry James and the Modern Reader*, p. 204), picks up these traits, and is more true to the novel than those who see Milly as a symbol of transcendental suffering from the first. As Kenneth Graham notes, 'Milly Theale's qualities . . . are not angelic but personal, and they are always shown to us within the context of her relationships with other characters' (*Henry James: The Drama of Fulfilment*, p. 162). Through the reported speech of the narrative here, Milly is brought within the superior intelligence of the ironic form, achieving a particularly close relationship with the authorial intelligence and with the reader, without being removed from the social sphere. Milly is American, therefore apart; American, therefore quick; but her Americanness becomes an entirely personal quality before this scene is over, and the poised frankness of her conversation with Lord Mark not only constitutes 'the various signs of a relation', but leads with a pace which testifies to Milly's intelligence even as it advances the narrative, to a further conclusion: 'that her doom was to live fast'. James's prose chokes, slows the reader, over this fact: the compression itself is significant:

It was queerly a question of the short run and the consciousness proportionately crowded.

These were immense excursions for the spirit of a young person at Mrs. Lowder's mere dinner-party; but what was so significant and so admonitory as the fact of their being possible?   (p. 133)

Following the dense allusiveness of this scene comes a section almost without direct speech or the dramatic rendering of experience. This slackens attention; but it also has another function: the indirection of this intercourse between Kate and Milly distances their friendship in imaginative terms before the plot requires it. It lends force to Milly's 'clear cold' realization in the next section 'that there was a possible account of their relations in which the quantity her new friend had told her might have figured as small, as smallest, beside the quantity she hadn't'. The 'other', the 'unspoken' becomes the 'great darkness' which was vaguely sensed before, and amidst the 'light literary legend' of Trollope, Thackeray, Dickens, which represents all Milly's knowledge of 'England', her speculations as to implications and motives in Kate's silence over Densher have an added potentousness. Mrs. Stringham's analysis, that 'it was seeing round several corners; but that was what New England heroines did', is both accurate and inadequate to the sense we have of Milly's anticipation of her own story. The recurrent themes of the worker and the worked, of money and the imagination, the 'imagination of dependence' which Kate supposes Milly lacks, the significance of silence, and of names: these are little more than portents here, stirring forces whose direction is not yet seen towards the 'abysses' in the 'labyrinth'. Milly's achievement is less in speculation as to the future than in appreciation of its intractability: as she tells herself,

She should never know how Kate truly felt about anything such a one as Milly Theale should give her to feel. Kate would never—and not from ill-will, nor from duplicity, but from a sort of failure of common terms—reduce it to such a one's comprehension or put it within her convenience. (p. 158)

There is an undemonstrative independence and a poignant ambiguity about Milly's refusal to pry: 'Milly, however, easily explained that she wouldn't have asked her for the world' (p. 168). The wealth of meaning, irreducible to Kate's terms, is all on Milly's side here.

The serious undertone is picked up at the beginning of the fifth book, though the context is social, and the questions of justice and injustice, confession, merit and caring, could be taken as social extravagance: the 'last gasp' of the season. The confusion of categories is conveyed in the imagery: 'impressions this afternoon having by a happy turn of the wheel been gathered for them into a splendid cluster, an offering like an armful of the rarest flowers'. Although 'their current consciousness' and 'light analysis' is still the approach to their experience, Mrs. Stringham's tendency to cliché, 'as Susie . . . phrased it again and again . . . so beautiful and interesting an experience', corresponds to some degree to Milly's more sophisticated formulations. The 'largeness of style' is impressionistically conveyed through lists 'of armour, of pictures, of cabinets, of tapestry, of tea-tables'; through the wash of colour: 'a tone as of old gold kept "down" by the quality of the air, summer full-flushed'; through 'murmurous' sounds. Milly sees these 'elements' as 'an assault of reminders that this largeness of style was the sign of *appointed* felicity'; but her analysis is dominated by the imaginative response, finding a symbol of the experience, then elaborating from this a series of metaphors whose connection is sensual rather than logical. The Watteau-composition, a pictorial formulation, a matter of colour and form, melts in its own atmosphere: colour becomes air; warmth, taste and sound are interfused. The picture is lost in its style, the style becomes a vessel, the experience a 'draught', 'the essence of which might have struck the girl as distilled into the small cup of iced coffee she had vaguely accepted from somebody'. The occasion is liquid, 'while a fuller flood, somehow, kept bearing her up'. The day, a 'high-water mark of the imagination', combines the charm of Strether's experience at Gloriani's garden party with a literary echo of the 'moment of real happiness' for Maggie Tulliver and Philip Waken:

It was one of those dangerous moments when speech is at once sincere
and deceptive—when feeling, rising high above its average depth,
leaves flood-marks which are never reached again.

(*The Mill on the Floss*, vol. II, Book 5, Ch. iv)

The richness of imagery, the use of synaesthesia, repetition
and variation, enable the author to present this 'flood' with
expansive power, yet in a short space: two pages. Thus the
narrative enacts for the reader the dense form attributed to
experience, whether by the author or by Milly herself, we are
not sure. The style is contained by an image of style:

It was to be the end of the short parenthesis which had begun but the
other day at Lancaster Gate with Lord Mark's informing her that she
was a 'success' . . .   (p. 173)

Only after this does it become clear that the image is Milly's: thus
she has the kind of advantage on the reader that the author
himself displays in the manipulative narrative. The syntactic
metaphor embodies a dramatic example of the structuring imagination, and Milly achieves an understanding inseparable from the
author's own.

Milly's imagination gives her a distance from her own experience through the power to appreciate it: a control which is not
manipulative. Thus 'in a sort of soft midsummer madness, a
straight skylark-flight of charity', she can see Kate as 'a beautiful
stranger . . . cut her connections and lose her identity, letting the
imagination for the time make what it would of them': Milly has
for others as well as for herself the ability to overcome 'the
imagination of dependence' which Kate loathes and fears. This is
a dangerous faculty: a 'real critical mind' used in play may dege-
nerate from toying with 'amusements of thought that were like
the secrecies of a little girl playing with dolls when convention-
ally "too big" ', to handling people in the same way; and Milly's
'odd beguilements of the mind' have a dangerous affinity with
Aunt Maud's 'great social uses'. Yet the 'more objective' view,
which can appreciate a person as 'the handsomest thing there', can
stand outside itself too, and recognize 'the image of the wonderful
Bronzino'.

The 'set-piece' Bronzino scene grows out of the narrative yet
is set apart from it. As in Strether's last interview with Marie de

Vionnet, there is a stage-managed 'approach' to the moment. Both the narrative of Milly's day and the account of her advance towards the picture, 'without haste, through innumerable natural pauses and soft concussions', contribute to the sense of occasion.

Amidst the 'carnival' it is Milly herself who seems to be on show, and there is danger, if not malice, in 'their accidents', though the hypnotic rhythm of Milly's thoughts disguises this: 'So it wasn't their fault, it wasn't their fault, and anything might happen that would, and everything now again melted together, and kind eyes were always kind eyes—if it were never to be worse than that!' The 'melting' of impressions, 'the beauty and the history and the facility and the splendid midsummer glow', like an operatic setting, makes 'a sort of magnificent maximum'. Through the style we have the impressions of the moment together with the later analysis of them, both contained within Milly. Consciousness momentarily ceases to divide experience from expression: an 'apotheosis' which is conveyed through the juxtaposition of experience and reaction without a logical framework in the narrative. Though there is some gesture towards exposition, this is rather a device of emphasis, conveying wonder, than an explanation: the 'Bronzino scene' relies on intuitive understanding. Phrases such as 'in fact', 'and the reason', and the use of deictic constructions, 'what . . . befell was', 'it was she herself who', 'and the reason was', are of little account beside the inexplicable extremes of 'nothing' and 'all', 'tears' and 'joy', and the terrible catalogue of delights in the Bronzino, which ranges from fleshly to material attributes, mummifying them all, until it culminates in the striking triple repetition:

The lady in question. . . with her slightly Michaelangelesque squareness, her eyes of other days, her full lips, her long neck, her recorded jewels, her brocaded and wasted reds, was a very great personage—only unaccompanied by a joy. And she was dead, dead, dead.   (p. 183)

The transcendence of logic in the narrative, a peculiarly direct linking of process and effect, which combines immediacy with an oblique tribute to Milly's intuitive understanding, is pointed through a triumphant paradox: 'Milly recognised her exactly in words that had nothing to do with her.' Whereas the process of looking at the portrait advanced through unspecified but distinct steps, juxtaposed without explanation, this sentence contains several layers of meaning concentrated into one expression. The reader's attention is drawn to it by the paradox of 'recognised' and 'that had nothing to do with her'; but not all the relationships of meaning are paradoxical. 'Recognised' implies at least three distinct but not conflicting processes: Milly's vision of the Bronzino, her tribute to the lady, and the perception of an analogy between the lady's case and her own. These could be seen as sequential perceptions; the hint of ambiguity in the pronouns, supported by the echoes of manipulation—Lionel Croy's 'do *for*', 'do *with*'—explicitly removed from the verb, would support this analysis, showing how Milly's attention moves away from the lady to herself, and how this represents a proper recognition of the qualities of both.

This distinction makes use of the likeness, the analogy, between Milly and the portrait, but transcends the 'categorizing' imagination which stops at the stage where 'she was the image of the wonderful Bronzino' (p. 180): a danger parodied in Lady Aldershaw's comical inversion: 'Lady Aldershaw meanwhile looked at Milly quite as if Milly had been the Bronzino and the Bronzino only Milly.' The progress beyond this 'identification' is marked through the manipulation of multiple meanings in the text. 'Recognised' brings together separate processes; 'better' contains a variety of judgements which must be distinguished. The possibilities are indicated, though not exhausted, by the conflict of interpretations between Milly and Lord Mark: the most celebrated example of James's manipulation of conversational incomprehension to express complexities of meaning. All Milly says is, 'I shall never be better than this'. The range of possibilities in her 'this', which could mean this moment, this state, this lady, or this portrait, and in Lord Mark's 'better . . . well enough . . . good', which moves from the physical to a moral judgement, is at once expansive beyond the text, and contained within it. Milly's thought: 'He hadn't understood', acknowledges the incompleteness of expression; but her next thought shows that understanding can be achieved: the physical and moral, the good, the beautiful and the right, momentary and absolute, can be united in experience:

It was perhaps as good a moment as she should have with any one, or have in any connection whatever. '. . . everything . . . has been too

beautiful, and . . . perhaps everything together will never be so right
again'.   (p. 183)

The descent from these heights, the acknowledgement of limitations of understanding and communication, is swift, in the
ralentando of a single sentence:

'Oh, we must talk about these things!'
Ah, they had already done that, she knew, as much as she ever
would; and she was shaking her head at her pale sister the next
moment with a world, on her side, of slowness.   (p. 184)

The 'world' is large, but not limitless; when Milly came down
from her Swiss mountain with 'the world all before her', it was
a confined choice, open to one without an eternal Eden. Lord
Mark's 'world of practice' corresponds to Densher's 'world of
thought', Susie's 'small world-space both crowded and enlarged',
to Kate's world, which Milly 'could quite see' was one in which
'dangers abounded'. At the end of this scene, Kate, in turn, is to
ask Milly with brusque directness, 'What in the world is the
matter with you?': the 'matter', for Milly, is that she is not 'in the
world' as the others are.

Milly's position is not, however, a 'given fact', in the fairy-tale,
arbitrary terms of a Susan Stringham. Her 'apotheosis' is an
extraordinary development, distinguished in style and mood
from the account of her time in London: extraordinary precisely
because Milly has the capacities of an ordinary girl, but moves
from one kind of existence to another. The interchange with
Kate at Matcham is a deliberate attempt at compensation on
Milly's part: she puts herself in Kate's power by asking for help
precisely because Kate is in her power since she knows Kate's
undivulged secret. The involved self-abnegation in Milly's
appeal is mirrored by the hyperbolic language of her request:
exaggeration neutralizing excess. It is an irony Kate picks up that
Milly asks her help 'to be wicked and false': 'And for cheating . . .
my powers will contribute? Well, I'll do my best for you' (p. 187).

Coming after the Bronzino scene, and illustrating Milly's
perceptiveness, tact, and the strength which will adopt weakness
as a policy, this passage heightens her extraordinariness by showing that it is not based on a lack of worldly wisdom. When Milly
enters 'quite another world', where Sir Luke Strett presides with
a mysterious power like that of Shakespeare's wise rulers in the late

romances, she does not become detached from the first world. Her stature as a character grows in terms of the new worlds in which she develops relations, 'the special trophy . . . an absolute possession, a new resource altogether'. Just as she conquers Boston after New York, London after Switzerland, and is to move on a triumphal progress to Venice, Milly moves in terms of mode between romance and naturalism, the symbolic drama and the social: no single setting, no one set of terms defines her. Nor does the complex whole: there is an eclecticism, rather than completeness, about the representation of Milly, aptly symbolized by the image of her relation with Sir Luke:

something done up in the softest silk and tucked away under the arm of memory. . . . she had it there under her cloak, but dissimulated, invisibly carried, when smiling, smiling, she again faced Kate Croy.

(p. 192)

The recurrence of this image, poignantly transformed, marks Densher's movement towards a similar attitude to experience: the thought, 'all his own', which 'he took out of its shared corner and its soft wrappings; he undid them one by one, handling them, handling *it*, as a father, baffled and tender, might handle a maimed child' (p. 569). It is through such links, and such transformations, such gaps, that Milly's world is constituted for the reader; and her ease, compared with Susie's anxiety or Densher's almost morbid longing to preserve what they see of it, is what distinguishes Milly. No one except Sir Luke has the same assurance; but the fact that he shares it guarantees its validity for the reader, and enables us to see certainty as an attribute of Milly Theale rather than as a condition within which only she can exist: 'there actually passed between them for some seconds a sign, a sign of the eyes only, that they knew together where they were' (p. 200).

The 'grey immensity' of this condition is expressed with a restraint notably unlike Susie's mountain scene. As Barbara Hardy points out, 'Milly converts the world of the park . . . into a subjective and transparent world of appropriate appearances, metaphors for her predicament which are not mere rhetorical identifications, conceited and convenient, but the literal identifications of genuine sympathy.'[1] The simplicity of this imaginative

[1] *The Appropriate Form* (1964), pp. 23–4.

identification does not wholly depend on the power of archetypal symbols: it is supported by the recurrent vocabulary of *The Wings of the Dove*, the images and phrases which link Milly's plight with the others we have seen. The utter simplicity of expression in 'she went forward into space', 'she went straight before her', 'the question of living', and 'grey immensity . . . furnished her world' has meaning by comparison and in contrast with Kate and Densher's wanderings, the questions that bristled in Chirk Street, and the heavy furniture of Aunt Maud's house. With this resonance, the style can be restrained here to a spareness fitting the extremity of the situation. Milly's speculations have a poise lacking from Susie's melodrama: she uses the impersonal pronoun, the balance and rhetorical questions of disinterested inquiry: 'It was wonderful to her, while she took her random course, that these quantities felt so equal: she had been treated—hadn't she?—as if it were in her power to live; and yet one wasn't treated so—was one?—unless it came up, quite as much, that one might die' (p. 206). The 'wonder' conveyed through the poise of this syntax is also represented imaginatively; but again it is the sense of the mind at work, rather than the imagery itself, which impresses the reader. From the delicate to the grotesque, Milly's symbols illustrate the baroque vigour of her imagination, so that if is neither 'the bloom' of the 'small old sense of safety' nor the 'military posture' of defence, but rather 'the beauty of the idea of a great adventure, a big dim experiment or struggle' which is constituted.

The almost clumsy manipulation of this imagery makes way for unpretentious prose and 'the real thing', the 'blessed old truth'. This is tentatively approached, through repetition, through the colloquialism of 'the same box', and the biblical tone of 'wanderers, anxious and tired'; but the 'smutty sheep', the 'idle lads at games of ball, with their cries mild in the thick air', are vividly realized. The atmosphere is tangible in 'this grim breathing-space', and the struggle for existence is 'a practical question'. The statement of the human condition, and the conversion of the claim that 'they could live if they would' into the 'old truth' that 'they would live if they could', is direct. Milly's understanding, 'directly divesting, denuding, exposing', works for the reader through style as well as theme, in the way that Sir Luke's appreciation does for Milly herself: 'It reduced her to her ultimate state'. Like Lear's stripped vision, Milly's attention moves from her own plight to the human state, and from this to the social being: 'that of a poor girl—with her rent to pay for example—staring before her in a great city'. This startlingly modern vision could scarcely be further from the pastoral romance of Susie's mountain scene.

Despite its thematic importance as a statement of the conditions of life, and hence of meaning, the passage in the park is so far from melodramatic emphasis that it is not even set apart by the narrative structure as a rhythmic climax. No break in the narrative divides this pause from Milly's engagement with the 'practical question of living': more specifically, her relation to Kate and to Kate in relation to Densher. The stark vision becomes a practical basis for conduct, the 'maze of possibilities' a 'revelation to herself that she absolutely had nothing to tell'. Milly's consciousness, not her actions, provides the drama, and it is her awareness of the disparity between her case and Kate's that 'inwardly danced their dance'.

There is however a pause before the confrontation with Merton Densher: the 'strange, indescribable session' with Mrs. Lowder over 'naming' Densher to Kate. Milly's reluctance to break her silence, her momentary withdrawal from the struggle, heightens the inexorability of the end. But her stubbornness is not all pathos. When Kate is 'just perhaps a shade perfunctory', Milly can read into it 'more of an approach to meaning'. Even while Kate explains the workings of English society to the American, it is through Milly's appreciation that we register her competence. While Kate images 'the monster', Milly supplies the 'technical term' for dealing with it: 'both analogy and induction, and then, differently, instinct, none of which were right'. The contrast between the young women is not in strength but in approach. It is 'the bold ironic spirit' that Milly admires; yet her own perceptiveness, objectivity, and poise are not related but demonstrated in the narrative. Both she and Kate find images for each other, and in doing so they attain a degree of independence of the narrative which they help to create. Milly meets Kate's image: 'on the instant as she would have met the revealed truth . . . *That* was what was the matter with her. She was a dove. Oh *wasn't* she?—it echoed within her' (p. 233).

It is this ability to adopt a suggested image, and to work it for herself as others work their companions, that Milly displays in the National Gallery when she comes upon Densher with Kate. After the long preparation, this meeting is anti-climactic; it is a recognition scene, rather than a confrontation: a double recognition, in that Milly 'knew herself handled and again . . . dealt with— absolutely even dealt with for her greater pleasure'. For the reader the extra twist is in Milly's awareness of how Kate is 'prodigious': this again makes Milly's the containing understanding. She is on a level with author and reader in her objective appreciation: 'The predicament of course wasn't definite or phraseable—and the way they let all phrasing pass was presently to recur to our young woman as a characteristic triumph of the civilised state . . .' (p. 243).

The scene is equally remarkable for its obliquity and its restraint, both made the subject of explicit comment: 'She was to wonder in subsequent reflection what in the world they had actually said, since they had made such a success of what they didn't say . . .' As in the significant silences of James's earlier novels, meaning is conveyed through the interstices of form: a paradox of expression allied to the quiet irony of social form which the characters see through, but nevertheless exploit: there is a suppressed pun in James's account: 'Whatever were the facts, their perfect manners, all round, saw them through.'

There are another hundred pages, a book and a half, before the move to Venice sets the scene for the next stage of the action, and the defeat of Milly: the climax of the novel, coming neither in the middle nor at the end, but like a third-act climax displaced to the position of the fourth act counter-action in Bradley's scheme of the Shakespearian tragedy. The displacement of Milly, ousting her from the position of structural pivot while she remains the thematic centre, begins in this interval between the 'apotheosis' of the Bronzino scene and the 'second apotheosis' in Venice. The counter-action of Kate and Densher usurps Milly's centrality, and she must react rather than instigate action.

For the first time since Milly's descent from the mountain, the centre of consciousness moves from her. The reaction to the National Gallery scene is for Kate and Densher. Their passion informs the vocabulary of their situation: 'The fact of their adventure was flagrant between them.' (p. 253). 'Their personal need of each other' is conveyed with an urgency quite alien to

Milly's vigour, which is a strength of mind and imagination. The imagery of their feeling is the archetypal snake and fire: the 'fifth wheel to the coach', which is respect, has no imaginative relation to them at all, and this odd assortment of images conveys the 'disconcerting' sense of their relationship. The disparity between their personalities, hinted through language and style in books one and two, becomes a symbolic conflict of the sexes here: 'one of those strange instants between man and woman that blow upon the red spark, the spark of conflict, ever latent in the depths of passion': D. H. Lawrence might have written this.

This change of mode helps convey how the relationship of the lovers is dramatic, not static: Densher's 'demands, desires had grown' (p. 256) during his absence; and for the reader, this is realized by his reappearance after a narrative absence, with feelings all the stronger for the interruption. From being a structural pattern, part of the eternal triangle, the relationship of the lovers has become an active force, affecting them and others. Densher 'had known more than ever . . . how ill a man, and even a woman, could be with it; but he struck himself as also knowing that he had already suffered Kate to begin finely to manipulate it'. (p. 256). His impersonal pronoun loses its delicacy in continued analysis, and Densher's consciousness, unlike Milly's, shrinks from expression: 'It had a vulgar sound—as throughout, in love, the names of things, the verbal terms of intercourse, were, compared with love itself, vulgar . . .' The unease is conveyed in the misnaming of things: the disparity of Kate's ability to 'manipulate' and Densher's actions: 'He laid strong hands upon her to say, almost in anger, "Do you love me, love me, love me?"' (p. 266). The hands 'speak' as clearly as the repeated demand, and Kate understands them: 'She closed her eyes as with the sense that he might strike her but that she would gratefully take it.' Her communication is equally physical, and uses the terms of conflict to 'the same tender purpose':

She came to him under the compulsion, again, that had united them shortly before, and took hold of him in her urgency to the same tender purpose. It was her form of entreaty renewed and repeated, which made after all, as he met it, their great fact clear.   (269–70)

Kate's control is shown in her language as in her actions: there is a double irony in her assurance to Densher, where her deliberate exaggeration is confirmed by an involuntary ambiguity: 'my cleverness . . . has grown infernal—I'll make it all right': the disparity between 'infernal' and 'right' is flagrantly ignored. The very rhythm of Kate's speech states her case: the monosyllabic deliberation of her determination is unarguable:

> 'I want . . . to make things pleasant for her. I use, for the purpose, what I have. You're what I have of most precious and you're therefore what I use most.'   (p. 292)

Densher's response to this is tangential, but to the purpose: 'He looked at her long. "I wish I could use *you* a little more".'

The urgency of Densher's sense of Kate, and his concern at the way Aunt Maud uses her, make the case of Milly unimportant here. While the terms of the drama become increasingly violent, Milly's fate is imaged with mawkish eccentricity: 'the oddity of a Christian maiden, in the arena, mildly, caressingly, martyred. It was the nosing and fumbling not of lions and tigers but of domestic animals, let loose as for the joke.' Compared with this comic grotesque, the sense of Kate is not only passionate, but recognizable in literary terms: her variety echoes Cleopatra's, and Densher's reaction is Othello's at its keenest:

> 'All women but you are stupid. How can I look at another? You're different and different—and then you're different again.' . . . He almost moaned, he ached, from the depth of his content.   (p. 300)

The hint of morbid passion in the echo of the 'weed/Who art so lovely fair and smellest so sweet/That the sense aches at thee' is ominous for Densher as for Kate, particularly in the Venetian setting.

Such echoes have an imaginative effect beyond their specific reference, however: their elevated tone creates space for the 'ground' of ambiguous words and phrases: the 'going straight' which is not, the 'proper lie', the 'difference between acting and not acting . . . that was not speaking the particular word', the distinction between the 'interesting' and the 'interested', and the ambiguity of the latter term. Representation becomes a matter of deliberate distortion and interpretation, as the perversion of the conditions of meaning mirrors the relationship between motive and action, cause and effect, in the narrative. The only 'straightness' is in the continued, though incomplete, consciousness of the main characters: the aspiration to understanding; and even this fits uneasily within the narrative process. Densher's awareness is remarkable:

> there were things she [Milly] seemed to say that took the words out of his mouth. These were not all the things she did say; they were rather what such things meant in the light of what he knew. (p. 313)

Yet the understanding of real sympathy is even greater:

> 'I'm not worrying, Milly'. And poor Susie's face registered the sublimity of her lie. . . . her companion went to her, met by her with an embrace in which things were said that exceeded speech. (p. 334)

The manœuvring between such indirections is difficult, however, and mistakes are not always clear. Susie supposes, and only the imagery hints that she may be wrong, that

> Discretion had ceased to consist of silence; silence was gross and thick; whereas wisdom should taper, however tremulously, to a point. (p. 337)

The 'case', the 'point', what one can 'do with' or 'do for' Milly: such phrases build up a sense of occasion, as well as the 'maze of possibilities' which are to be worked out in Venice. The meanings themselves are active, while Milly becomes increasingly passive: the object worked upon, worked round. The lead in to the Venice section comes at the end of Milly's interview with Sir Luke Strett, when she explains how little the 'world's before' her. In relation to Mr. Densher, she says, 'I'm afraid there's really nothing one can do'.

The narrative mirrors Milly's passivity as the 'set-piece' description of her palazzo stills conversation and action. Like an overture, Chapter XXIV creates a tonal setting and hints the main theme, but without insistence. The Venetian Rococo, 'embossed and beribboned, all toned with time and all flourished and scolloped and gilded about'; the *commedia dell'arte* figure of Eugenio, 'forever carrying one well-kept Italian hand to his heart and plunging the other straight into her pocket, which, as she had instantly observed him to recognize, fitted it like a glove' (p. 359); the triumphal progress to Venice: all this high ceremony and surface, and not less the echoes of 'some dim scene in a Maeterlinck play', are insistently artificial. The separation of surface and depth is clarified, in preparation on the one hand for the drama of deception, and on the other for Milly's transcendence of 'the world'.

Silence for Milly herself is an opportunity for communion with her world, 'when things spoke to her with penetration. It was mostly in stillness that they spoke to her best; amid voices she lost the sense' (p. 361). Between Milly and Kate, however, silence is dangerous concealment, loaded with hidden or disguised meanings, when 'face to face, they wearily put off the mask' (p. 363). This is a ritual as artificial as any social gesture; as the nominalization of the verb, the slightly stilted singular 'mask', the involved logic of complement, verb, and abstract subject, reveals in the sentence structure: 'These puttings-off of the mask had finally quite become the form taken by their moments together.' James uses the familiarity of the omniscient author in contrast to the inflationary abstraction of their pretence: 'Strangely enough, we say, for the volume of effusion in general would have been found by either, on measurement, to be scarce proportional to the paraphernalia of relief.' The shifts of stance, indirections rather than simply the removal of layers of concealment, involved in the 'theory of intimate confessions, private, frank ironies that made up for their public grimaces' are conveyed to the reader in such modulations of mode and tone. Where 'there could be no gross phrasing to Milly', 'the broken talk, brief and sparingly allusive, seems more to cover than to free their sense'. There is a consciousness of pretence: Kate 'grasped with her keen intelligence the logic of their common duplicity', and Milly's shifts are open to the reader:

Strange ... yet lawful, all the same—weren't they?—those experiments tried with the truth that consisted, at the worst, but in practising on one's self.   (p. 366)

The main theme is not only immanent in the imagery of this passage, the ark of the deluge, the imagery of traps and warfare, but, like the 'experiments tried with the truth', it is carried within Milly's own mind. It is Milly who recognizes Eugenio for a Venetian counterpart to Sir Luke, Milly who sees the dramatic function of Susie:

She could see Susie, in the event of her death, in no character at all,

Susie being insistently, exclusively concerned in her mere make-shift
duration. (p. 360)

Milly alone, on her stage, also recognizes the dramatic moment of
Lord Mark's arrival:

He had waited then, Lord Mark, he was waiting—oh, unmistakeably;
never before had he so much struck her as the man to do that on
occasion with patience . . . (p. 367)

Lord Mark's tour of the palace, with 'something of the grace of
amends made', balances, in a minor key, the 'hour at Matcham'.
The recognition of 'their excluded, disinherited state' is dramatically possible in this context; though it is made immediate in
Milly's image: 'an image of never going down, of remaining
aloft in the divine, dustless air, where she would hear but the
plash of the water against stone'. The spatial dimensions of the
drama are defined here: for Kate and Densher's horizontal
wanderings, there is Milly's suspension: 'I don't move, in fact
. . . I stay up.' Milly's 'whirlwind of suggestion' lifts Densher
briefly to the same freedom:

It wasn't . . . within such walls, confinement, it was the freedom of all
the centuries: in respect to which Densher granted good-humouredly
that they were then blown together, she and he, as much as she liked,
through space. (pp. 393–4)

Unfortunately, however, it is only these upper regions that are
free to Milly. What her rejection of Lord Mark reveals is a complexity of worldly wisdom and unworldly aspirations. Milly sees
through him: she is not helpless; but it is not clear whether she
sees through herself:

there was a beautiful reason—indeed there were two—why her companion's motive shouldn't matter. One was that even should he desire
her without a penny she wouldn't marry him for the world; the other
was that she felt him, after all . . . concerned for her. (p. 373)

The balance, which is not equivalence, between the Palazzo
Leporelli and Matcham, is a reverberation of the balance between
Lord Mark and Densher in respect to Milly. Densher enters: to
a stage where the limits of 'freedom', the possibilities of deception, have both been bluntly stated, though scarcely accepted,
between Milly and Lord Mark.

The shift of the centre of consciousness to Merton Densher in the eighth book is the first of a series of abrupt changes which act as 'foreshortening' devices accelerating the pace of intrigue around Milly, while her existence is sustained in a sort of calm centre. Not at her death, but before it, Milly moves outside time, while time, for Densher, undergoes important changes. 'Double time' helps create an impression of haste: from the morning of Densher's visit to the midday meeting in the Piazza, dinner in the evening to the assignation with Kate, the imaginative time-span is a single day, for the intervening spaces are of no account. The slowing down from this climax to the period left in Venice, caught by the memory of Kate's coming, then lingering for Milly's end, introduces the dreadful final spell in London, where time is measured not in mealtimes or in days but in seasons of the year, dragging as the days shorten.

There is an effective poignancy in the importance of these developments for Densher, which leave Milly untouched. His 'necessity of making the best', of holding together 'the whole queer fabric that built him in', is for himself, and for Kate. His sense of place is reduced from abstract form to practical balance, with a half-echo of Othello's 'gulfs': 'He was walking, in short, on a high ridge, steep down on either side, where the proprieties— once he could face at all remaining there—reduced themselves to his keeping his head.' Densher's control is heard in his language: the abstraction, passivity, impersonality of his suppressed urgency:

an exasperation, a resentment, begotten truly by the very impatience of desire, in respect to his postponed and relegated, his so extremely manipulated state.   (p. 395)

The 'real meaning of it' can be more succinctly put: 'he was perpetually bent to her [Kate's] will'. It is not only a matter of 'just where he was', but also 'just *how* he was': Densher is determined now to move on his own account. His terms are the recurrent elements of the novel: question, matter, knowledge and will:

His question . . . was the interesting question of whether he had really no will left. How could he know—that was the point—without putting the matter to the test?   (p. 396)

Like Kate, or like Kate's father at the outset, Densher can see 'his mature motive' objectively; but the motive grows to an independence reflected by its syntactic position, where the elements of the story, personified abstracts, seem more powerful than the actors they manipulate:

His mature motive ... had thus in an hour taken imaginative possession of the place: that precisely was how he saw it seated there, already unpacked and settled, for Milly's beauty, no matter how short a time, to be housed with. (p. 399)

Densher's objectivity is not the poise of Milly, able to appreciate her own case and others, nor of Kate, who can control the scenes in which she acts: it is rather a reluctance to engage with himself than the distance of understanding. This confusion, not of motive but of interpretation, is reflected in the change from involved diction to simplicity; as logic breaks down in Densher's thoughts, a pose of philosophical interest gives way to unanalysed colloquialism or simple physical imagery:

This awkwardness of his conscience, both in respect to his general plasticity, the fruit of his feeling plasticity, within limits, to be a mode of life like another—certainly better than some, and particularly in respect to such confusion as might reign about what he had really come for—this inward ache was not wholly dispelled by the style, charming as ever, of Kate's poetic versions. Even the high wonder and delight of Kate couldn't set him right with himself. (p. 400)

Densher's strolls 'through dusky labyrinthine alleys and empty *campi*' provide an image for this wandering in the mind; the peculiarly 'inward' geography of Venice, where even the Piazza, like a great drawing-room, seems a contained, domestic space, blurs the distinction of imaginative and physical setting, and makes the city an outward image of the mental state of the drama: more intimate and more dramatic than the Paris of *The Ambassadors*. The 'grim breathing-space' of Milly's world is claustrophobic. Even her 'beatific mildness' is frighteningly pervasive: airless and silent:

There was a deeper depth of it, doubtless, for some than for others ... he [Densher] seemed to stand in it up to his neck. He moved about in it, and it made no plash; he floated, he noiselessly swam in it; and they were all together ... like fishes in a crystal pool. (p. 424)

When Milly's deception is revealed and the weather in Venice changes, it seems no coincidence, no elegant pathetic fallacy, but the perturbation in nature inevitable at a tragic catastrophe.

Meanwhile the effect of abrupt transition is achieved through narrative economy in relating Densher's development. The recognition of Milly's qualities, 'an eloquence, an authority, a felicity—he scarce knew by what name to call it', for which 'he had not consciously bargained', is given almost no space, but comes, significantly, before Densher's bargain with Kate: an irony which precludes his claiming again, 'Well, that he had been rather taken in by not having known in advance!' (p. 402).

The vocabulary of barter associated with Kate's family relations is not used for the bargain between Kate and Densher. This is not a financial but a moral affair: though their 'give' and 'take' also have a physical sense. The intimacy of relations between the moral and physical, and the corresponding power of the moral itself over action, is seen in the play with words, applied first to one then the other sphere, and ambiguous in both. Densher's simplicity is deluded: 'Idea for idea, his own was thus already, and in the germ, beautiful.' His grasp of Kate's arm is symbolic: 'possessing himself of her arm' seems a guarantee that 'what he was possessed of was real—the fact that she hadn't thrown over his lucidity the horrid shadow of cheap reprobation'. Yet 'mad in pursuit and in possession so/Had, having, and in quest to have', lust possesses him: there is a fine irony about the understatement, riddled with ambiguities: 'He was already, in a sense, possessed of what he wanted.' At Milly's party, her 'second apotheosis' is elided because of our concentration on the lovers. Milly is seen only through the eyes of Susie, Densher and Kate: they notice her pearls, symbols of her wealth, rather than the girl. She is lost in the atmosphere of strategic manœuvring, verbally consummated with swift irony in a terse catechism fusing physical and moral prostitution:

'Well, I understand.'
'On your honour?'
'On my honour.'
'You'll come?'
'I'll come.'   (p. 438)

The elision of their meeting itself, like the turning from Milly's deathbed, is not an evasion by James, but a way of directing the reader's attention to what is important for the novel: the 'sense of . . . sense *for* . . . adventures' (*The Art of the Novel*, p. 56) without which they would not be interesting. It is the effect of this meeting on Densher, and possibly the lack of any witnessed effect on Kate, which matters; and this is seen in Densher's dwelling on it. The narrative captures an action which has different meanings in prospect and retrospect, and which combines the qualities of lingering and impermanence. Kate's coming, 'what had come to pass', is an obsession which will not endure. The event affects Densher: 'a conscious, watchful presence, active on its own side'; and though we do not see Kate, the ambiguity of 'what survived of her' points its importance for her too. The deed is absolute, dominating even the actors: 'there might be for a man almost a shade of the awful in so unqualified a consequence of his act. It had simply *worked*, his idea, the idea he had made her accept . . .' (p. 442).

The *doubles entendres* of this passage are not frivolous but obsessive: 'so intensely there that, as we say, no other act was possible to him than the renewed act, almost the hallucination of intimacy'. The obsession is such that it 'shut her in. Shut her out —it came to that, rather . . . Kate was *all* in his poor rooms' (p. 444). The same verbal figure, playing with prepositions, becomes positively contortionist when Densher meets Milly and must come to terms with his own position:

He couldn't stand up to lie—he felt as if he would have to go down on his knees. As it was he just sat there shaking a little for nervousness the leg he had crossed over the other.   (p. 447)

The acceptance of his position frees Densher to move; but the echoes of *Othello* in *The Wings of the Dove* hint the danger in an ability to 'turn and turn and then go on/And turn again':

When he had turned about, to Milly . . . on the question of the impossibility he had so strongly felt, turned about on the spot and under her eyes, he had acted . . . as a consequence of seeing how little, how not at all, impossibilities mattered.   (p. 454)

The physical embarrassment becomes an imaginative possibility: 'When people were at *her* pass everything was allowed'. But this possibility is based on deception and self-deception, pointed for the reader in linguistic ambiguities or contradictions: 'the perceived truth that he might on any other system go straight to destruction' (p. 455), where 'straight' could have a moral as well as a temporal meaning; 'he best kept everything in place by not hesitating . . . to let himself go—go in the direction, that is to say, of staying' (p. 456), where an inverted morality demands a looking-glass approach to movement.

The highly formalized complicity between Densher and Milly is enacted in its expression, which demands attention to verbs re-echoing with alternating subjects, indicated only through pronouns. Following this offers little reward to the reader, but generates an impression of superficial order based on tension:

> They really, as it went on, *saw* each other at the game, she knowing he tried to keep her in tune with his notion, and he knowing she thus knew it. Add that he, again, knew she knew, and yet that nothing was spoiled by it, and we get a fair impression of their most completely workable line.   (p. 457)

Three weeks pass by full of such empty forms: they are noted in one page. But when Densher is turned away from the palazzo, time, as well as setting, atmosphere, character itself, changes. Densher's three minutes on the steps are measured exactly. And even Pasquale, hitherto a non-speaking figure, develops depth: 'he would have been blank, Densher mentally observed, if the term could ever apply to members of the race in whom vacancy was but a nest of darknesses—not a rich surface, but a place of withdrawal. . . .' The 'Venice all of evil' is a threatening environment. While 'the air had made itself felt as a non-conductor of messages', it also makes itself felt physically: 'where the wind was higher, he fairly, with the thought of it, pulled his umbrella closer down'. The immediacy of sensation quickens the pace of this passage, and the 'few seconds' for which Lord Mark's face is glimpsed are almost overtaken by their own significance: 'had already made the difference'. The pressure of interpretation is beyond logic. What the reader experiences are the leaps of recognition Densher makes, not explanations. An 'answer' is as real as a character: 'He held it close, he hugged it, quite leaned on it as he continued to circulate'. It is *because* of Lord Mark', not only that the palace is closed to Densher, but, before this, that 'the weather had changed, the rain was ugly, the wind wicked, the sea impossible, *because* of Lord Mark'.

The use of Densher as the centre of consciousness here is masterly: it pre-empts Eugenio's mute criticism, and places Lord Mark as the evil genius, in a way that could scarcely have been conceived from any other point of view. Densher is shown as ready for self-criticism, but rejecting it, and our interpretation meets his in 'a kind of exhilaration'. Every element of the narrative contributes to this persuasion: 'The exhilaration was heightened fairly, besides, by the visible conditions—sharp, striking, ugly to him—of Lord Mark's return.' We are not invited to speculate as to Densher's guilt: all queries are directed toward the mystery of a melodramatic evil 'sinister even to his own actual ignorance'. Thus the transition is effected 'to the reflection ... that the only delicate and honourable way of treating a person in such a state was to treat her as he, Merton Densher did'; and the narrative, through Densher, congratulates itself on the fortunate evolution of the plot:

It was for all the world ... as if a special danger for him had passed. Lord Mark had, without in the least intending such a service, got it straight out of the way. It was *he*, the brute, who had stumbled into just the wrong inspiration, and who had therefore produced, for the very person he had wished to hurt, an impunity that was comparative innocence ...

Freed of guilt by Lord Mark's 'anticipation of his dread exploits', Densher is gradually freed now as a moral being from his ties with Kate. He thinks of 'the two women', Kate and Milly, without his earlier affiliation. Kate 'was out of it, by her act, as much as he was in it'; and the deeper Densher is in, the greater, by implication, the stature of Milly, and the alignment of these two against Kate. Milly's withdrawal has a different quality from that of Kate, whose going has changed from a bond to a separation, and symbolizes the imaginative distance between her and Densher:

they had practically wrapped their understanding in the breach of their correspondence. He had, moreover, on losing her, done justice to her law of silence ...   (p. 468)

When Susie Stringham comes to Densher's rooms, even though

she is an unauthorized deputy, and no substitute, for Milly, Densher recognizes that Kate's influence has gone. It is an intellectual, not an emotional recognition, expressed in abstract and strangely impersonal terms:

> She was as absent to his sensibility as she had constantly been, since her departure, absent, as an echo or reference, from the palace; and it was the first time, among the objects now surrounding him, that his sensibility so noted her.   (p. 478)

This impersonality stands in unstated contrast to Milly's silence; and Kate's distance sets off Susie's sympathy, which is felt as a reverberation of Milly's influence: 'She hadn't come to judge him; had come rather, so far as she might dare, to pity'. The conversation between Susie and Densher, a tissue of misunderstandings, but based on confidence, establishes the possibility of communication between Milly and Densher, without actually expressing or anticipating their relations. The repeated phrases, 'Then *you* know——', 'How you *do* know!', 'I *can* piece it', convey the struggle for understanding, and its incompleteness. Barbara Hardy has noted the symbolic effect of the growing darkness through this interview:

> 'Shall we have lights—a lamp or the candles?'
> 'Not for me.'
> 'Nothing?'
> 'Not for me.'

Understanding is not an answer, but an acceptance of mystery.

The progression of the narrative from this interview to London without any representation of the meeting between Densher and Milly, teases the reader the more for the reappearance of Sir Luke. The expectation of a deathbed scene is aroused but not fulfilled, and the pressure of interest is diverted instead to the continuing narrative. The first words of the last book play upon this elision: 'Then it has been . . . a whole fortnight?—without your making a sign?' (p. 503) Only after this speech is it attributed to Kate, and thus set in London. The *trompe l'œil* effect is to make it seem as if Kate is in some way responsible for the defeat of the reader's expectations, and robbing Milly of her last scene. The slight shock of understanding also has the imaginative effect of defining the distance between the lovers: a distance per-

ceived by Densher, so that the reader is drawn into sympathy
with him. J. A. Ward has noted that 'it is not only Milly who is
remote from the reader's apprehension, but also Kate. . . . Kate's
mind is closed to us throughout all the final nine books'[1]: though
this is an exaggeration, it is true of the final section, and crucial
to its effect.

The 'difference' marks Densher's imaginative progression in a
way that asserts the importance of the Venetian experience and
functions as an oblique tribute to Milly: Densher and Kate 'met
. . . even as persons whose adventures, on either side, in time
and space, of the nature of perils and exiles, had had a peculiar
strangeness'. In this retrospective view, Densher savours the
quality of the story much as Milly was able to do in prospect at
Matcham. Yet the detachment of irresponsibility is gone. It is a
gallant gesture, little more, when he offers Kate to take equal
blame with her:

'It isn't a question for us of apportioning shares or distinguishing
invidiously among such impressions as it was our idea to give.'

It isn't a question at all any more: the 'possible' has now become
fact. The peculiar quality of this book of *The Wings of the Dove* is
in this mingling of the impossibility of further development with
the incompleteness of knowledge.

The balance of stasis and impatience in Densher's anticipation
fits a narrative in which the protagonists themselves act as readers
of their own story, analysing the plot, the motives, the possibilities, and recognizing the roles they have played. Kate's earlier
manipulation gives way to objective appreciation:

'She never wanted the truth . . . she wanted *you*. She would have
taken from you what you could give her, and been glad of it even if she
had known it false. You might have lied to her from pity, and she have
seen you and felt you lie, and yet . . . have thanked you and blessed
you and clung to you but the more.'   (p. 514)

Her monosyllabic clarity, and the repetition of the pronoun, 'you
. . . you . . . you', which centres her speculations, convey her
analysis of an uncanny detachment. In contrast with Densher's
reticence over his interview with Milly, Kate says 'so many

[1] *The Search for Form* (1967), p. 173.

things'. The overriding impression is of an intellect more powerful than sympathetic; and her half truths are indistinguishable from his. The recurrent word 'work' draws attention to this, when Kate claims, 'What I've worked for' is that Milly should be satisfied. But the most telling irony comes at the end of Chapter XXXIII, where syntactic elision matches partial communication between the two, and the gap becomes more significant than what is said:

> 'She won't have loved you for nothing.'
> It made him wince, but she insisted.
> 'And you won't have love me.'   (p. 519)

Milly will have loved Densher disinterestedly, that is, 'for nothing', but not 'for nothing', without marking the fact by her generous bequest. It is the second of these possibilities that Kate picks out. The dark side of this is 'nothing for Milly, everything for Densher (and hence Kate)'. But the other interpretation suggests a reward beyond financial interest. This is what Milly will both have given and got from her love, and Kate's blindness to it shows the limitations of her own. The further 'for nothing' implied by Kate when she insists to Densher, 'And you won't have loved me', is indeed, ironically, most present in its omission: lacking the dimension of disinterest, their love will indeed have been 'for nothing', negated by its development, in vain, and unrewarded.

Again the ambiguity is obliquely acknowledged by the narrative *reprise*, which demands both retrospective and onward attention: 'He was to remain for several days under the impression of this inconclusive passage' (p. 520). The 'aftersense that wasn't real' is professed and denied by turns: 'The queer turn of their affair made it a false note.' The measure of Densher's distance from Kate is seen in his relative closeness to Aunt Maud. The futile meetings between Kate and Densher elaborate this theme, merely impeding the progression to an end which the reader longs for, with their dramatic insistence on the situation accessible to 'mere cold thought'.

The development of Densher is conveyed in his imaginative recognition and transformation of this 'fact' and its 'consequences': 'his intelligence and his imagination, his soul and his sense had never, on the whole, been so intensely engaged'. This activity is

combined, however, with a sense of tedium familiar in the rhythm
of Shakespeare's tragedies, particularly when one partner has
died and the survivor is merely waiting for the end: 'He stared
at the buried day and wore out the time . . .'. The recognition
of the death of Milly, not from any direct communication, but in
the knowledge that Sir Luke has left Venice, is in keeping with
this low-keyed avoidance of climax. That Aunt Maud should be
the one to find the words which 'fitted an image deep in [Densher's]
own consciousness' for Milly as a dove with wings spread wide,
is ironic. Such is Milly's transcendence now that her image
emerges unscathed even from such handling; though Densher
does 'warn her off'.

Milly's position is now so well established that it gives scope
for a further thirty pages treating the relations between Densher
and Kate, Densher and Aunt Maud, even Kate and her family,
without threatening the dominance of the heroine. While the
world narrows around the survivors, Milly is outside its constraints, and every meanness of Condrip Street or grossness of
Lancaster Gate is an oblique confirmation of her freedom. This is
dramatized in the treatment of Milly's will, when James's 'slow
motion' representation of Densher's interview with Kate, the
tiptoe pace of the narrative, noting each look, the turned back,
the turning round, the distinctness of speech, creates a sensuous
apprehension so precise that the failure of Densher to kiss Kate
when she expects it becomes a narrative event, as clearly recorded
as his later 'yielding to the impulse' to touch her. The attention
on the letter, taken from the pocketbook in the breast of Densher's
waistcoat, carried 'with a movement not the less odd for being
visibly instinctive and unconscious' behind him, finally drawn out,
taken, is painfully acute. The 'jerk' with which Kate throws it
into the fire breaks the rhythm as abruptly as her action destroys
the link between Densher and Milly: the process and the effect of
representation are finely matched.

The contrast between Kate's destruction and Densher's
cherishing of 'the thought' of his experience is what finally
distances them irrevocably. The image of Densher's thought,
done up in 'soft wrappings' is a strange one, made recognizable
by its links with Milly's image for her relations with Sir Luke, and
perhaps too by its seasonal appropriateness, at Christmas; but
with a suspicion of morbidity inherited from its earlier use, by

Thackeray, of Amelia in *Vanity Fair*.[1] The 'ache' for the loss of Milly, the loss of her letter, the loss of the right to complain, and the loss of closeness to Kate, is undistinguishing. It sounds like a sentence, but means little, that 'he had given poor Kate her freedom': the relations between the lovers are no longer within their control. In the structure of relations theirs is over:

> It had come to the point, really, that they showed each other pale faces, and that all the unspoken between them looked out of their eyes in a dim terror of their further conflict.   (p. 574)

Their politeness is appalling, a recognition of their loss of familiarity:

> 'I don't understand. It seems to me in your place——'
> 'Ah' he couldn't help from breaking in, 'What do you know of my place? Pardon me' he immediately added; 'my preference is the one I express.'

Their final bargain is a question of forced renunciation, and the evasion of choice, of statement even. The elision increases towards the end, so that the last interchange is no new expression, but a summary of the position already established, and Densher's is a counterpart to the reader's attention: 'He heard her out in stillness, watching her face, but not moving.' The consummation is an elegy: 'she turned to the door, and her headshake was now the end. "We shall never be again as we were." '

The elegiac note at the close of *The Wings of the Dove* is final because it implies an appreciation of what has gone before: it is the note of understanding and acceptance, and as such the only 'answer' to the problems raised by the work. These are as much questions of understanding, concerned with the perception and expression of a situation, as problems of dramatic action. Milly is doomed, and so are Kate and Densher, from before the start of the novel: no action can save them from death or degradation. What redeems them from the squalor of their world can only be awareness. This is what Milly enjoys, at Lancaster Gate and the National Gallery as well as at Matcham and on her deathbed in Venice. Densher finally attains something of the same quality

---

[1] 'Oh these women! They nurse and cuddle their presentiments, and make darlings of their ugliest thoughts, as they do of their deformed children' (*Vanity Fair*, 1848; rpt. 1968), p. 163.

through her example; but Kate, struggling for a more practical triumph, is limited to worldly achievement, and here there can be no success.

The development of understanding, as opposed to the quest for success, is obliquely conveyed through the style of *The Wings of the Dove,* and worked out with remarkable immediacy in the expression of the novel. This process is occasionally accorded recognition, as when technical terms from grammar, such as 'word', 'sentence' and 'parenthesis'; overtly artificial literary modes or genres: the romance, the detective story, the play, or social forms and ploys: the dinner party, the mask, are used to image or express the human and social relations in the novel. The characters themselves create and recognize their own stories: Kate with active manipulation, Milly with effective appreciation of others. These processes indeed represent their only apparent control over their own destiny: and it is because Milly's is the more comprehensive imagination that she achieves a paradoxical success, while Kate, with all her manipulative vigour, fails utterly.

The process of representation is both effective and affective in *The Wings of the Dove.* In one capacity it conveys the workings of society and personal relations, where 'the workers in one connection are the worked in another'; in the other it draws attention to itself, demonstrating its own procedure, and thus implying an analogy between the process of the novel and those it depicts. The curious balance of lingering appreciation and pressing discovery in this novel, where the conclusion is twofold: a death to be dreaded, and an 'apotheosis' of sympathy to be appreciated, is perfectly caught in this double use of the techniques of representation, at once a moving process and a self-regarding effect. The Bronzino scene is the most remarkable example of this use of form to set up and go beyond the expressive limitations of its own technique: 'Milly recognised her exactly in words that had nothing to do with her.'

Unlike *The Ambassadors, The Wings of the Dove* has no guiding rule of technique dominating every expressive element. Instead of duality there is multiplicity; instead of 'central perspective', a continually shifting stance, a teasing manipulation of technique maintaining the reader's interest while undermining easy assumptions of authority and control in the approach to experience. The consistency of relations between author, characters, and reader, like those between the actor and the deed, the fact and the interpretation within the novel, is repeatedly challenged, and attempts to impose rather than perceive order are thwarted. Milly, Susie, and Kate, Lionel Croy and Aunt Maud, as well as Densher, are all, to some extent, authorial characters; but how different their authority and reliability, and how little relation this bears to their worldly position!

The metaphors of place and the structural principle of pace, or effective time, in the novel, provide a novelistic counterpart to this highly technical demonstration of the novel process. Though a key vocabulary repeatedly draws attention to these notions of 'placing', the imaginative world is as unreliable, as subject to varying interpretations, as the narrative, social one. The irony of Milly's wealth and her unworldliness points the inadequacy of social 'codes' to experience.

On every level of subtlety and overt statement, *The Wings of the Dove* stimulates attention to its own proceeding, and promotes uncertainty in our relation to the experience it offers. It is a more extravagant, more problematic and disturbing novel than *The Ambassadors*. Its terms include the extremes of passion and death, yet even these 'absolutes' are effectively annulled. The narrative structure of the plotting, manipulative world gives way to imaginative acceptance, where selfless appreciation alone 'makes sense' of a grotesquely disordered moral universe. In some sense this passivity undercuts the forces of narrative, and the assumptions through which an author creates and reader interprets character. Yet this is a question never overtly presented in *The Wings of the Dove*: the morality of the creative imagination is a responsibility for the living Maggie Verver, not for Milly Theale, who is absolved by death, though her bequest allows the survivors to determine their own response.

V

The Bath and the Goldfish bowl: Immersion and Observation in The Golden Bowl

I *The Prince*

The Golden Bowl, though written shortly after *The Wings of the Dove* and *The Ambassadors*, differs from them not simply in degree but in kind. Those novels share a highly developed but conventional relationship between what is attempted and what is suggested by the novel form. The 'ideal' lies beyond the limits of the novel, though it is indicated within it: Strether's 'There we are', or the recognition by Milly's survivors that 'We shall never be again as we were'. In each novel there is a completion of form: the 'hour-glass' (as E. M. Forster called it) of *The Ambassadors*, and the triangle of *The Wings of the Dove*, where Milly in ascension covers the conspirators with her wings. The concluding sentences seem to acknowledge this containment, accept the implied defeat. But in *The Golden Bowl* there are two basic figures: the square of the relationship between four main characters, and the rounded bowl which is to symbolize their perfect happiness. The bowl may be broken into three angular pieces, the protagonists realigned in triangular phalanxes of relationship and conspiracy, understanding and design, but the fundamental impossibility of accepting both bases at once, of blurring the distinction between them, is not belied. While Maggie works with what she has to hand, and the ideal, in *The Golden Bowl*, is conceived in terms of the world of the novel, the conclusion of this work rejects complacency. There are two important statements: the first indicating an achieved possibility of significance:

Stillness . . . might have been said to be not so much restored as created; so that whatever next took place in it was foredoomed to remarkable salience.   (*The Golden Bowl*, II, 375)

Yet it is the hint of silence, rather than the triumph of meaning, which is taken up:

> All she now knew, accordingly, was that she should be ashamed to listen to the uttered word; all, that is, but that she might dispose of it on the spot forever. (II, 377)

At the very limits of the novel form, it is a wry acknowledgement of its inadequacy to the boundless quality of experience itself. Instead of gesturing towards an ideal beyond form, yet resting upon the achieved work, this novel attempts an achieved ideal, but finally, with a humility like that of Maggie re-entering the arms of her husband, admits that all it has done is all it can. It is *The Golden Bowl* which most clearly exemplifies the achievement Conrad attributed to James:

> One is never set at rest by Mr. Henry James' novels. His books end as an episode in life ends. You remain with the sense of life still going on.[1]

The 'interest' of the novel is no longer in the virtuoso display of novel languages, of different modes, with which *The Wings of the Dove* teased the literary reader, highlighting the pathetic inevitability of its end. In *The Golden Bowl*, the reader's activity is as difficult, and as important, as that of Maggie Verver; or, to put it another way, the heroine's consciousness is as fully exercised as that of the reader; and both show 'something of the glitter of consciously possessing the constructive, the creative hand' (*The Golden Bowl*, II, 151). The hand, that is, of the author. The characters of *The Wings of the Dove*, with the important exception of Milly, whose imagination was appreciative, receptive, on the whole passive, put forward various fictive interpretations and projections of the plot, but failed to perceive their own story until it was over; but Maggie creates, or re-creates, her plot, through redefining the 'basis' of relationships. She goes 'behind' expression to do this, to the conditions of meaning itself, and is not afraid to use silence and inaction besides active manipulation to establish what she believes to be right.

The absolute moral confidence which can use a lie and not be used by it demands of the reader a degree of trust in the fiction and in its creator which exceeds the conventions of the novel

[1] 'Henry James: An Appreciation', p. 46.

form; just as the delicate and difficult, the occasionally vigorous, baroque style of *The Golden Bowl*, makes unusual, some would say inordinate, demands on his patience and intelligence. These obstacles to easy pleasure both select an audience[1] and establish the conditions for the kind of 'interest' associated with *The Golden Bowl*: an exhaustive exploitation of the novel form. The exhilaration of difficulty overcome in reading *The Golden Bowl* in turn 'demonstrates' the triumph of Maggie, and indirectly vindicates her role within the novel. The corollary of this, however, is that all the difficulty of accepting Maggie's activity, the qualifications to her rights, reflect back upon the form itself, in an unease for the reader about the way the novel works.

This is a circular argument of interdependence between the novel and its heroine. Critics who attack Maggie for her callousness can be refuted by those reading carefully enough to discriminate between crass materialism and ironic blatancy. But does James depend too heavily on the reader's good faith? Maggie eventually recognizes, in the imminent separation of the two couples, 'the note of that strange accepted finality of relation . . . which almost escaped an awkwardness only by not attempting a gloss' (II, 369). Does that acceptance beg the question, or in fact avoid doing so, precisely by refusing to formulate the question in a way which would dictate the terms of an answer?

Close reading can approach this problem through the more limited concern with the operation of the novel: how does it work and what does it do? Relating whatever is striking in the reading to James's exploitation of the novel form provokes a further question: that of the 'location' of the reader's interest. Two figures from the novel illustrate the possible extremes.[2] Luxurious, yet claustrophobic, they are not concluding symbols. They image existence as it is through much of the novel: one constrained against its nature. It would be misleading to suggest

---

[1] Seymour Chatman, in *The Later Style of Henry James* (1972), p. 85, suggests that various rhetorical effects in the late James 'are ways of pre-selecting the audience'. Adrian Poole, in 'Transactions Across the Abyss' *T.L.S.*, No. 3, 891, p. 1272, makes a similar point more poetically: 'The intricate, mesmeric courtship of the language sifts out only the choicest of victims.'

[2] They also occur elsewhere in late James, e.g. in Strether's Paris, where he and Waymarsh regarded each other 'with the round impersonal eye of silent fish', or in Venice, where Densher finds Milly's benevolence 'up to his neck': 'He moved about in it, and it made no plash; he floated, he noiselessly swam in it; and they were all together, for that matter, like fishes in a crystal pool' (p. 424).

that they could stand at the end. But for an idea of the novel in operation, the bath and the goldfish bowl, immersion and observation, provide analogies whose very disturbing qualities are important.

> They had built her in with their purpose ... in the solid chamber of her helplessness, as in a bath of benevolence artfully prepared. ...
>
> (*The Golden Bowl*, II, 45)

Maggie's early perception parallels that of the reader, accepting the luxuriance of the form, but unable to control experience, to see motives, perceive the basis of relationships, change perspectives. Later, however, Maggie sees the party at Fawns in terms of immersion and display, which implies an audience. In this airless environment,

> Maggie grew to think again of this large element of 'company' as of a kind of renewed water-supply for the tank in which, like a party of panting gold-fish, they kept afloat. (II, 296–7)

There are many other images, from the building to the web, the golden cage to the telescope, which figure both experience itself and the approach to experience; then there are frequent representations of the situation by the characters in terms of elements and form, which have a near-metaphorical quality within the novel structure. The uneasy balance between immersion and observation, passivity and active interpretation, and the hinted parallel with a precarious stance in relation to art and experience, a mistrust of forms, and an acknowledgement of their power: these are tensions and concerns underlying not only Maggie's experience, but that of the reader in relation to the novel itself; and the assurance and humility of the end of *The Golden Bowl* may be taken as confirmation that they are preoccupations shared, from his different standpoint, by the author.

It is in the Preface to *The Golden Bowl* that James writes of 'the process and the effect of representation'; and the context is a discussion of the responsibility of authorship. Unlike *The Ambassadors*, where Strether's consciousness supersedes the narrator's as the dominant point of view, or *The Wings of the Dove*, where continual shifting between points of view effects modulations in tone, rather than in 'reality', *The Golden Bowl* exploits two different approaches to the centre of consciousness and its relationship to reality, and in this way explores the question of creative responsibility. James makes the claim that 'the Prince, in the first half of the book, virtually sees and knows and makes out . . . everything that concerns us . . . The function of the Princess, in the remainder, matches exactly with his' (*The Art of the Novel*, p. 329). This is not a wholly satisfactory account. Leo Bersani sees it differently: 'Reality in *The Golden Bowl* consists in the novelistic arrangements of the first half; the second half gives us the correction, the unashamed radical revision which Maggie then makes of her own work.'[1] This is also too sweeping. There is in effect a change from one sort of consciousness, that noted by James, to another, more akin to Bersani's analysis. The question of loyalties and blame towards Prince or Princess from the reader is evaded through a shift of terms between the two halves of the novel: there is not merely a different centre of consciousness, but a different kind. The approach to experience changes, and with it the quality of experience, and the nature of the relationship between the perceiver and what is perceived.

This might seem like the undercutting irony of the manipulative style in *The Wings of the Dove*. But in *The Golden Bowl* each character is introduced, constructed, with leisurely amplitude, and without superficial pretensions. Not only the Prince but Adam Verver is given a significant share of the consciousness in the first volume. Charlotte is seen with some understanding: at the Embassy party, we share her point of view briefly as she comes 'to the right assurance, to the right indifference, to the right expression, and above all, as she felt, to the right view of her opportunity for happiness . . .' (I, 247). Fanny Assingham's exhaustive analysis establishes the *status quo* and partly interprets it. Not until the second volume, where Maggie alone enjoys the dominant consciousness, are these 'arrangements' challenged, and their way of ordering reality recognized as 'Evil'. The eventual victory is not an intellectual *frisson*, but a triumph of the creative imagination, deconstructing as Strether did, but also reconstructing reality, as Milly Theale could not.

Leo Bersani points out that though *The Golden Bowl* is immensely different from *The Ambassadors* and *The Wings of the Dove*, 'the questions which it succeeds in making irrelevant give it a thematic continuity with the two earlier novels' (op. cit. 67). The introduc-

---

[1] 'The Jamesian Lie', *Partisan Review*, 36, 1969, p. 73.

tion of the Prince, of Adam and Maggie Verver, and of Charlotte, raises issues of race and cultural conventions, language, the hereditary and financial aristocracy, 'natural' and conventional relationships and the rights they demand or confer. James's 'international theme', his 'money' theme, and the concern with power and the exercise of power, which recur throughout his major works, besides the aesthetic question, a mode of considering the relationship of art to morality in a social context, are all presented in the first volume of *The Golden Bowl* with a dramatic immediacy, subtlety, and imaginative power which preclude easy dismissal. It is in this sense that *The Golden Bowl* can be seen, as it is by Dorothea Krook (op. cit. 199), as a 'palimpsest' of James's earlier novels. By the end of *The Golden Bowl*, however, such questions as these are transcended. The relation of personal to social being, and all the cultural and artistic questions which provide the setting for a 'false position', are either resolved or made irrelevant, depending on whether one finds the ending satisfactory or not. When Maggie finds her right place in the Prince's arms, and hopes for no more words, it must be seen either as grateful oblivion, snatched at the expense of all other relations, or as a proper consummation achieved through the exercise of all her powers in support of her personal and social role: she loves him both as a woman and as his wife.

Clearly it is the second of these alternatives which James intends the reader to accept, and this could only be achieved through an admission of all contrary possibilities which is more than perfunctory. No superficially witty dismissal, the elegant irony of *The Ambassadors,* or the exuberant activity of *The Wings of the Dove,* could provide for the reader a counterpart to Maggie's own process of understanding and creative re-ordering of experience which was sufficiently demanding, in imaginative, as well as intellectual terms, to earn the reward of satisfaction.

Opening *The Golden Bowl* with the Prince, and ostensibly devoting the first half of the novel to him, is bolder than giving Kate Croy the stage in *The Wings of the Dove*. Amerigo is not a figure who can eventually be left behind. He must be worthy of Maggie's devotion, yet capable of entering a position so false as to justify her measures to set it right. James's treatment of the Prince at the outset from his own centre of consciousness is followed by several episodes in which he is dramatically seen from the outside, or analysed by Fanny Assingham, before the volume under Maggie's control, where he seems curiously near, though separated by silence from the central consciousness. The distance between the Prince and the reader is controlled, yet flexible, and assures Amerigo of respect even while he cannot be given approbation.

The Prince's foreignness partly excuses, though it does not justify, his mistaken conception of the role he is to play. By admitting his difference, and showing Amerigo himself as intrigued by the cultural questions it provokes, James suggests a certain concern in the Prince, counterbalancing the irresponsibility of foreignness without actually negating it. In this context, foreign languages provide a shorthand notation of entire cultural systems; and it is significant that the Prince is fluent in English. Yet it is not his native language: merely the one 'he used'. In this hint of manipulative ability is the rationale for Amerigo's other linguistic choices, notably his use of French for 'discriminations, doubtless of the invidious kind, for which that language was most apt' (I, 6). He uses French of Charlotte—'Est-elle toujours aussi belle?'—and to her, in his telegram: '"*A la guerre comme à la guerre,* then"—it had been couched in the French tongue' (I, 294). There is an ironic distance between this cool, and dangerous, ease, and Fanny Assingham's amateur aspirations to equal poise: her American bluffness is unconquerable, as she briskly tells her husband: 'You give me a *point de repère* outside myself—which is where I like it. Now I can work round you' (I, 288).

James's use of languages as signals establishes a level of expression distinct from the narrative, allowing for different, even contrary, responses. At the same time the sophistication of this technique evokes a kind of respect for a character who requires such poise, and himself displays it. Amerigo is far from naïve. Indeed, his critical interest evokes our sympathy.

The opening of *The Golden Bowl* has a transparency of style, placing the reader with the Prince, and wilfully concealing neither his perceptiveness nor limitations of vision. The ironic perspective is introduced through him, quizzically: 'Capture had crowned the pursuit—or success, as he would otherwise have put it, had rewarded virtue'. Polarities for judgement are established without ostentation; but a Jamesian precision of reference inevitably entails a thickening of style, corresponding to the complexity of experience. Surface simplicity reveals depths of complex association when 'Miss Verver had told him he spoke English too well—it was his only fault, and he had not been able to speak worse even to oblige her. "When I speak worse, you see, I speak French" . . .'. Such paradoxes foreshadow the great riddles posed and explored throughout the novel: simple to express, but for solution requiring a moral vision beyond the exactitude of syntax. The relations of the serious and the curious, of youth and age, of the sexes, explored in Maggie's relationship with her father, are brought together economically and simply by the Prince, using terms which combine moral scope with the social fluency of cliché:

> Only the funny thing, he had respectfully submitted, was that her father, though older and wiser, and a man into the bargain, was as bad—that is as good—as herself. (I, 11–12)

There is no urgency about defining these terms, which only the whole work can secure: for the moment, Maggie simply accepts Amerigo's reference with generous ease: ' "Oh, he's better," the girl had freely declared—"that is he's worse." '

While this word-play introduces recurrent Jamesian preoccupations with colloquial simplicity, the process of rendering irrelevant those themes familiar in James's earlier novels, or at least of transforming the quality of their relevance, is begun. The 'international theme' receives something of a setback, in a rejection of the opportunity to elaborate on a well-established paradigm. The Prince comments on Mr. Verver,

> 'No, it's his *way*. It belongs to him.'
> But she had wondered still. 'It's the American way. That's all.'
> 'Exactly—it's all. It's all, I say! It fits him—so it must be good for something.' (I, 7)

The precedence of personal over national character is here firmly asserted. And indeed critics[1] who query James's success in creating an 'American robber baron' with philanthropic tendencies in Adam Verver are surely attributing to him an intention implicitly disavowed. James strenuously avoids the easy prejudice of

---

[1] Mildred E. Hartsock, 'Unintentional Fallacy Critics and *The Golden Bowl*', *Modern Language Quarterly* 35 (1974), p. 274, gives a useful summary of the 'Adam-haters' and where their criticisms can be found.

national types; though, as we have seen with Amerigo, he does not deny the importance of cultural background in determining social and moral codes.

The disturbance of accepted categories, an attitude not gratuitously destructive, but responsibly sceptical in an empirical tradition, pervades the opening of *The Golden Bowl*, characterizing the introduction of important themes, and preparing for Maggie's questioning and experiment later on. At the outset, Maggie is shown as accepting, the Prince as eager to learn: this helps redress the balance of responsibility between them in the book as a whole. When the transition is made from national to financial categories, and Maggie describes the Ververs as 'like a pair of pirates' (I, 13), exaggerating the acquisitive *coup* of the marriage with Prince Amerigo, her blatant exuberance disposes of the question, for all but those critics who find the rich irredeemably to blame.[1]

The stereotypes of character and role are set aside rather than ridiculed, for cheap wit would prejudice the real triumph of understanding. Not every gesture, therefore, is negative at this stage. The use of imagery by Amerigo and Maggie both demonstrates and encourages imaginative vigour, though it also shows incidentally how inadequate our preconceptions as to national characteristics are: the Prince's ability with the forms of a foreign culture are shown in his laughing opposition of the *quattrocento* staircase to a '"lightning elevator" in one of Mr. Verver's fifteen-storey buildings', while Maggie's images include the ancient volumes of family history besides those terms 'drawn from steamers and trains, from a familiarity with "lines" . . . from an experience of continents and seas, that [Amerigo] was unable as yet to emulate'. While our minds are cleared of the habits of thoughtless response, such imagery shows the creativity of the characters and fosters a complex of accurate expectations.

The balance between empty forms and those elements, such as ability with imagery, which have imaginative force and therefore contribute to what Maggie eventually recognizes as 'remarkable salience', pivots on character in *The Golden Bowl*. Character is both a form and a force, embodying and shaping 'representation'. Just as language is used for a sign, the operation of the imagery is

---

[1] Such as F. R. Leavis in *The Great Tradition*, p. 160 (see below, p. 147), or C. T. Samuels in *The Ambiguity of Henry James* (1971), p. 219, who finds Verver 'selfish and exploitative'.

frequently overtly recognized, so that the narrative moves on to a higher level of abstraction, as when Adam Verver 'spoke . . . as if he grasped the facts, without exception, for which angularity stood' (I, 138). Character can be grasped in equally abstract terms, as Fanny Assingham discovers: 'she wanted to leave well behind her both her question and the couple in whom it had, abruptly, taken such vivid form' (I, 275). Yet this very awareness raises the characters above mere form. Fanny's curiosity and speculation, fallible as they are, correspond to the Prince's consciousness of cultural patterns, in offering a faltering prefiguration of Maggie's eventual understanding of how personal and formal characteristics are properly to be integrated.

The close parallel between our interest in process and effect and that amongst the characters in understanding form and force, role and character, social and personal motivation, grows from the opening of *The Golden Bowl*. It is not only Maggie who appreciates such matters. The Prince wonders about Fanny's role in bringing about his marriage—and in admitting his dependence on her judgement, strengthens the correspondence between his role and ours: we also need Fanny's commentary and analysis in this volume. Dependence, however, need not be naïve. Selective interpretation is recognized within the narrative but extends beyond it to the reader, wary of forms:

It fairly befell at last, for a climax, that they almost ceased to pretend— to pretend, that is, to cheat each other with forms. The unspoken had come up, and there was a crisis . . . during which they were reduced, for all interchange, to looking at each other on quite an inordinate scale.   (I, 34)

How far the Prince is from *naïveté*, or Fanny from *insouciance*, is demonstrated in the announcement of Charlotte's imminent arrival. The Prince, 'with conscious inconsistency', is seen selecting an appropriate response, the correct word. After changing colour and hesitating, he ventures to speak:

'Oh,' he promptly declared—'charming!'
But this word came out as if, a little, in sudden substitution for some other. It sounded accidental, whereas he wished to be firm. That accordingly was what he next showed himself.   (I, 40)

He asks, too openly, 'Has she come with designs upon me?' and retreats, as he supposes, to a distance we recognize ironically as dangerous proximity: 'Est-elle toujours aussi belle?' The Prince cannot quite handle the situation, and Fanny's responsibility appears frighteningly large; but they both realize this: the unspoken is near the surface:

It had been said as a joke, but as, after this, they awaited their friend in silence, the effect of the silence was to turn the time to gravity . . .

When Charlotte comes in, the Prince's mental assessment of her, a 'catalogue of charms', provides a feeling account of her person; but his danger is hinted in this 'cluster of possessions'. This last is the word Fanny has used of the relation between Amerigo and Maggie. But the Prince's repetition—'He saw . . . He saw . . . He knew . . . he knew . . . he knew . . . he knew' (I, 49)—appropriates Charlotte verbally, just as it hints at a physical possession. When Charlotte is asked by Adam for her hand in marriage, her response will recall this: 'Do you think you've "known" me?' (I, 224). Meanwhile, however, this web of irony is on the edge of the narrative consciousness. Of the 'facts' of Charlotte's person and presence, Amerigo recognizes that 'If they had to be interpreted, this made at least for intimacy' (I, 48). The distance of formality, its poise, is subverted to a means of manipulation now. The Prince fully understands the significance of his staying with Charlotte, and she, in her turn, 'would see what he would do—so their queer minute without words told him; and she would act accordingly' (I, 53). Though Fanny's approval of their planned meeting makes her complicity equal their own, 'And it was really so express a license from her, as representing friendly judgment, public opinion, the moral law, the margin allowed a husband about to be, or whatever' (I, 64), in the excess of epithets, the narrative ironically disengages from the trio, disavows their complicity, and thus dramatizes through style itself the departure from integrity which their plan, so careful of its façade, represents.

It is the passage between the Prince and Charlotte, the first meeting and the rendezvous, which marks the departure from transparency to manipulation in the narrative that alters the character of Volume I and prepares the position which Maggie will be justified in destroying. When Maggie speaks to her father of Charlotte's greatness, it is he, ironically, who cautions her.

She is content with an impression unsupported by knowledge, echoing in this Jamesian heroines from Gertrude Wentworth to Isabel Archer, who have a romantical partiality to veils not unlike Catherine Morland's in *Northanger Abbey*. Maggie says

> 'I don't think I want even for myself to put names and times, to pull away any veil. . . .'
> Mr. Verver deferred, yet he discriminated.
> 'I don't see how you can give credit without knowing the facts.'
>   (I, 187–8)

These facts are what the novel gives us, and withholds at this stage from Maggie. When the bowl itself reappears to betray the interlude on the eve of her marriage, this will be enough to signal the adulterous relationship which followed it; though before that, Maggie will have begun to watch and interpret events much as the reader does. The novel draws attention, through Maggie's consciousness, to its own method of proceeding:

> It fell, for retrospect, into a succession of moments that were *watchable* still; almost in the manner of different things done during a scene on the stage . . . Several of these moments stood out beyond the others . . . These were parts of the experience—though in fact there had been a good many of them—between which her impression could continue sharply to discriminate.   (II, 11)

This process of watching, a discriminating response, from outside, as it were, the goldfish bowl, begins long before Maggie's recognition, avoiding an absolute rift between the two parts of the novel and preparing for an eventual reconciliation. Fanny Assingham's analysis takes up where the Prince's amused curiosity as to the processes in which he is involved lapses. But from that point there is a change in the quality of the narrative, discernible in effects as broad as the structural distinction between scenes of analysis and those of action, and their respective characters, as oblique as the manipulation of narrative modes and as minute as the pressure of precision in verbal effects, as small as single words or as dramatic as mismatched conversations. Not all these techniques come into operation at once; but their cumulative effect, from the strangely fairytale quality of the Bloomsbury dealer's shop and the episode in it, to the comedy of interludes between Fanny Assingham and the Colonel, and from

Adam Verver's unexpected penchant for romance to Fanny's melodramatic suspicion of 'Evil—with a very big E' (I, 394), besides the operatic histrionics of the escapade leading Amerigo and Charlotte to Gloucester, amounts to an uneasy narrative extravagance which in itself conveys the loss of integrity, the loss of a common basis of understanding.

The distortionary effect of compressing process and effect in summary again obliquely indicates their real subtlety. Only on the brink of adultery does Amerigo desire, and achieve, a '*situation nette*'. The 'images and ruminations of his leisure, these gropings and fittings of his conscience and his experience', which prefigure Maggie's, are matched in the first volume by Adam Verver's mental activity. Like the Prince, Adam has not yet achieved 'Negative Capability, that is when a man is capable of being in uncertainties, mysteries, doubts, without any irritable reaching after fact and reason' Keats, op. cit. 43). The narrative of Verver's 'groping' and its resolution in his unfortunate marriage dramatizes in stylistic terms the 'false position' where integrity becomes impossible. The deceptions of the narrative mirror his false consciousness at this stage, and we are more deeply involved than in *The Ambassadors* or *The Wings of the Dove* in a confusion from which Maggie's determination will eventually extricate both herself and us.

The 'general golden peace' of a Keatsian, as well as Kentish, October is full of the sense 'of all the pleasure so fruity an autumn there could hold in its lap',[1] as Adam's house opens to Charlotte. This is a prelude comparable with Susan Stringham's mountain scene in *The Wings of the Dove*, and through confusion of the senses and the appearance of 'warning' words, as in *The Ambassadors*, we are alerted to Adam Verver's unwariness. Yet the opposition between appearances and implications is not a matter of ironic polarity: to some extent the 'attentive and gratified' responses are compatible:

---

[1] A more explicit reference to Keats is Adam's reflection on the sonnet mentioning Cortez. Stephen L. Mooney suggests that 'Thematically, the Keats sonnet is central to the novel; it provides, through Adam Verver's sensibility, a revealed meaning for the whole system of exploration images. . . . Both Keats and James are concerned with the discovery of wealth through exploration . . .' He goes on to suggest one resolution of the conflict here: 'By associating him with Keats, James gives Adam the right to be rich, for his wealth is of the spirit'. 'James, Keats, and the Religion of Consciousness', *Modern Language Quarterly* XXII (1961), pp. 399–401.

The note of reality, in so much projected light, continued to have for him the charm and the importance of which the maximum had occasionally been reached in his great 'finds'—continued, beyond any other, to keep him attentive and gratified.	(I, 199)

The tone of this passage is light, and Verver alert to his 'acquisition' of Charlotte and of the Prince. But amidst such deliberately preposterous similes for these 'finds' as the Bernadino Luini and 'an extraordinary set of oriental tiles', some of the imagery—notably the extravagant likening of Verver to a pleasure-loving bachelor—apparently unwittingly exceeds its context. This difficulty is recognized in the text, which admits, 'That figure has . . . a freedom that the occasion doubtless scarce demands, though we may retain it for its rough negative value.' Here, indeed, the disintegration of Adam Verver, as a collector and as a lover, seems to have provoked a collapse of the fictional stance of the kind James condemned in Trollope.[1]

It is remarkable that this occurs precisely at a time of such luxuriant acceptance at Fawns, and in response to an image only excessively vivid. If this episode points to anything in terms of its own proceeding, it can only be to an authorial refusal to offer a comprehensive vision resting on his own control and ordering of effects. A breakdown in narrative consistency is, in this view, a tribute to the scope and power of the form itself: a refusal to set the whole novel within a larger frame of reference—that of the mind of the producer—and an acknowledgement of the effort which sets *The Golden Bowl* apart from its predecessors, as the form itself is expanded in the attempt to determine within the novel itself the issues raised there, rather than appealing to a notional ideal beyond it. A lapse of tone at this point is a tribute to the unruly autonomy of the characters. In the golden luxury of a Kentish October at Fawns, the narrative itself sits up to its neck in a bath of opulence, and is helpless to move or see.

This reading is based on the premiss that James's control is unflawed, and even an anomaly is designed to achieve a specific effect. The alternative is to claim that James did not intend or

[1] In 'The Art of Fiction', where James writes on Trollope's 'want of discretion . . . In a digression, a parenthesis or an aside, he concedes to the reader that he and this trusting friend are only "making believe". . . . Such a betrayal of a sacred office seems to me, I confess, a terrible crime; it is what I mean by the attitude of apology . . .' (*Selected Literary Criticism*, p. 80).

perceive any confusion in the presentation of Verver. But even then, as Susie's limitations 'contained' the stray implications of the mountain scene in *The Wings of the Dove*, so the narrative context sets limits here. The autumnal haze at Fawns is important. To define the influence of time, place, circumstance exactly would clarify the situation before the characters themselves do so, and they would have to be judged negligent or culpable. Only by maintaining a vagueness before Adam's proposal can James retain the possibilities of both guilt and innocence, for every character. When the situation becomes clearer, it is Verver, or our view of him, which changes. Seen from the outside, he becomes remote and mysterious: we cannot judge how much he knows, or from what point. The burden and reward of discovery is for Maggie alone; and Adam Verver's arbitrary dealings, whether out of love for Maggie or respect for the form of marriage, serve to highlight her humanity, since from her we see sympathy, and value for others as people, even while she regards impersonal social forms as proper embodiments of this value.

The exact placing of each observation of Verver before his marriage is important, for what seems inconsequential at the time may be interpreted in retrospect. The interruption of the narrative of immersion which provoked our digression is followed in the novel itself by a shift of subject. But in the imaginative reading there is no break. The image of the 'serenade' which lures Amerigo away will reappear much later in the context of his escapade with Charlotte: and it will indicate the inevitability of a liaison between the former lovers, predating the marriages which make it practicable.

On the departure of Amerigo and Maggie, Verver and Charlotte are left together in charge of the Principino: a domestic situation of equal intimacy and simplicity. Now Adam finds

She was directly and immediately real, real on a pleasantly reduced and intimate scale.   (I, 205)

The difference in tone between this and the collector's recognition of 'the real thing' (I, 198) is striking; but it is not clear which is the more accurate account of Charlotte in relation to Adam. It is when his intellectual defences are lowered in response to her domestic immediacy that he is most susceptible to those arts appealing to his 'aesthetic principle'. Charlotte seems to enter his affections somewhere between the two: the exact nature of her personal appeal is not pinpointed. Instead, the impressionistic luxury of the golden autumn is recreated, in night tones, with Adam smoking, watching Charlotte playing the piano, lit by candles:

the picture distinct, the vagueness spread itself about him like some boundless carpet, a surface delightfully soft to the pressure of his interest.   (I, 206)

It is a beguiling image: a brilliant reworking in the Jamesian canon of that scene at Gardencourt where Isabel Archer comes upon Madame Merle at the piano and is charmed by her.

The 'picture', blurred with smoke and candle haze, is orchestrated with

a full word or two dropped into the still-stirring sea of other voices— a word or two that affected our friend even at the moment, and rather oddly, as louder and rounder than any previous sound . . .
                                                                   (I, 206)

It is now that Adam thinks 'in a loose, an almost agitated order, of many things', and gropes for 'some mere happy word perhaps'. Immersed in the scene, his search is that of the narrative itself for words, for one word, which will restore order. It seems that 'There had in fact been nothing to call a scene, even of the littlest, at all': but this is the social 'scene': an interlude with recognizable moves and implications. Charlotte's words about their forthcoming journey almost constitute a gambit in one. She is all but prompting Adam to 'speak', in the technical, social sense: to make a scene by speaking the word.

It is at this point that Amerigo's name comes up again for Adam Verver. The significance of this sequence is neither obtrusive nor explicit; it is a withheld irony, just as Adam's knowledge is restrained, on the brink of discovering the relationship which would prevent his marrying Charlotte. The two perceptions come close, without meeting in 'some mere happy word':

It had struck him, up to now, that this particular balm was a mixture of which Amerigo, as through some hereditary privilege, alone possessed the secret; so that he found himself wondering if it had come to Charlotte, who had unmistakably acquired it, through the young man's having amiably passed it on.   (I, 208)

Instead of pursuing this enquiry, Adam Verver leans on the parapet, 'losing himself in a far excursion'. He is capable of sensing and of analysing Charlotte's expertise:

> She made use, for her so quietly grateful host . . . of quite the same shades of attention and recognition, was mistress in an equal degree of the regulated, the developed art of placing him high in the scale of importance. (I, 208)

He can conceive the form of the future:

> in forming a new and intimate tie he should in a manner abandon, or at the best signally relegate, his daughter. He should reduce to a definite form . . . the idea of his having incurred an injury, or at the best an inconvenience, that required some makeweight and deserved some amends. (I, 209)

Yet this curiosity over form, the subtleties of significance and interpretation, glides over the interim states, the immediate forces. The impatience for an overall view is in keeping with the reader's curiosity: it is a process very like our own. But the imagery continues to warn against this sophistication. It is too ambitious for clarity; too many senses are involved, too many boundaries between the abstract and the concrete ignored. The contrast between Verver's sensations and the tortuous thoughts around them betrays their escapism; but intellectual research is abandoned as 'Light broke for him at last'. The longed-for 'fusion' comes in a merging of mental labyrinth and physical scenery. The sense of discovery is breathtaking. But in the moment of triumph James allows us several warnings about its validity. The very order speaks against a disorder presented in the same breath: a sequence of impressions culminates in an unnatural climax:

> the autumn night seemed to clear to a view in which the whole place, everything round him, the wide terrace where he stood, the others, with their steps, below, the gardens, the park, the lake, the circling woods, lay there as under some strange midnight sun. (I, 210)

The heightened 'distinctness' of familiar objects is twice described as 'inordinate'. What might have been seen as a revelation is actually called a 'hallucination'; and its effect is devastating: 'brief, but it lasted long enough to leave him gasping'. The hyperbole, in other words, mirrors a disproportion of thought. Although order is swiftly re-established, it is founded on a dangerous misapprehension. We, like Adam, are liable not to notice this flaw: it is tempting to believe that

> the cool darkness had again closed round him, but his moral lucidity was constituted.   (I, 212)

Yet we are warned against oversimple solutions. The word is no formula for success; mechanical aptitude is inappropriate to human situations. This is pointed alike by the riddling sense and the facile sound of the sentence which purports to sum up the achievement of 'lucidity' won through such imaginative and intellectual endeavours:

> It wasn't only moreover that the word, with a click, so fitted the riddle, but that the riddle, in such perfection, fitted the word.
>   (I, 212)

The inadequacy of 'the word' is pointed by this mismatch of simplicity and complexity: a misapplication of formal rigour which recurs in the proposal itself. The clichés of behaviour would constitute admirable restraint if the situation conformed perfectly to type, but this ease may be too alluring:

> He liked . . . to feel that he should be able to 'speak' and that he would; the word itself being romantic, pressing for him the spring of association with stories and plays . . .   (I, 213)

The echoed image of mechanical association, the setting apart of the cliché 'speak', as a formula, both more and less than a word, together with the artifice of fiction: all these points of style mark a distinction between Adam's behaviour and his understanding. Beyond this exposition, immediately available through a precise, ironic style, there is also a more remote ironic allusion to warn us. Mr. Verver's enjoyment here—'He liked . . . to feel that he should be able to "speak" and that he would'—recalls a similar pattern of words in a different context. The exercise of power is similar in process, though different in effect, from that more uncompromising statement:

> He should be proposed to at a given moment—it was only a question of time—and then he should have to do a thing that would be extremely disagreeable. He almost wished, on occasion, that he wasn't

so sure he *would* do it. He knew himself, however, well enough not to doubt: he knew coldly, quite bleakly, where he would, at the crisis, draw the line. (I, 135)

To say no to Mrs. Rance, and to invite Charlotte to say yes, can be seen as related examples of Adam's own power. That he recognizes this of the first, and not of the second proposal, is in itself significant, for this marks a diminished self-awareness.

Such effects are subtle and complex. But the text does not rely too heavily on the luxuries of researched implications. The proposal scene itself is presented with a dramatic immediacy weighted with imagery which recalls various symbolic themes, from exploration to the pillage of piracy. There is a striking correspondence of 'real' and 'imagined' worlds, achieved partly through the concrete rendering of figures of speech, partly through the abstraction of immediacies of sensation. As Mr. Verver gazed over the terrace at Fawns, night became day, but the strangely highlighted landscape was in fact a 'hallucination'. Now, from Brighton, it can be seen that 'Fawns . . . was out of the world' (I, 214). But Brighton, for all its 'actual' force, 'so plump in the conscious centre', has a kind of realism quite foreign to the world of the novel as it generally appears through the consciousness of the characters. This is an episode as grotesquely 'realistic' as the escapade of Charlotte and the Prince in Blooms-bury; and it has a similar function, in that it brings to life, to a strangely excessive life, what functions elsewhere in the novel as a symbol. In Bloomsbury it is the golden bowl itself; here it is these tiles Adam Verver wanted to acquire very much as he wanted Charlotte. The strange equivalence between person and thing is grotesquely confirmed as he does both: buys the tiles and obtains Charlotte's consent to marriage. There is a kind of imaginative transgression about this transposition of the figurative to the dramatic which matches the moral outrage. When Verver 'burns his ships', Charlotte sits blushing; yet even this intimate physical reaction is appropriated, as it were, and set to the credit of Mr. Verver:

All that she was herself, moreover, was so lighted, to its advantage, by the pink glow. (I, 224)

There are hints that Charlotte has played her part in manœuvring this proposal, and that it is disastrous for Adam; but the dominant tone here, only qualified by the mystery which we are given to understand he feels too, is the sense of activity on his part which endows him with a large share of responsibility for the outcome of the marriage. The narrative strategy of point of view becomes a moral question of advantage and manipulation: a great deal rests on interpretation, precisely because it is this, rather than the primary level of activity, which attracts our interest. There is a shocking ease in the facility with which Adam proposes to Charlotte what is effectively a marriage of convenience for Maggie. It is Charlotte's acute yet inexplicit assessment that the reader follows here, while Adam congratulates himself on the achievements of a selfishness adopted on his daughter's behalf:

> 'Our keeping together will help you perhaps to see. To see, I mean, how I need you.'
> 'I already see . . . how you've persuaded yourself you do.'
> . . . . . .
> 'Well then, how you'll make Maggie right.'
> ' "Right"?' She echoed it as if the word went far. And 'O-Oh!' she still critically murmured as they moved together away.   (I, 230)

The technique used here, of picking out in inverted commas a word of ambiguous significance, is one device to focus both the plurality of meanings and the importance of various distinct attitudes to words themselves, as units of meaning, expression, or communication. Just as whole languages may signal cultural distinctions, or the very technique of quotation, whether from Keats or Edgar Allan Poe, indicate something of the cast of mind as well as the literary knowledge of its speaker, so individual words may be mechanical devices, fitting with a click, puzzles or solutions. Adam Verver, having found phrases, has 'times of using these constantly, as if they just then lighted the world, or his own part in it, for him—even when for some of his interlocutors they covered less ground' (I, 138): the word for him may be a formula, or an icon, rather than a unit of expression or communication. His tendency is to fit experience into a discovered pattern. Fanny Assingham has something of the same tendency, though with less deliberation, to take refuge in 'that good right word about the happy issue of his connexion' (I, 138). We have already noted the Prince's sensitivity to language, and its fallibility. Charlotte's ability is unlike this: a cavalier manipulation of speech and silence, which 'would see what he would do ... and ... act accordingly'; but Charlotte's intelligence is sufficient for her to appreciate words quite as well as to interpret silence, as her precise, distinguishing response to Adam's proposal demonstrates. Maggie alone in the first volume seems to have an appreciation of what cannot and what ought not to be expressed in words, as well as what can, to her father, about Amerigo and herself.

On a smaller scale, the range of attitudes to expression appears if we catalogue the uses of a particular word. Our example is prompted by James, through repetitive use, frequent unusual stress, and an exploitation of alternative meanings so pronounced as to amount to gross manipulation of the word itself. Adrian Poole suggests that James is not so much an 'intimate adversary' for the reader as a seducer (op. cit. 1272). While the seductive elaboration of style may be most highly developed in passages of imagery, and in long, intricate sentences, it is also most evident there. The greater danger, or persuasion, is when language itself becomes the material of seduction; and this is liable to happen at those points more noticeable for their 'contentious' proceeding. Such difficulties may only distract attention from the 'insignificant' word which is actually the pivot of significance.

One such word is the preposition 'for', stressed through repetition and selected through emphasis, despite surrounding riddling patterns of words. Gradually a cumulative emphasis draws attention to this word as a point where the themes of motive and the strategies of substitution, whether benevolent or hypocritical, come together, knitting process and effect both within the novel, on conscious and subconscious levels, and in the operation of the whole, where similar concerns and techniques mediate through the work between author and reader. The accretion of significance also works in the other direction, heightening and drawing together points in the narrative whose thematic connections might not otherwise be apparent. Thus there is a similarity of attitude, a resolution, in common between Charlotte's assertion to the Prince, 'I came back for this. Not really for anything else. For this' (I, 92), and Adam Verver's reflection: 'To think of it merely for himself would have been ... yes, impossible.

But there was a grand difference in thinking of it for his child' (I, 212). In the latter statement, 'for' could mean 'in the interests of' or 'in place of'; then it could be, he in her place, or she in his. These convolutions lead to a growing understanding for the reader of a fundamental impropriety. The strategy of substitution in the word 'for' may be acceptable in the linguistic or symbolic ploy of analogy—'He spoke . . . as if he grasped the facts . . . for which angularity stood' (I, 138)—but it must be suspect when people are the materials to be manipulated. This is at least a potential meaning, even if not the overt intention, when Adam says to Charlotte of Maggie, 'She'll speak to you *for* me' (I, 229). The cavalier disregard of personal dignity and the irreducible quality of otherness is even more flagrant when he subordinates the Prince's reaction to his daughter's; nor is this modified by Adam's bluffness, for we are told that his tone is 'grave': 'That [Maggie's accepting] . . . will have to do for him' (I, 236). The repeated neglect of significance builds up an ominous force in the word which makes Charlotte's response peculiarly dark when she asks Adam, of waiting to call their 'little question' a 'catastrophe', 'What would you like, dear friend, to wait for?' (I, 238). There is then an understated irony in Verver's subsequent explanation to Charlotte of their position. The word has no warning stress, merely the familiarity of recurrence, when he explains of Amerigo, 'Why, our marriage puts him for you, you see—or puts you for him—into a new relation . . .' (I, 244). One further example may bridge the two volumes. To Adam Verver's 'What my child does for me!' (I, 244) corresponds Maggie's dreadful realization: 'He did it for *me*, he did it for me . . .' (II, 83).

Selecting specific verbal effects to suggest the degree to which Adam is, or fails to be, conscious of and responsible for the implications of his marriage is no falsehood: but it does not explain the effect of the novel. Adam's responsibility is qualified by his own ignorance and well-meaning, but it is also set against the responsibility of every other party involved.

Our first, and abiding, impressions of Maggie's father are those of his own self-analysis, long before the proposal. Immediately after the Bloomsbury episode and before the reintroduction of Amerigo and Maggie as man and wife, the statements of Chapter VII convey a contemplative depth in Adam Verver incompatible with simple tyranny. Though his attitude to others and to their claims on him is not submissive, it has a degree of detachment and control, together with a certain weariness of responsibility, which are not unlike our attitudes as readers. If Amerigo at the outset enjoyed our poised curiosity, Adam seems involved in much the same way as we are by now, and his resistance to 'immersion' shows an attractive restraint, an implied criticism of the Jamesian method as effective as Colonel Assingham's jocularity, though quite different in tone. We can well understand the sensation that 'such connection as he enjoyed with the ironic question in general resided substantially less in a personal use of it than in the habit of seeing it as easy to others' (I, 131), and the resistance in Verver's feeling: 'Everyone had need of one's power, whereas one's own need, at the best, would have seemed to be but some trick for not communicating it' (I, 182). Yet if Verver constitutes to some extent a force alien to expression, one whose 'lips, somehow, were closed—and by a spring connected moreover with the action of his eyes themselves' (I, 132), he also carries within himself his own 'intimate adversary': 'He feared not only danger—he feared the idea of danger, or in other words feared, hauntedly, himself' (I, 134).

The Golden Bowl abounds in words which draw attention to themselves as language, in phrases which seem to offer comments upon the novel process, in characters who intermediate between author and reader in relation to their own story; but to extract and interpret these elements as a paranarrative working independently of the rest of the book is to ignore the cohesive impulse toward interpretation within the framework of the whole, and to invent an emasculated structure which is not the novel James offers. The manipulative technique of *The Wings of the Dove* relies on the reader's poised reaction to local effects in context and in sequence; though *The Golden Bowl* makes less play with stylistic manipulation, the novel demands a balanced appreciation of process and effect which takes account of the placing of each element. Selective response is fallible and may be misleading, for it presupposes a mechanics of character and action rather like Adam Verver's riddle and word, where things click into place and spring into action. What Maggie learns to see in Verver, and what is summarized for us through her, is 'a reminder of all he was' (II, 280). The perception of outward character, Verver's 'impression', is combined with an appreciation of the inner being. This poise of

activity and passivity of response is what 'placed him [Adam] in
her [Maggie's] eyes as no precious work of art probably had ever
been placed in his own' (II, 281). This is the perfection of that
appreciation which in Adam's response to Charlotte appeared
qualified by a suspicion of acquisitiveness. For Maggie,

There was a long moment, absolutely, during which her impression
rose and rose, even as that of the typical charmed gazer, in the still
museum, before the named and dated object, the pride of the catalogue,
that time has polished and consecrated.   (II, 281)

The transition from the first view of Adam Verver as perhaps
only excessively passive, through the episode of the proposal in
which he is suspected of too active and too proud an attitude,
towards this last analysis by his daughter of 'simply a great and
deep and high little man' (II, 282) is not to be made in terms of
character analysis and perceptive sympathy alone. What Adam
Verver is as a character is partly made up of what he does: both
how he acts and what function he fulfils in terms of the novel
structure, particularly the function he has in relation to Maggie,
how far his stature deserves her tenderness and pride.

This is as much a question of process as of effect. A sense of
the person corresponding to human dignity evolves through the
narrative. To see how this works, we must pay attention, not to
words, phrases, actions, characters, in isolation, but to all these
things in relation to each other, and in relation to the whole
work, in the novel process. To arrive at Maggie's estimation of
her father, we are taken through not only her thoughts and his
actions, but the narrative of those nearby standing in relation to
them both. Through a system of contrasts and analysis, and
through a sense of the forces of relationship, whether domineer-
ing or absorbent, the 'immersion' of the 'bath' becomes the
balance of involvement and detachment, being and display, of
the 'goldfish bowl' novel.

One approach to this narrative drama of interaction is through
a device developed in *The Golden Bowl* beyond the satirical comedy
in *The Ambassadors,* the grotesque distortion of *The Wings of the
Dove*: the mismatched conversation. Dialogue, the most immediate narrative device, apparently permitting the easiest and fullest
intercourse between characters within the novel, and between
novel and reader, works as a type of the novel process, and reveals

the inherent dangers and imperfections of this kind of communication.

This is of particular interest in the treatment of Charlotte: a character whose consciousness we scarcely enter, but who is given away in her relations with the other characters. The obliquity of this method of presentation is strangely effective in throwing the emphasis on the consciousness in which we have most interest: Maggie's. F. R. Leavis's assertion that

> Actually, if our sympathies are anywhere they are with Charlotte and (a little) the Prince, who represent what, against the general moral background of the book can only strike us as decent passion; in a stale, sickly and oppressive atmosphere they represent life.
>
> (*The Great Tradition*, p. 160)

gives a reaction so far from the novel's demands that it can only be seen as the outcome of inappropriate methods of analysis: those based on the old stable idea of character in the novel. What Leavis's comment incidentally betrays is that amongst the protagonists of *The Golden Bowl* Charlotte, though not the most sympathetic, is simply the most easily recognizable in the terms of a novel world which this work has left behind.

From her first appearance, Charlotte shows a familiarity with the social forms which correspond in their orderliness to the decorum of that world. She can assess and manipulate appearances, and conversely, her behaviour is open to interpretation, particularly ironic interpretation, according to those forms:

> She could have looked at her hostess with such straightness and brightness only from knowing that the Prince was also there ...
>
> (I, 46–7)

When Charlotte speaks, her words take a good deal for granted, but they assume nothing that could not be put into words. They presuppose Amerigo's shock at seeing her, and defy him not to respond with pleasure. Her first verbs taunt him with their dismissive colloquialism, while her epithet for Maggie mocks the conventional in its clichéd propriety: 'You see you're not rid of me. How is dear Maggie?' (I, 49) Though Charlotte may use the unspoken, there is little hint, in her assured propriety or poise, that she finds the forms of expression inadequate to her purpose. As the Prince sees it, with a curious blend of male chauvinism and sophisticated abstraction,

She was the twentieth woman, she was possessed by her doom, but her doom was also to arrange appearances, and what now concerned him was to learn how she proposed.   (I, 52)

There is a nice irony in his unawareness of the reversal of roles implied in 'how she proposed'. The degree of Charlotte's control is captured in her visit to him at Portland Place, when she dismisses comments which might prove embarrassingly incisive, in the very phrase which ostensibly pays tribute to the unspoken: 'There it all is—extraordinary beyond words' (I, 307). What Charlotte does is hurry past the threat which words might pose: 'Haven't we therefore to take things as we find them?'

It is not that Charlotte cannot see the significance of words, but rather that they act for her like Adam Verver's clicking riddle worked by a mechanical spring. Charlotte's social fluency merely highlights the distinction between what can and what cannot be reduced to form and practically communicated. There is a suspicion of glibness as well as coy manœuvring in her interchange with the Prince in Bloomsbury, when Charlotte tries to make their rendezvous seem more indiscreet, more improper, than need be, and to set aside the question of a wedding gift as the blatant pretence she undoubtedly meant it to be. Inverted decorum, a knowledge of propriety which is so distinct as to be open to manipulation, continues to characterize Charlotte's scenes with the Prince after her marriage. It is a perversion to which form is susceptible when it is divorced from a sense of what is beyond form: and it is as a matter of form that Charlotte's consciousness, as well as her strategy, is discussed:

There were hours when she spoke of their taking refuge in what she called the commonest tact . . . there were others when it might have seemed, to listen to her, that their course would demand of them the most anxious study and the most independent, not to say original, interpretation of signs.   (I, 292)

The divorce between motive and appearance in this misuse of signs is revealed by James with a delightful counterpoint of hyperbolic pomposity and bathetic simplicity:

She talked now as if it were indicated, at every turn, by finger-posts of almost ridiculous prominence; she talked again as if it lurked in devious ways and were to be tracked through bush and briar; and she even, on occasion, delivered herself in the sense that, as their situation was unprecedented, so their heaven was without stars. ' "Do" ?' she once had echoed to him as the upshot of passages covertly, though briefly, occurring between them . . .   (I, 293)

Such exuberance is partly for the entertainment of the reader. But there is a serious point to be made. This misuse of expression involves a duplicity which it grows to match perfectly in the adulterous 'elopement' scene. There the false tone of the operatic diction—'a moon, a mandolin, and a little danger', ' "Vengo, vengo!" ' (I, 365)—depends on a complicity as tawdry in moral terms as the intellectually slipshod communication of the cliché. It is only in this ironic sense that

The quality of these passages, in truth, made the spoken word, and especially the spoken word about other people, fall below them . . .

(I, 347)

The outcome of such liberties with words is the embarrassingly false tone of Amerigo's exulting 'Gloucester, Gloucester, Gloucester':

this place had sounded its name to him half the night through, and its name had become but another name, the pronounceable and convenient one, for that supreme sense of things which now throbbed within him.[1]   (I, 365–6)

Extravagance of diction and a false tone, as in this 'elopement', and the dwelling on a particular word, a particular speech act, as in Adam Verver's proposal, are two examples of stylistic tensions in the novel which both extend and threaten the novel form. Another strategy with this double force, promoting the analytical alertness which will discredit the means by which it was aroused, is the use of the Assinghams. Their critical voice within the narrative is the most accessible level of analysis and appreciation; but its effect is complex. Since Fanny is scarcely a reliable commentator, and a large part of Bob's function is to make this clear, before he tries to supplement her interpretation, their efforts promote the attempt at understanding, rather than achieving it. Fanny's fallible analysis and Bob's dismissal of curiosity seem to provide extremes of the range of narrative awareness in the novel corresponding to the interest shown by the reader from outside,

[1] A speech the more ludicrous, as the American James must have realized, in the mouth of any but a native English speaker—for 'Gloucester' is precisely one of those names that foreign visitors find unpronounceable and inconvenient.

and bridging the gap between self-awareness in the characters and the reader's detached perceptions. To some extent this kind of interest would support a hierarchy of character, situation, and narrative, where boundaries could be drawn between the various elements of the novel as they could between, say, character and reader: even if in this instance such boundaries were obscured, or even transcended, by sympathetic understanding. The strategy of analysis and commentary would precipitate one solution into a mixture of distinct elements; just as in the process of representation, the scenes of analysis punctuate those of action or developing consciousness. Instead of this, however, James gives us an unreliable, though well-meaning, chorus: a stimulus to understanding which is so imperfect that it not only stops short of usurping the reader's interpretative function, but actually brings that activity into question. Indirectly, Fanny Assingham's incompetence is a measure of Maggie's challenge; and in relation to the process of narrative, her most important function is in demonstrating to the reader how complete an immersion in the novel process is required.

The introduction of a character whose function is perhaps more complex than her nature, begins somewhat enigmatically, with elliptical economy, through Prince Amerigo. The detachment of Fanny's power, and its uncertain allegiance, are rapidly established: 'She had *made* his marriage . . . though he could scarce see what she had made it *for* . . .' (I, 21). The implications of such detachment are stated with equal brevity. If Fanny has had no gross remuneration for her matchmaking, 'then . . . her disinterestedness was rather awful—it implied, that is, such abysses of confidence'. Within the novel this bears on the plot; beyond this, the implications for a view of character, the relations between people, even between character and reader, are far-reaching. In these early stages of the novel, the assault on accepted notions of explanation and responsibility is conducted with remarkable astringency. To the Prince's circling round the meaning of her 'beautiful . . . charming and unforgettable . . . still more mysterious and wonderful' (I, 30) act, Fanny's reply is a brief but comprehensive challenge, setting the pattern not only for him, but for the reader too:

'If you haven't . . . found out yourself, what meaning can anything I say have for you?'   (I, 30)

The second stage of the exposition of the function of a choric character comes with the entrance of Colonel Assingham. As the Prince is present, partly, in order to exercise a cultivated curiosity, Colonel Assignham exists in the novel to have things explained to him. He is a foil to Fanny, but also to some extent a counter-point to the Prince, in ignorance, and to Adam Verver in reluc-tance to enquire: 'He disengaged, he would be damned if he didn't ... his responsibility' (I, 66). His outspokenness is abrasive, but a relief to the reader, amidst the toils of words. The winning of his interest demonstrates both the sympathetic nature of the protagonists and the power of the narrative process, the scope of the novel form to contain remarkable tensions. Colonel Assingham, like the most reluctant reader, while refusing to be immersed, becomes fascinated by the process he witnesses.

The activity of Mrs. Assingham, however, puts her in a different relation to the central events and development of the plot: a relation which is not constant, but varies according to the changing understanding of personal responsibility on the part of the protagonists: a responsibility which is both a consequence and a measure of their individuality as persons. While relations between people diverge further and further from conformity with accepted social and moral patterns, the centres of these relationships, each personality in itself, are refined and streng-thened, though not in an easily recognizable way. The evasive-ness which would protect Maggie—

'She wasn't born to know evil. She must never know it' (I, 80)—

will give way to the facts:

'To what's called Evil—with a very big E ... To the discovery of it, to the knowledge of it, to the crude experience of it.'   (I, 394)

From a containing, protective consciousness, Fanny will with-draw to the position of an onlooker, witnessing the larger opera-tions of Maggie's understanding. This does not require the nega-tion of her first premiss, that

'Our relation, all round, exists—it's a reality, and a very good one; we're mixed up, so to speak, and it's too late to change it. We must live *in* it and with it.'   (I, 89)

This is the premiss on which the novel functions, and on which the reader's interest is founded. Fanny simply needs to redefine 'our relation': a process which involves increasing distance, and critical reappraisal of such moral judgements as her early claim that 'stupidity pushed to a certain point *is*, you know, immorality. Just so what is morality but high intelligence?' (I, 90) The motive may be no higher than entertainment, though it need not rest there: Fanny's clichés have dark overtones: 'Besides, it's all, at the worst, great fun' (I, 91).

The Assinghams are not present throughout the first volume of *The Golden Bowl*, although Fanny's knowledge of the secret between Amerigo and Charlotte, her promotion of Amerigo's marriage, and approval of Adam Verver's, give her a pervasive influence. Her involvement gathers momentum when Charlotte's position as Amerigo's 'mother-in-law' gives the former lovers a new intimacy which only Fanny amongst the representatives of society is qualified to suspect. In Chapters XIV to XVI, during and immediately after the Embassy party, Fanny's close questioning of Charlotte and the Prince, followed by her discussion with her husband, outlines the unspoken position which Charlotte is to turn to her own advantage when she visits Portland Place, taking the initiative.

Charlotte's intrepidity, as she oversteps the social boundaries, has a certain hardness. Amerigo stares at her tone in dismissing Fanny Assingham, protesting that 'she would do anything for us' (I, 313); but Charlotte's response is incisive, if elliptical: 'We're beyond her.' Action, the promotion of the relationship between Amerigo and Charlotte, has overtaken analysis, the process by which Fanny attempted to interrupt, or at least slow it down. Charlotte sees their relationship to Fanny in terms of strategic advantage:

'What in the world can she do against us? There's not a word that she can breathe. She's helpless; she can't speak . . . It all comes back to her. . . . She made your marriage.'

Her 'high reasoning' is not only unsympathetic to Fanny, but incompatible with the workings of the novel, for Charlotte's triumph puts plot above personality in a way alien to the form:

'I only say that she's *fixed*, that she must stand exactly where everything has, by her own act, placed her.'   (I, 348)

If Maggie is a heroine partly by virtue of powers like those of the author and an understanding as great as the reader's, then by the same canons this speech alone marks Charlotte as something of a villain, and Fanny as her victim.

In opposition to this, Fanny's role is defined as a brave little echo of Maggie's. Maggie will supersede Fanny as the 'all-knowing' character whose interpretation of conduct and motive helps bind together the characters whose normal social affiliations are strained; but because Maggie herself is at the centre of those relations, she has a basis for instigating action, and her role grows with the central development of the novel.

The close relation of the two roles is hinted in certain common turns of mind, suggested in scenes of contemplation, and in the developing perceptions captured in attention to verbal, as well as visual impressions. Thus Fanny fastens on the word 'arrange' in her conversation at the Embassy party with Charlotte. When Charlotte speaks of Maggie's 'arranging for' seeing her father— 'she likes to arrange', 'To-night has been practically an arrangement' (I, 260)—Fanny, with discriminating, if not ironic, sympathy, 'picked out, after consideration, a solitary plum. "So placed that *you* have to arrange?"' (I, 261). On Charlotte's assent Fanny continues, her insistence stressing the tones of strategic manœuvre in the term:

'And the Prince also . . . does he arrange' Mrs. Assingham asked, 'to make up *his* arrears?'

Charlotte parries the insinuation with a counterplay on 'otherwise':

'He might so well, you know, otherwise. . . .
"Otherwise"—yes. He arranges otherwise.'

But already the ground is laid for Maggie to notice how

Ah! Amerigo and Charlotte were arranged together, but she—to confine the matter only to herself—was arranged apart. (II, 46)

And when she overcomes their manœuvres, Maggie has to use their chosen weapons: there is a wry tone in her admission: 'I live in the midst of miracles of arrangement . . .' (II, 114).

Fanny's vision, however, is only an attempt at what Maggie's perfects: where Fanny falters at what she sees, evades a name, or declines to proceed without one, Maggie makes the progression from imagined to achieved reality which works in a way similar to the reader's process of understanding: a 'willing suspension of disbelief' followed by an apprehended imaginative truth. The bravura which dares dispense with certainty and use working hypotheses lays Maggie open to the charge of being arbitrarily managing; but the alternatives James offers are the passivity of the gentle wife who sews while her husband is engaged in an adulterous, almost incestuous affair, or the hesitant understanding which Fanny Assingham voices with a syntax to match imperfect mental agility, full of contradictions and interrupted with parentheses:

'If he had been afraid he could perfectly have prevented it. And if I had seen he was—if I hadn't seen he wasn't—so,' said Mrs. Assingham, 'could I. So,' she declared, '*would I*.'   (I, 282)

It is not that Fanny has no interest in the questions at issue, but that she has no desire to instigate action: 'Asking is suggesting—and it wasn't a time to suggest.' Charlotte's original involvement is one of obscure responsibility: 'She had come, frankly, into the connection, to do and to be what she could, "no questions asked" . . .' (I, 322). But as Fanny tells the Colonel, Charlotte has become part of 'the question':

'The question isn't of what I think. The question's of the conviction that guides the Prince and Charlotte—who have better opportunities than I for judging.'   (I, 379)

The Prince's volume ends with a lengthy discussion between the Assinghams of the present situation, how it came about, and how it is likely to develop. Though their terms are the absolutes of innocence and Evil, nothing and everything, their consideration is so open, and ranges so freely, that it prejudices none of their questions. This passage is pivotal in the novel, summing up the first volume and introducing the second. In the overall structure, it nicely balances the conclusion of 'The Princess', for instead of an explicit, though inconclusive, discussion between two observers, that volume ends with the Prince and Princess themselves, in a wordless embrace.

A consideration of the first volume of *The Golden Bowl* is lengthy, complex, and scarcely shapely in the disparate questions it provokes as to the process and effect of the novel. A simple plot based on a single secret, shared by three people but unknown to two more, and on the formation between these people of alliances which the revelation of the secret would preclude, is almost melodramatic machinery for the construction of a complex situation which will provide for an exploration of character within the novel. The relation of social form to personal ambitions, understanding and responsibility is established, though to a degree as yet unclear, as a novelistic counterpart to the relations between literary form, sympathies and imaginative involvement on the part of the reader. The first volume of *The Golden Bowl* does not flaunt stylistic exuberance in the way that *The Wings of the Dove* does; but the reader's attention is drawn to the process of the novel both through such common devices as recurrent words and phrases, verbal ambiguity and dialogue in which several levels of meaning and implication are exposed, and through a remarkable number of enigmatic, aphoristic comments or reflections by the characters upon those concerns common to them and us: comments which have a direct bearing on the understanding of character, or reflections which seem open to interpretation as commentaries upon the novel process itself. The questioning is more radical than anywhere except perhaps *The Sacred Fount*, and much more determined and serious than in that *jeu d'esprit*. Words such as 'question', 'form', and 'word' itself, and the distinction between appearance and reality, perception and involvement, irony and power, recur with an insistent stress; but the cohesive forces of curiosity over plot, the impulse to link scenes in which the same characters reappear, and the structural rhythm grouping scenes of analysis and of action, all strengthen the 'wholeness' of the volume, preventing any facile answers to its problems.

II *The Princess*

Maggie's volume of *The Golden Bowl* opens with an intimacy between heroine and reader which is near, but not quite, identification. Her experience and ours are modulated through third-person narration, which sets both in relation to some third perspective. Gabriel Pearson has suggested that the pagoda image which serves to introduce the second book 'at the same time becomes a pictorial analogy of its action . . . Perhaps the pagoda suggests everything, which is clearly too much'.[1] But the second volume actually opens:

It was not till many days had passed that the Princess began to accept the idea of having done, a little, something she was not always doing, or indeed that of having listened to any inward voice that spoke in a new tone. (II, 3)

We are drawn in, in fact, by our sense, in common with Maggie, of an unwitting and already prolonged involvement in extra-ordinary activity, by our experience of that distinct voice of the first volume, and by our anticipation of a new phase of imaginative activity. This proleptic reconnaissance leads beyond the image of the pagoda, which the narrative, miming the very development it has been relating, now moves back to take in. A switch to the precise pluperfect tense marks an intrusion, emphasizing the strangely reflexive powers of the grotesque pagoda symbol. And in keeping with its strangeness, the situation is an inversion of what we have been led to expect. The Princess, the besieged consciousness, listening to an inward voice, and thinking of an 'unattackable' situation, is not inside, but shut out from the fortress. The exoticism of the pagoda represents in imaginative terms an alien quality which goes deeper than surface aspect:

This situation had been occupying, for months and months, the very centre of the garden of her life, but it had reared itself there like some strange, tall tower of ivory, or perhaps rather some wonderful, beautiful, but outlandish pagoda, a structure plated with hard, bright porcelain, coloured and figured and adorned, at the overhanging eaves, with silver bells that tinkled, ever so charmingly, when stirred by chance airs. (II, 3)

The image is not impossible to place in the context of the novel. There are links with the garden at Fawns, which was so strangely illuminated for Adam Verver by the idea of a proposal to Charlotte, the garden where Maggie has the conversation with her father which leads to her invitation to Charlotte, and where a series of meetings and confrontations with both Adam and Charlotte will mark the stages of their unspoken understanding of the situation all have helped to create. The pagoda also

[1] 'The Novel to End All Novels: *The Golden Bowl*', p. 343.

recalls various images of buildings: principally Adam Verver's 'Palladian church' (I, 136), of Amerigo; but also perhaps his museum, a 'house on a rock . . . compact as a Greek temple was compact' (I, 147), in America. More ominously, the pagoda pre-figures the prison Maggie will shortly perceive in the practice of Charlotte and the Prince:

> They had built her in with their purpose—which was why, above her, a vault seemed more heavily to arch; so that she sat there, in the solid chamber of her helplessness, as in a bath of benevolence artfully prepared for her, over the brim of which she could but just manage to see by stretching her neck. (II, 45)

Many other images of buildings and of building, of the foreign and the exotic, the decorative yet oppressive, appear in the narra-tive, with an elaborate, if accurate, analogy to states of feeling, characters, or, most frequently, situations. Their lapidary self-consistency and brilliance, their very obtrusiveness, threatens to dominate the narrative, converting the novel into a mosaic made up of many tiny, distinct parts, and conceivable only as a total impression, not a process. Just as the pagoda seems to embody Maggie's situation yet exclude her consciousness—the bath leaving only the head above the water—so the technique of symbolism distances imaginative apprehension from intellectual interpretation, setting them apart as distinct stages of perception.

Philip Grover traces in James's 'aestheticism' the influence of various French writers, from Flaubert to the Goncourts, and finds the culmination of this in 'concentration, elimination and the total subordination of parts to the whole' in *The Golden Bowl*.[1] He stresses the use of 'internally consistent' imagery, pervading the words of the novel both in ostensibly descriptive passages and in figures of speech, and finds that 'the world of *The Golden Bowl* is self-contained and self-enclosed—an objective ardently pursued by Flaubert' (p. 187). This serves well as a commentary on the use of imagery examined above, but it fails to capture the range of qualities in the imagery of *The Golden Bowl*: the obstreperous excess of many symbols, from the pagoda to the bowl itself, which demands attention to their artificiality; the unevenness which gives the pagoda image quite a different quality from the 'house of quiet on a Sunday afternoon', or the golden cage from

---

[1] *Henry James and the French Novel* (1973), p. 152.

the 'roomful of confused objects' (II, 15), which image the mind as a prison and a lumber-room respectively.

Gabriel Pearson claims that 'If one reads along the line of imagery right through the book one can extract an exotic Conrad novel, where the metaphors all become acts' (op. cit. 354); but the experience of *The Golden Bowl* is not, though it may include, that of a Conrad novel, any more than it is *Madame Bovary* or *Salammbô*. One of the exercises of the reader's imagination is the integration of weird and wonderful imagery into a text which contains elements of domestic comedy and comedy of manners, as well as exotic melodrama; but it is not the fact of this exercise, but the process itself, which matters. For this modulation of perceived and achieved experience is what links the reader by analogy with Maggie, and this is our guarantee of the propriety of her procedure: a 'decorum' which goes beyond formality, but includes it, in the exercise of the imagination.

The development by analogy of imaginative activity into a moral guarantee depends on James's use of Maggie as the centre of consciousness in the 'Princess' volume. In the Preface, James writes that

the Princess, in addition to feeling . . . and to playing her part . . . duplicates, as it were, her value and becomes a compositional resource, and of the first order, as well as a value intrinsic.

Leo Bersani argues that 'The novels are a constantly dramatic struggle *toward* the security of the Prefaces' (op. cit. 58); and this Preface supports Bersani's claim that 'the crucial question raised by James's work has to do with the relation between structuring processes and personality in art' (p. 54). J. H. Raleigh takes this notion to the extremes of abstraction:

The fluid nature of the action, combined with the passivity of the characters, almost gives one the feeling that the only objective and solid entity is the problem itself . . .[1]

But this is misleading. A good deal of the preparation for the 'Princess' volume of *The Golden Bowl* has to do with this approach to experience: the 'formulaic', or even iconographic use of

---

[1] The Poetics of Empiricism', in Tanner, ed., *Henry James: Modern Judgments,* p. 67.

language, from entire languages to single words, by the Prince, Adam Verver and Fanny Assingham; the manipulation of the social code by Charlotte; the stress of recurrent words such as 'position', 'arrangement', 'difference' and 'basis', all serve to delineate what Amerigo, on the point of adultery as a means of creating a *'situation nette'*, longs for: 'the small intellectual fillip of a discerned relation between a given appearance and a taken meaning' (I, 362–3). What the first volume offers 'the inquiring mind', however, is not this satisfaction, but 'a mere dead wall, a lapse of logic, a confirmed bewilderment' (I, 363). The persuasion of the book is against fixed forms, which are both intrinsically and functionally inadequate to experience. It remains for Maggie, as an isolated consciousness, to discern and restore order without being bound by the simplicities of form.

This is not to suggest that Maggie has no recourse to patterning. On the contrary, her first need is to see this surface, before she can see beyond it:

it came to her . . . that if she could only get the facts of appearance straight, only jam them down into their place, the reasons lurking behind them, kept uncertain, for the eyes, by their wavering and shifting, wouldn't perhaps be able to help showing. (II, 54)

But her techniques for controlling confusion are at best tactical manœuvres. There is an implicit recognition of their arbitrary nature at the very moment when Maggie, aware that 'Charlotte was in pain, Charlotte was in torment', might be expected to take refuge from responsibility in the idea of fixed form. Instead of moral cowardice, Maggie displays something which may look suspiciously near unfeeling triumph, but she faces this risk with brave honesty: the acceptance of personal responsibility for the use of impersonal form. Maggie puts herself in the Prince's place to see Charlotte's position and her own:

Charlotte was in pain, Charlotte was in torment, but he himself had given her reason enough for that; and in respect to the rest of the whole matter of her obligation to follow her husband, that personage and she, Maggie, had so shuffled away every link between consequence and cause, that the intention remained, like some famous poetic line in a dead language, subject to varieties of interpretation. (II, 353)

The last simile here, mysterious and powerful, is a tempting analogy for *The Golden Bowl* itself; but in context its imaginative power is used to a specific end. The image is refracted through at least three consciousnesses—four including the narrator's—before it reaches the reader: it does not simply image the process of representation, but demonstrates it, and in the course of doing so, also shows character functioning in the narrative. The boundaries between character and opinion, theme and action, and narrative itself, are indefinable, and the analogy with a poetic line in a dead language is in fact the reverse of appropriate to the novel process.

The 'Princess' volume of *The Golden Bowl* works rather in terms of Maggie's 'succession of moments that were *watchable* still' (II, 11). There is nothing divisive about the process, as Maggie, somewhat to her exasperation, discovers: names, attitudes, evasions, 'whatever it did for her', cannot suppress the dramatic life of the novel, which resists simplification. This volume, though interlaced with verbal and imagistic patterns as complex as those in the first, and often related to them, is more open to analysis in terms of scene-sequences, each involving Maggie and one other person, or the group of four. Maggie's character, Maggie's understanding, the story and our understanding, grow through this narrative sequence of encounters and analysis. The novel is full of the consciousness of its own operation; but these clues to the reader are complex statements. As Maggie's discoveries they have a dramatic validity which counterbalances the distancing effect for the reader of their attention to form. These insights both contribute to the intensity of imaginative life and assail it from outside, so that it is very difficult to determine the effect of such dual awareness as this:

Sharp to her above all was the renewed attestation of her father's comprehensive acceptances, which she had so long regarded as of the same quality with her own, but which, so distinctly now, she should have the complication of being obliged to deal with separately.

(II, 32–3)

The precarious balance between Maggie's perceptiveness and her control, like the poise of form and force in 'The Prince', pivots on the question of character. Maggie is absolved of tyranny by the very insight most characteristic of her imaginative power: the recognition of the intractability of every individual. Though all the main characters have some sense of the mystery of otherness, none demonstrates Maggie's ability to accept the existence of another point of view than their own: a curiously liberating perception:

> Once she was convinced of the flitting wing of this last impression—the perception, irresistible, that she was something for *their* queer experience, just as they were something for hers—there was no limit to her conceived design of not letting them escape. (II, 52)

Like Milly Theale recognizing that 'she should never know how Kate felt about anything such a one as Milly Theale should give her to feel' (*The Wings of the Dove*, p. 158), Maggie is able to admit,

> Yes, it was one of the things she should go down to her grave without having known—how Charlotte, after all had been said, *really* thought her stepdaughter looked under any supposedly ingenious personal experiment. (II, 14)

This is not authorial omniscience, but an awareness of the limitations of consciousness. It is by recognizing the nature of her position, not by presuming upon her knowledge, that Maggie becomes a dependable character within the novel: quite unlike Charlotte, whose dismissive attitude to Fanny Assingham showed the opposite use of knowledge. In Maggie's figure of the goldfish bowl, she herself is amongst the fish; but her understanding is outside the bowl, watching the whole spectacle. The narrative shows her acting out her scenes, but looking back on them too.

The first encounter, after the 'tap or two' upon the pagoda which symbolizes Maggie's situation, is that with the Prince. This echoes the opening of Volume I, and unobtrusively begins to restore the pattern of their rightful relationship. The reversion from a symbolist approach to the dramatic mode also anticipates the restoration of normal human relations 'in renewed circulation'.

The first analysis of this move, however, is so formal as to screen human in social relations: Maggie's reflections are full of phrases such as 'named', 'figured the arrangement', 'extension' and 'form', which echo the dangerously formulaic words of the first volume. There is an air of tortuous logic about 'Maggie's actual reluctance to ask herself' the meaning of her changing reactions to her pagoda image. Her 'false position' involves the very syntax in a complexity from which a lively simile[1] offers a welcome relief:

> she reflected that she should either not have ceased to be right—that is, to be confident—or have recognised that she was wrong; though she tried to deal with herself, for a space, only as a silken-coated spaniel who has scrambled out of a pond and who rattles the water from his ears.   (II, 7)

The digression into elaboration of this image, however, only leads through a series of feverish analogies to one 'which, might I so far multiply my metaphors, I should compare to the frightened but clinging young mother of an unlawful child'. At this point the narrative voice cannot be identified with Maggie herself. Like the 'gentlemen of pleasure' with whom Adam Verver was compared, this image acknowledges its own embarrassment. In its compromising tone, it can also be linked with Maggie's surprisingly excessive account of her own devotion to Amerigo in Volume I:

> she going so far as to put it that, even should he some day get drunk and beat her, the spectacle of him with hated rivals would, after no matter what extremity, always . . . suffice to bring her round. (I, 168)

The sensationalism of these images obtrudes in the narrative, as James's ear must have warned him, and as their rather awkward apologies betray. Nevertheless they are allowed to stand in the text, stretching the novel form to the limits of melodrama, and rejecting the bounds of the conformable, in order to make through tone the point Maggie recognizes: that 'any deep-seated passion has its pangs as well as its joys, and that we are made by its aches and its anxieties most richly conscious of it' (II, 8). When the late James is accused of stylistic excess, it is usually his convolutions of measured perception and statement that are attacked; but these melodramatic images show something of the extremes to which he could go to avoid that artificiality, and suggest the violence of sexuality.

---

[1] Ruth Bernard Yeazell gives an extended analysis of this simile in *Language and Knowledge in the Late Novels of Henry James* (1976), pp. 41–6, making an illuminating comparison between Maggie and the metaphysical poets, and suggesting that such incongruous images create 'a world in which connections are not easily made, one in which the imagination must strain to see the resemblances of things.'

The relationship between Maggie and her husband is not, however, normally characterized by such extremes. It is the 'small variations and mild manœuvres' of domestic and social life which are followed, 'with an infinite sense of intention' (II, 9): the very exactitude of manœuvre conveys Maggie's embattled sense that 'she was no longer playing with blunt and idle tools, with weapons that didn't cut' and her explicit rejection of 'the impulse to cheat herself with motion and sound'.

The poise of dramatic immediacy and the detached awareness of form and meaning which characterizes their encounter is preserved through the fiction of memory. As so often in the late James, the perceiving consciousness finds the dramatic scene 'The great moment, at any rate, for conscious repossession' (II, 12). In this perspective the distinction of tenses, conveying the relationship of intention and analysis to experience, is not blurred; but a clarity important for the reader is attributed to the consciousness of Maggie herself, so that there is no lessening of imaginative intensity: the 'compositional resource' and 'value intrinsic' support each other.

James's use of third-person narration has a similar effect. The narrative flow is maintained, and contained, by this device; yet a scrupulous attention to the source of judgements, while alerting the reader to the importance of this awareness, only prompts him to see where it is not finally satisfied. It is the difficulty of maintaining an alertness adequate to the narrative process which prepares the reader for the much deeper difficulty of confronting the problems raised within the narrative by Maggie's position and those inseparable from the use of the novel form itself. As James wrote in the Preface to *The Wings of the Dove*:

The enjoyment of a work of art constituting, to my sense, our highest experience of 'luxury', the luxury is not greatest, by my consequent measure, when the work asks for as little attention as possible.

The 'accumulations of the unanswered' (II, 14), conceived through Maggie's gathering awareness are constituted through the indirections of a complex syntax; but they are given immediate presence in a concrete image: 'They were *there*, these accumulations; they were like a roomful of confused objects, never as yet "sorted", which for some time now she had been passing and re-passing, along the corridor of her life'. The simile, though it has none of the exoticism of the pagoda, is an interesting one. The image of a locked door recurs frequently in James's work, from that at Isabel Archer's American home to those at which Maisie dares not knock for fear of the laughter which shuts her out; from the spying keyhole of *The Sacred Fount* to the terrifying doors of 'The Jolly Corner', which are open and shut by Spencer Brydon's ghostly double.[1] Within *The Golden Bowl* itself, the metaphors of siege and labyrinth are linked through this image of a locked room off the corridor of life with the pagoda symbol, the simile of the 'spying servant on the other side of a barred threshold' (II, 44), and the 'bad-faced stranger surprised in one of the thick-carpeted corridors of a house of quiet' (II, 243). In these analogies James creates an almost claustrophobically dense imaginative context for related incidents in the action of the novel, and it is not easy to separate the two levels.

In Maggie's mind, impenetrability is attributed at this stage rather to other persons than to experience itself. The lumber-room image is domestic, not portentous, and though it is developed at some length, the tone remains casual, the diction colloquial:

she passed it when she could without opening the door; then, on occasion, she turned the key to throw in a fresh contribution. So it was that she had been getting things out of the way.   (II, 15)

The distinction between imaginative validity by analogy and 'simple' expression is lessened by this technique; but there is no confusion as to which kind of representation is actually offered: though the 'mental act' becomes a dramatic one, it remains essentially a symbolic drama, dealing with abstract concepts in a vivid and familiar way:

What she should never know about Charlotte's thought—she tossed *that* in. It would find itself in company, and she might at last have been standing there long enough to see it fall into its corner.   (II, 15)

[1] With an effect interestingly close to Maggie's experience in this scene. Brydon 'saw, by the fact that the vestibule had gaped wide, that the hinged halves of the inner door had been thrown far back. Out of that again the *question* sprang at him, making his eyes, as he felt, half-start from his head, as they had done, at the top of the house, before the sign of the other door. If he had left that one open, hadn't he left this one closed, and wasn't he now in *most* immediate presence of some inconceivable occult activity?' (XII pp. 223-4) Maggie's 'question' takes the form of the Prince, Brydon's, the ghostly form of his other self.

Though there is no pretence, however, about the technique of representation being used here, the simple diction and dramatic action disarm the reader. It is a surprise, an intellectual 'fillip' comparable with Maggie's emotional sensation, when by a sort of literary *coup* the figurative actually becomes dramatic:

> It made her in fact, with a vague gasp, turn away, and what had further determined this was the final sharp extinction of the inward scene by the outward. The quite different door had opened and her husband was there.
> (II, 15)

The device is an effective one, and James uses it again. On the re-entry of Amerigo after his going to dress, Maggie

> looked about her, from the middle of the room, under the force of this question, as if *there*, exactly, were the field of action involved. Then, as the door opened again, she recognized, whatever the action, the form, at any rate, of a first opportunity. Her husband had re-appeared . . .
> (II, 25)

How is this just perception, represented through the figurative made dramatic, different from the deceptive 'hallucination' of Adam Verver on the terrace at Fawns, or from the 'structuralist' obliteration of personality in Fanny Assingham's wishing 'to leave well behind her both her question and the couple in whom it had, abruptly, taken such vivid form'? It must be that 'in such a matter, a shade of difference is enormous' (I, 268), and that the heightened sensibility stimulated in the reader of *The Golden Bowl* is required for precisely such distinctions as these between degrees of artificiality, patterning and drama, and for the exact use which is made of these imaginative strategies. What Adam and Fanny, in their different ways, take as the 'answer' to uncomfortable questions, remains for Maggie an approach, the issue from a 'repeated challenge' into 'a first opportunity'.

The narrative structure of 'The Princess' volume of *The Golden Bowl* fosters such discriminations through the use of repetitive sequences with important differences. In the first volume the impulse for the reader was to interpret an accumulation of imperfectly understood revelations by assimilation and analogy, like with like, which could be figured by the web or the patchwork quilt. Now the reading process demands a different approach: distinguishing between similar occurrences. Maggie's understanding, growing through time, is analogous to this heuristic progress through the novel:

It had made for him some difference that she couldn't measure . . . and back and back it kept coming to her that the blankness he showed her before he was able to *see* might, should she choose to insist on it, have a meaning—have, as who should say, an historic value—beyond the importance of momentary expressions in general   (II, 16–17)

This 'back and back' enquiry is balanced, however, by the restraint from a voiced meaning. A great deal is done in this volume through the unspoken, the withheld assertion. At the first encounter of Maggie and Amerigo, it is her 'break with custom', his *not* being 'able to see' what she means by it, which threatens their 'precious equilibrium' (II, 18). At this stage the narrative is explicit:

Some such words as those were what *didn't* ring out, yet it was as if even the unuttered sound had been quenched here in its own quaver. It was where utterance would have broken down by its very weight if he had let it get so far.   (II, 19)

Instead of words and explanations, there is the Prince 'smiling and smiling', and an embrace, 'close and long in expression of their personal reunion'. But the danger of the wordless embrace is shown by the discrepancy, not stressed in the narrative, between the explicit challenge which does not ring out from the Prince (p. 19), and the demand from Maggie which is not even conceived of, as he leaves to dress (pp. 20–1). All we see here is Maggie's gentle appeasement, and a failure to insist on what might indeed have been a revelation.

It is in the light of this suspended consciousness that Maggie's developing awareness can be judged. The inadequacy of her formulations is suggested by the loose syntax of Maggie's accumulated impressions, where co-ordination is used rather than a complex structure expressing cause and effect: it is left to the reader to make the connections which Maggie, for all her analysis, leaves unquestioned:

The dazzling person was upstairs and she was down, and there were moreover the other facts of selection and decision that this demonstration of her own had required, and of the constant care that the equilibium involved; but she had, all the same, never felt so absorbingly married, so abjectly conscious of a master of her fate.   (II, 22–3)

The narrative concisely picks up the irony which Maggie ignores, while the syntax leaves an ambiguity between direct and indirect narration which allows this effect without insisting on it:

He could do what he would with her; in fact what was actually happening was that he was actually doing it.   (II, 23)

A distinction between direct and reported speech, however, brings the ironic awareness nearer the surface; though the typically late-Jamesian ambiguity of the 'brightness of high harmony' still obscures overt comment, and a delicacy over explicit discussion of Amerigo's sexual power is deftly, even comically manipulated:

'What he would,' what he *really* would—only that quantity itself escaped perhaps, in the brightness of high harmony, familiar naming and discussing.

There is a mounting accumulation of meanings both unexpressed by and hidden from Maggie, which reaches its ironic climax in her own word 'literally':

If he had come back tired, tired from his long day, the exertion had been, literally, in her service and her father's.

When the Prince reappears, 'the form, at any rate, of a first opportunity', the terms, 'form', 'plan' and 'light', and the confidence of 'knowing . . . what to do', sustain Maggie's illusion of understanding. But the irony is covertly maintained in the rhythm of Maggie's reflections, until it is voiced in the inversion of an answer which comes as a question. It is Maggie, not the reader, who is deluded by the incantatory rhythm, the illusion of progress which masks an oscillation. Her sensation is one of floating:

It was, for hours and hours, later on, as if she had somehow been lifted aloft, were floated and carried on some warm high tide beneath which stumbling blocks had sunk out of sight. This came from her being again, for the time, in the enjoyment of confidence, from her knowing, as she believed, what to do. All the next day, and all the next, she appeared to herself to know it. She had a plan, and she rejoiced in her plan: this consisted in the light that . . . had come to her as a question— 'What if I've abandoned *them*, you know?'   (II, 26)

Maggie's unfounded assumption of a common base with her husband is caught in an ironically apt verb: 'She wanted him to understand how her scheme embraced Charlotte too' (II, 29).

The course of simple tolerance, misplaced 'in the darkening shadow of a false position', is ironically undercut through the narrative rather than through Maggie. Her active correction of the situation, when she embarks upon it, will be seen as a necessary course, not gratuitous vindictiveness. The ironic process of representation prepares for a situation in which directions and moral judgements are predetermined, with the indirect sanction of the author and the support of any reader who has interpreted his ironic hints. Though Maggie bears responsibility for her actions, she did not create the whole situation in which this had to be so: she works as a responsible agent within a fixed moral code.

The false position, whatever Maggie's part in permitting its development, is at this stage an imposition on her. She feels herself 'present at a process taking place rather deeper within [Amerigo] than the occasion, on the whole, appeared to require'. The domestic scene is a drama of motive and interpretation: an affair of intention rather than feeling: 'He had guessed that she was there with an idea, there in fact by reason of her idea'. The embracing 'scheme' of Maggie is obliterated by the Prince's embrace: 'She gave up, let her idea go, let everything go; her one consciousness was that he was taking her again into his arms'. Maggie's later interpretation of this act—how it 'operated with him *instead* of the words he hadn't uttered' shows an awareness of gesture akin to the sense for foreign languages as signs which marked the opening of Volume I. The detachment of the narrative here, neither showing nor telling so much as expounding, is in keeping with this deliberate manipulation of expression, though the softening use of balance and repetition in phrasing corresponds to the chosen means of expression: a persuasive demonstration of affection. How far the embrace comes from the heart, and how far from the head, need not be dictated through explicit irony. A lulling repetitive rhythm is followed by the counting of embraces, and whatever there is of manipulation in the Prince's action is met by Maggie's analytical awareness.

The rhythmic structure may be clarified by setting down the phrases in sense-units:

Her acceptance of it,
her response to it,
inevitable,
foredoomed,
came back to her,
later on,
as a virtual assent
to the assumption he had thus made
that there was really nothing
such a demonstration
didn't anticipate
and didn't dispose of,
and that the spring
acting within herself
moreover
might well have been,
beyond any other,
the impulse legitimately to provoke it.
It made,
for any issue,
the third time
since his return
that he had drawn her
to his breast . . .   (II, 30)

But the rhythm of weakness is not far from the urging to strength
which goes on in Maggie's thoughts. The shift from determination through capitulation and back to resolution again is eased
by this prose rhythm, which preserves a certain psychological
identity through superficial changes of direction. Thus the mind
which accepts that

He had been right,
overwhelmingly right . . .

is recognizably the same as that which knows

that she mustn't be weak for this,
must much rather be strong.

It is at the thought of Charlotte that the spell is broken and the
rhythms of reason return, broken with parentheses and hesitating
over qualifications. The difference of Maggie's relation to

Charlotte from that she has with her husband is expressed in this rhythmic break as much as in her words:

She recovered soon enough, on the whole, the sense that this left her Charlotte always to deal with—Charlotte who, at any rate, however *she* might meet overtures, must meet them, at the worst, more or less differently.   (II, 31)

The deliberation of Maggie's tactics in demanding Charlotte's version of the visit to Gloucester is noted 'almost ostentatiously' in phrases such as 'Maggie took the ground that . . .' and 'to proceed with the application of her idea'. But on a different level her approach is more intuitive and imaginative. In the reverse of the process by which a series of 'pictures', broken down into formulations of 'questions', were interrupted, or made real, by the appearance of Prince Amerigo, when Charlotte appears to Maggie 'in the light, strange and coloured, like that of a painted picture, which fixed the impression for her', the visual image becomes a metaphorical one:

It was the effect of her quickened sensibility; she knew herself again in presence of a problem . . .

This 'circular' process which works through one use of imagery into its opposite, like the incantatory rhythm which begins by lulling the consciousness but ends by inciting an increased effort, is a complex narrative device. Maggie's wavering with the Prince has the effect of softening the suddenness of her resolution to set their affairs in order. It allows her to be seen as the victim, however briefly, of his manipulation: an interlude which actively demonstrates the justice of her subsequent determination. There is also scope for distinguishing between relations with Amerigo, who can persuade Maggie against her will, and Charlotte, who does not. This not only places Maggie's relations with them, but discriminates between them in a way which imaginatively sets them apart from each other.

James's use of imagery and rhythm thus supports a point which might be asserted, but could scarcely be demonstrated, directly; the reader, like Maggie, 'works through' the circular process. The Prince, facing the facts of Charlotte's presence just before his marriage, understood that 'if they had to be interpreted, this made at least for intimacy'. At their final meeting, the intimacy between Maggie and her father will also be demonstrated through an act of interpretation; as they gaze together at a picture. It is an intimacy of this kind that the reader shares with Maggie, in interpreting the experience she interprets. This forms the basis of an understanding upon which the author draws for a continuing sympathy over actions which have, which for Maggie necessarily have, an extraordinary degree of arbitrariness.

It is Maggie's recognition of this quality which to some extent pre-empts a reader's condemnation: 'Maggie went, she went—she felt herself going'. Maggie's emotional and imaginative endeavours are fused, and the dramatic is brought very close to the artistic. Thus it is for the reader as well as Maggie that 'one rule of art' obtains: 'to keep within bounds and not lose her head' (II, 35). But this triumph is both extended and tested by each analytical formulation and each imaginative element in the narrative. It is because the balance between them remains precarious that we continue to feel Maggie's consciousness as an active force, for this preserves an equilibrium. The need to maintain a balance in her situation determines a reserve: 'for her to ask a question, to raise a doubt, to reflect in any degree on the play of the others, would be to break the charm' (II, 35). But Maggie's outward composure is poised for the reader against the questions she faces alone. Expressions of analysis permeate the text, yet the kind of consciousness they promote is dramatically, as well as thematically, in keeping with the narrative. Maggie's need for concealment gives her a degree of detachment from the situation corresponding to the reader's, and both can share an analogous interest. While the analysis can reach extraordinary abstraction, this has the effect of deliberate tact in the expression of raw perception, as Maggie considers the likeness of Amerigo's and Charlotte's reactions:

This analogy in the two situations was to keep up for her the remembrance of a kinship of expression in the two faces—in respect to which all she as yet professed to herself was that she had affected them, or at any rate the sensibility each of them so admirably covered, in the same way.   (II, 36–7)

The stylistic mannerism conveys an emotional sensation: the itch 'to play with it, in short, nervously, vaguely, incessantly' which is common to Maggie's reactions and the reader's. For both, the 'high pitch' is

enhanced, furthermore—enhanced or qualified, who should say which? —by a new note of diplomacy, almost of anxiety . . . of intensity of observance, in the matter of appeal and response . . . that resembled an attempt to play again, with more refinement, at disparity of relation.

(II, 38–9)

Maggie's observation of the 'silver tissue of decorum' disposed by Charlotte has much in common with the reader's appreciation of the author's style. The narrative is not directly discussing itself, but indirectly offering analogies for its mode of proceeding, and the literary sophistication of this manœuvre in turn conveys the pitch of Maggie's consciousness.

This 'sense for the equilibrium' and 'instinct for relations' is not, however, confined to Maggie or directed unequivocally for the reader. The most delicate poise is not that between experience and expression, but between the unspoken and the unspeakable: the nature of suppressed expression. Maggie has two conceptions of Charlotte's attitude: one given as an imagined monologue, the other never directly voiced. These correspond to the words which '*didn't* ring out' between Maggie and Amerigo, and those which did not even occur to her. To suppress comment is not the same as forgoing expression: this is not 'decorum' in the classical sense of appropriate poise, but in a corrupted sense: 'The word for it, the word . . . was that they were *treating* her' (II, 43). The delicacy of judgement required for the situation is sufficiently signalled by James's use, for the Princess's indignation, of the term picked out by Amerigo in 'The Prince' for the Ververs' relation to him. As he waited in vain for Maggie to appear, and just before Charlotte called, he savoured 'the particular "treat", at his father-in-law's expense, that he more and more struck himself as enjoying' (I, 296). The selected expression, 'the word for it', picks up a process, but also strikes an attitude in relation to it: even a chosen word is no fixed truth.

The language of analysis, once Maggie has seen that Charlotte's decorum is slanted, and depends on an exclusive understanding with Amerigo, gives way to the intensity of images. Maggie's lack of perspective on the situation is a stifling, though rich, immersion:

under the dizzying, smothering welter—positively in submarine depths where everything came to her through walls of emerald and mother-of-pearl . . .   (II, 44)

The 'bath' and the 'gilded cage' are hers long before the others are trapped in the goldfish bowl, or Charlotte in the cage. The occurrence of the image here will prove Maggie's authority when she sees Charlotte's sufferings and recognizes that 'The cage was the deluded condition, and Maggie, as having known delusion—rather!—understood the nature of cages' (II, 236).

Maggie's imagery conveys to the reader not only the immediacy of her developing sense of the situation, but the power this exerts over her consciousness. Just as the Principino, by a sort of imaginative transposition, turns into the figurative child of the family's 'infant project', and acquires something of the muscular power of Macbeth's 'naked new-born babe/Striding the blast', having

kicked its little legs most wildly—kicked them, for all the world, across the Channel and half the continent, kicked them over the Pyrenees and innocently crowed out some rich Spanish name   (II, 48)

—so Maggie's analytical perceptions take on a vigorous, almost grotesque, life of their own. A distance is established between Maggie's situation and her sense of it. Some of her responsibility is, as it were, absolved by her very recognition of it, for her freedom is limited by her knowledge:

and what it compelled her to say to herself was that to behave as she might have behaved before would be to act, for Amerigo and Charlotte, with the highest hypocrisy.   (II, 49)

The importance of consciousness, and the inevitable responsibility it brings, is conveyed subtly. There is a close parallel between Maggie's situation now and her father's before his proposal to Charlotte: the same word, 'speaking', is picked out in inverted commas in both cases. But Maggie, unlike Adam on the previous occasion, refrains from 'speaking', resists 'the charm'. The analogy is not a closed one, however, designed to make a simple point, that Maggie's consciousness is greater than Adam's. For he now preserves their silence, and a mysterious bond between them is created by this common restraint:

Day after day she put off the moment of 'speaking', as she inwardly and very comprehensively called it—speaking that is to her father; and all the more that she was ridden by a strange suspense as to his himself breaking silence.   (II, 50)

As the 'golden mist' of Eaton Square attenuates to a 'silver mist' which becomes 'sensibly thin', Maggie's determination to make something of this silence strengthens. Confronted with the shared secret of Amerigo and Charlotte's memories of Matcham, her efforts become almost hysterical; but the exaggeration is shown as a deliberate technique on her part Not only the cry, 'They're paralysed, they're paralysed!' (II, 54), but the 'intensity of her consciousness', the 'theory' of having attracted attention, characterize her attitude.

The departure from any 'custom of delicate approach—approach by the permitted note, the suggested "if", the accepted vagueness' (II, 54–5) is both necessary and blatant. In summary, the aim, the cost, and the achievement of this approach are put in abstract terms; but the approach itself is expressed simply in an image of extraordinarily unsophisticated physicality: Maggie's *moue*, or her loud-mouthed talk—the image could mean either—have the éclat of a mime or a clown:

And the profit of her plan, the effect of the violence she was willing to let it go for, was exactly in their *being* the people in question, people she had seemed to be rather shy of before and for whom she suddenly opened her mouth so wide.   (II, 55)

It is Adam Verver's breaking his silence which relieves Maggie of the necessity to do so. But Maggie's immediate reaction is not to consider the fact of his speaking, but to register the reactions of Amerigo and Charlotte. This she achieves 'secretly, almost breathlessly', with an apprehension as far removed from actual examination as her previous 'going and going' was distant from the effects she wanted to measure. The affair is indeed a drama of relations and of structure, intensely vivid, but not at all naturalistic:

Everything now so fitted for her to everything else that she could feel the effect as prodigious even while sticking to her policy of giving the pair no look. There were thus some five wonderful minutes during which they loomed, to her sightless eyes, on either side of her, larger than they had ever loomed before, larger than life, larger than thought, larger than any danger or any safety. (II, 56)

These grotesquely distorted fish-eye images convey the surrealistic quality of a text where drama comes out of inaction, expression out of withheld speech, and the theme seems to materialize where the narrative becomes abstract. Maggie's developing consciousness is both a means and an end: the substance of the novel depends on this balance, and if this is lost, nothing remains. In this moment of discovery, the blind trust we must have in Maggie is revealed with an uncanny exactitude in a sensation of emptiness: the absolute negation of time, space, and substance is the gap to be leapt in the act of perception:

There was thus a space of time, in fine, fairly vertiginous for her, during which she took no more account of them than if they were not in the room.

The achievement of this perception is demonstrated forthwith, as Maggie and the Prince travel home, in her response to the embrace 'that such opportunities had so often suggested and prescribed' (II, 58). The pattern established with the first entry of the Prince in this volume, of the abstract subsumed into his concrete presence, is precisely reversed here, with a move into metaphor which demonstrates the power of will over feeling:

Yes, she was in his exerted grasp, and she knew what that was; but she was at the same time in the grasp of her conceived responsibility, and the extraordinary thing was that, of the two intensities, the second was presently to become the sharper.

A new pattern of embrace is established here: to be repeated very near the conclusion of this volume, when relations are all but restored. The 'passionate' kiss of Amerigo and Charlotte, which purported to be a pledge of fidelity, but actually marked the beginning of their adultery, is melodramatic by comparison with this impending embrace, described with sensual exactness and rhythmic urgency, but confined within a tight syntactic structure, conveying the mental effort to restrain a physical response:

He was so near now that she could touch him, taste him, smell him, kiss him, hold him; he almost pressed upon her, and the warmth of his face—frowning, smiling, she mightn't know which; only beautiful and strange—was bent upon her with the largeness with which objects loom in dreams. She closed her eyes to it, and so, the next instant, against her purpose, she had put out her hand, which had met his own and which he held. Then it was that, from behind her closed eyes, the right word came 'Wait!'   (II, 361)

Maggie's will is strong, but she is not without feelings. Coming back from Eaton Square, her singleness of purpose is poignantly contrasted with the distinct sensations of pain: her physical being is dissected by the narrative:

She was making an effort that horribly hurt her, and, as she couldn't cry out, her eyes swam in her silence. . . . her lips helped and protected her by being able to be gay.   (II, 59–60)

From the moment of annihilating perception, the narrative is rebuilt with Maggie's bravery: 'Touch by touch she thus dropped into her husband's silence the truth about his good nature and his good manners'. The need for restraint having been established its effect is now appreciated: 'the act grew important between them just through her doing perceptibly nothing.' Maggie waits for the Prince to break through her silence; but since he does not, the responsibility for this procedure is transfered to him:

They had silences at last, that were almost crudities of mutual resistance—silences that persisted through his felt effort to treat her recurrence to the part he had lately played, to interpret all the sweetness of her so talking to him, as a manner of making love to him.   (II, 63)

The 'question' is not one of Maggie's deepest feelings and responses, but of his: 'Ah, it was no such manner, heaven knew, for Maggie; she could make love, if this had been in question, better than that!'

John Bayley compares *The Golden Bowl* with Shakespeare's *Othello*, suggesting that 'In both of them knowledge confronts innocence; the world of definition is met by the world of incalculability' (*The Characters of Love*, p. 210). It is the Prince who seeks a '*situation nette*', in which 'he would have known what to think' (I, 362); but what he discovers, as Bayley points out, is that 'the nemesis of wrong-doing is the final stupidity of clarity and definition' (op. cit. 239). The more precise the misunderstanding, the lower the comedy: a fact James picks out through the use of personal pronouns and of numbers. When Maggie proposes to the Prince that he should go with her father while she stays with Charlotte, so that 'the two of [them] were showing the same sort of kindness' (II, 66), his misunderstanding is betrayed through an attribution of antecedents which would be syntactically impossible, just as they are improper. For his wife's 'the two of us', one must be Maggie herself, but 'Amerigo thought. "The two of us? Charlotte and I?"' The difference between the husband and wife could be defined in terms of the triviality and 'stupidity' of this question, and the largeness of those Maggie has been wondering about. She corrects Amerigo without overt comment; but the rhythm of conversation between an estranged couple is economically conveyed: 'Maggie again hesitated. "You and I, darling"' (II, 66).

The misunderstanding is more serious when Maggie confronts the Prince with the broken bowl. The symbolic three pieces stress the significance of number; then there are 'these three months' of Maggie's growing certainty:

'Counting,' as she put it 'from the night you came home so late from Matcham. Counting from the hours you spent with Charlotte at Gloucester. . . .'   (II, 197)

Her accusation turns on a number:

'. . . of your having, and of your having for a long time had, *two* relations with Charlotte.'

It is the same number as in their earlier misunderstanding, and the Prince's confusion is equally damning:

He stared, a little at sea, as he took it up. 'Two—?' Something in the tone of it gave it a sense, or an ambiguity, almost foolish—leaving Maggie to feel . . . how such a consequence, a foredoomed infelicity, partaking of the ridiculous even in one of the cleverest, might be of the very essence of the penalty of wrong-doing. 'Oh, you may have had fifty—had the same relation with her fifty times! It's of the number of *kinds* of relation with her that I speak—a number that doesn't matter, really, so long as there wasn't only one kind, as father and I supposed. . . .'

It seems that the converse of this 'foredoomed infelicity' is to be conveyed through Maggie's relations with her father: their wordless understanding. But this is nearer a parallel than a co-trasting situation, 'groping' for security as Verver did before his proposal, and as the Prince did after his 'pledge' with Charlotte. Maggie's relationship with her father is uncomfortably close: and though her innocence is underwritten by the narrative, our sense that this represents a refusal to see dark implications brings the novel itself into question. Only the dangers Maggie faces can be overcome, while her consciousness guides the narrative: but it is the danger of separation from her father, rather than incestuous proximity, that she thinks of as 'the possible peril' (II, 74). The sense of excessive intimacy aroused by ambiguous phrases such as 'groping, with sealed lips' (II, 74), 'their intercourse as a whole' and 'the clutching instinct' (II, 75), is scarcely disposed of by the determined propriety of pedantry, cliché and archaism in one sentence, particularly as this is a negative definition:

The merely specious description of their case would have been that, after being for a long time, as a family, delightfully, uninterruptedly happy, they had still a new felicity to discover; a felicity for which, blessedly, her father's appetite and her own, in particular, had been kept fresh and grateful.   (II, 75)

The text challenges the reader with this imperfect poise, to believe in a relationship which is not expressed. To refuse that belief will damage our trust in Maggie and our acceptance of the conclusion of the novel. The reward for trust, on the other hand, is not immediately apparent: it is simply a matter of being able to go on. We have only the images Maggie imputes to Adam for an idea of the value of their situation: 'up in a balloon and whirling through space, or down in the depths of the earth, in the glimmering passages of a gold-mine' (II, 75). Maggie, with the implicit endorsement of the narrator, may term it a 'precious condition'. The reader has only their word for that; but he has his own experience of the difficulty of the situation: 'forbidden, face to face with the companion of her adventure, the experiment of a test'. The narrative demands a patience which it does not woo: the reader has no advantage on Maggie:

If they balanced they balanced—she had to take that; it deprived her of every pretext for arriving, by however covert a process, at what he thought.

But we do have the reward Maggie shares with her father, 'supremely linked . . . by the rigour of their law' (II, 75).

The exact nature of this link remains hard to establish, however. James is evidently aware of the possibility that the relationship between Maggie and her father could be interpreted as incestuous, and he arouses the reader to a similar recognition through frequent stress on their extraordinary closeness. Maggie, however, in her 'milk-white fog', is as invincibly innocent as Daisy Miller in James's early novella, surrounded by unfortunate scandal. Maggie must recognize 'Evil' where it does exist, between Amerigo and Charlotte; but she is not the lesser in our estimation for her lack of false, low suspicions. She comes to see that her ties with her father are too close, and that these must be sacrificed if their marriages are to survive. In the last interview with Adam at Fawns (II, Chapter XXXVII), Maggie characteristically takes the sting out of this by exaggerating it: she is 'frozen stiff with selfishness' (II, 273), and will 'sacrifice' her father. This recognition of their essentially different interests is the basis of her proper 'belief' (II, 282) in Adam, for it is in accordance with the dignity of both father and daughter.

The account of Maggie's consciousness growing through the silences that surround her is neither intellectually nor imaginatively easy to follow. The elements of judgement, of action, of reflection, the retrospection and the hypotheses, the weight of narrative and dramatic authority in the text are distinguished by different styles, but they are not ordered for the reader. There is an uneasy balance of analysis and impressionism, which suggests the workings of Maggie's consciousness rather than its results; and there is more than a hint of violence, however oddly it is manifested:

She had made anxiety her stupid little idol; and absolutely now, while she stuck a long pin, a trifle fallaciously, into her hat—she had, with an approach to irritation, told her maid, a new woman, whom she had lately found herself thinking of as abysmal, that she didn't want her—she tried to focus the possibility of some understanding between them in consequence of which he should cut loose. (II, 84)

It is the imagery attributed to Maggie which has the most disturbing effect. She sees her father, fancifully,

slowly and vaguely moving there and looking very slight and young and,

superficially, manageable, almost as much like her child, putting it a
little freely, as like her parent . . .   (II, 85)

Adam is 'like some precious spotless, exceptionally intelligent
lamb' and Maggie imagines his supposed 'bleating'; but he is 'all
accommodating': 'Sacrifice me, my own love; do sacrifice me, do
sacrifice me!' With all due allowance for the exaggeration of her
fancies, the cry is almost obscenely masochistic, and 'the positive
effect of the intensity of this figure' is far from unambiguous.

It is Adam Verver who voices the accusation against himself
and Maggie of 'a kind of wicked selfish prosperity perhaps' (II,
94). Acquisitiveness, the collector's instinct, laziness, are all
charges he expresses; and in doing this refutes at least the criticism
of unconsciousness. By this strategy, James is able to place the
attacks so as to suggest the terms of defence. The development
of the charge is more subtle, however, for their 'sense of difficulty'
is what enables them to fall into this failing:

'But we're selfish together—we move as a sort of selfish mass. . . . We
want each other,' he had further explained, 'only wanting it, each
time, *for* each other. . . .'   (II, 95)

An overdevelopment of such circumspect self-abnegation creates
'the happy spell; but it's also, a little, possibly, the immorality'.
To refute this would be to fall into a simpler fault; but Maggie
simply echoes her father: '"The immorality"?' The vague unease
simply does not stand up to examination. The disquiet, once
formulated, can be allayed:

'Well, we're tremendously moral for ourselves—that is for each other;
and I won't pretend that I know exactly at whose particular personal
expense you and I, for instance, are happy.'

The investigation becomes an opportunity for a reaffirmation,
not of the situation of the Ververs, which is as yet precarious, but
of Maggie's activity and Verver's in support of her: that is to
say, of the process of the novel:

'But the beauty of it is . . . that we *are* doing; we're doing, that is, after
all, what we went in for. We're working it, our life, our chance, whatever you may call it, as we saw it, as we felt it, from the first. We *have*
worked it, and what more can you do than that?'   (II, 95)

The tribute to Maggie and himself from her father, couched in terms which could be applied to the novel, has a detached, almost disinterested tone, which makes it persuasive. But from the same source comes another of those disquieting peculiarities of diction we have hitherto associated with Maggie's imaginative exuberance: Maggie as a pirate, Maggie beaten by a drunken husband, Maggie sacrificing her lamb-like father. When Adam phrases his remarks with the same sort of jocular extravagance, it is Charlotte who becomes the victim:

'Whenever one corners Charlotte,' he had developed more at his ease, 'one finds that she only wants to know what *we* want. Which is what we got her for!' (II, 98)

The cavalier tone of the owner is picked up by Maggie: 'What we got her for—exactly!' And although the narrative comments on 'a certain effect of oddity in their more or less successful ease', this admission is not enough to 'contain' the effect of their phrase. It is more than odd; it is shocking.

The question of tone thus becomes an important moral problem in the novel. It is not simply that Adam Verver changes from being 'bad' to 'good', nor even from a mistaken man to one who learns from his mistake. On the one occasion when the Assing-hams confer in this volume, this is one of the questions they raise. Colonel Assingham half complains, half asks, again the surrogate reader: 'What I can't for my life make out is your idea of the old boy' (II, 140). Fanny's reply is scarcely illuminating: 'Charlotte's too inconceivably funny husband? I *have* no idea.' This the Colonel seizes upon as a formulation of his character; but Fanny argues, as it were, for the author,[1] in rejecting such an inadequate judgement:

'he may be, for all I know, too inconceivably great. But that's not an idea. It represents only my weak necessity of feeling that he's beyond me—which isn't an idea either. . . .'

She puts alternative suggestions: 'You see he *may* be stupid too. . . . Yet on the other hand . . . he *may* be sublime: sublimer even than

---

[1] Of whom T. S. Eliot wrote, in his essay 'On Henry James' (1918) (rpt. in Dupee, ed., *The Question of Henry James,* p. 110), 'James's critical genius comes out most tellingly in his mastery over, his baffling escape from, Ideas; a mastery and an escape which are perhaps the last test of a superior intelligence. He had a mind so fine that no idea could violate it.'

Maggie herself.' Finally the dispute is put aside: 'He may in fact already have been. But we shall never know'. But it does not end on this evasion. Maggie, we learn, '*She'll* know—about her father; everything. . . . But she'll never tell us.'

It is this prognostication which brings the question which is 'beyond' Fanny within the novel. Adam raises the problem of his position and Maggie's; she allows him to elaborate it to the point where he offers the answers to his own difficulties. The question arises again once an 'odd' tone throws Adam's judgement into question. His character is discussed by the Assinghams; but Fanny tells us, as it were from the author, that we can never know the answer to this riddle. Only Maggie will know. Thus whether Adam is fallible or not, whether he is 'stupid' or 'sublime' his value is ultimately a function of Maggie's. By a circular argument, a kind of novelistic sleight of hand, the moral problem raised by the situation of characters is turned in upon itself as a demonstration of their relation to each other, and becomes an affirmation of the moral insight of the protagonist. Absolute morality is subordinated to the process of perception: a process closely linked with that by which we as readers apprehend the novel as a whole. Thus our own activity becomes Maggie's guarantee: if we could not follow her insights, we should not have been able to see the problem; since we have, she must equally have been capable of conceiving it.

This forms the basis of the narrative confidence in Maggie at Fawns, when, alone with her father, she revels in a situation ambiguously phrased. It is only for other people that this ambiguity exists: their relation to each other is simple for them. Taken out of context, our quotation acquires an ambiguity it does not have in Maggie's thoughts, since for her, 'It was positively as if . . . the inward felicity of their being once more . . . simply daughter and father had glimmered out for them' (II, 262). Only for others were they 'oh, so immensely!' 'husband and wife'. Whose husband and whose wife is not stated. For Maggie, wistful for a childlike innocence, the incestuous relation is not thinkable; for 'other persons' it is not speakable. At this point, perhaps, though scarcely overall, C. T. Samuels's criticism of *The Golden Bowl* provides a partly accurate description, 'as a novel whose wisdom is qualified by nostalgia for immaturity' (*The Ambiguity of Henry James*, p. 224). Yet even this must be qualified; for the novel, here,

is not wholly identified with Maggie's 'nostalgia': her weakness
is 'contained' by her own consciousness of it.

The recognition that 'they *had*, after all, whatever happened,
always and ever each other' (II, 262), is thus seen as a comfort
rather than an evasion. Their having each other is not the main
point. Conscious of this, Maggie now raises the question of their
position, much as Adam did before, but at a further level of
sophistication. Is their sublimity itself 'fatuous'? Her concern is
careful, and this is its answer. But the whole inquiry, it now
appears, is only a way of 'avoiding the serious, standing off,
anxiously, from the real' (II, 264). Looking at themselves in
relation to each other is easier than examining their relations
with Charlotte and Amerigo. How far is 'sublimity' an evasion?
The problem cannot be answered by a statement: it requires the
whole process of the novel to represent it, and to do this is no
guarantee of an answer. If the reader's examination of Adam's
role ended in a formulation of it as a function of Maggie's, the
circling around Maggie's true role sends us back to the novel
itself. Character exists in relation to other characters, and by
virtue of action; conversely, both structure and representation
contribute to a sense of character, and it is not enough to say, as
Raleigh does (op. cit. 67), that 'the only objective and solid entity
is the problem itself'.

The history of Fanny's responsibility for the situation, and the
hint of guilt in 'the physiognomic light' which Maggie notices
in her as she has done in Amerigo and Charlotte respectively, is
briefly summarized in justification of this highhandedness.
Maggie's conjecture is phrased with the cliché and hyperbole of
melodrama, in order to 'voice' what is called the 'cunning' of her
restraint, and give Maggie in narrative terms a frankness impracti-
cable in the dramatic situation. It is Maggie's conjectural outspokenness which redeems her, for indignation and appeasement
cancel each other out, allowing for a more temperate judgement,
in our reactions to such fancied outbursts as this:

'Don't cry out, my dear, till you're hurt—and above all ask yourself
how I can be so wicked as to complain. What in the name of all that's
fantastic can you dream that I have to complain *of*?' (II, 108-9)

Any ambiguity which remains in the reader's reaction to
Maggie is not ignored but exploited, by being redirected as

another perspective on the heroine, of which she herself is conscious,

by the aid of her wondering if this ambiguity with which her friend affected her wouldn't be at present a good deal like the ambiguity with which she herself must frequently affect her father.   (II, 109)

Maggie's honest self-consciousness contrasts with Fanny's evasions. But Fanny's determined refusal to face the idea of Charlotte's reaction to a long visit by the Assinghams to Fawns is in itself 'a fact of the highest value for Maggie'. Through her our interest is directed, not into judgement of Fanny, but towards the light such assessments shed on those who make them, and the implications this has for the relations between the protagonists: relations in which Fanny's part is merely incidental.

It is this fact, the externality of Fanny's relation to the main situation, which provides the constant for her role throughout this volume. Fanny can lie to Maggie 'Upon my positive word as an honest woman' (II, 124), with as much narrative justification as she can show her the truth, in the scene with the golden bowl. Though one dialogue seems to claim naturalism, with the attendant conventions for the reader of character interpretation and moral judgement, while the other is more overtly, even melodramatically, symbolic, both are really to be judged by the same canons of non-naturalistic artifice. The intensity of Maggie's statement of faith—'I can bear anything. . . . For love . . . For love . . . For love' (II, 120)—is not really more naturalistic than the hypnotic repetition of the bowl scene, with Fanny's gasping chorus. The common revelation of these two scenes is that 'With time . . . Fanny could brilliantly think anything that would serve' (II, 118): serve Maggie, that is, as she embodies the attempt to establish a balance which is beyond the 'truth' of naturalism. While Fanny recognizes that 'There are many things . . . that we shall never know' (II, 182), for Maggie, 'Knowledge, knowledge was a fascination as well as a fear' (II, 145). It is not the extent of their knowledge but the quality of their apprehension which is different. The distance between Fanny's hesitations and contradictions and Maggie's 'sublime' exploration in this volume heightens Maggie's pre-eminence, so that when 'seeing herself finally sure, knowing everything, having the fact, in all its abomination, so utterly before her . . . she felt the sudden split between conviction and action' (II, 193), Maggie's daring is justified in taking off from the fact to where 'action began to hover like some lighter and larger, but easier form . . .' (II, 193), and she can insist to the Prince, as the novel does to the reader, 'Find out for yourself!' (II, 211). This independent exploration can only show 'a new need of her' (II, 193).

Once Maggie's initiative is justified, Fanny is there, as Bob Assingham was in the first volume, mainly to have things said to her. The limits of speech between Maggie and Fanny are those of conversation, rather than the larger boundaries of expression itself, and because of this the reader is able to accept statements from Maggie to Fanny which would be too cryptic as general statements.

The use of absolutes marks a new freedom from equivocation and circumspection which is a relief to the reader, and imparts a fresh impulse of energy halfway through this volume. As Maggie confronts Amerigo over the pieces of the bowl so melodramatically contrived and shattered,

There it was that her wish for time interposed—time for Amerigo's use, not for hers, since she, for ever so long now . . . had been living with eternity, with which she would continue to live.   (II, 191)

Like silence as a means of expression, it is the abolition of time which carries significance. On a more practical level, Maggie sees Fanny's presence as a social 'seal of approval', denying that anything is wrong: 'as a value for the clear negation of everything'. Fanny's is the ear to which Maggie can say that '*Nothing* . . . explains!', and once such terms have been introduced, they can be used more contemplatively, less as a challenge: 'he had, in so almost mystifying a manner, replied to nothing, denied nothing, explained nothing, apologized for nothing . . .' (II, 226). The Prince's conduct is, paradoxically, open to interpretation as the deepest tribute to Maggie's understanding:

It was as if she had passed, in a time incredibly short, from being nothing for him to being all . . .   (II, 234)

The extremes of 'nothing' and 'all' bound a range of expression within which the interviews between Maggie and Charlotte may be seen as extraordinary without being ridiculously exaggerated. In Chapter XXVI, while the party of six sit after dinner, 'the facts of the situation were upright' for Maggie, more real than the sitters themselves: the word 'fact' recurs five times in consecutive clauses, realizing, with rhetorical insistence, a scene in which the pattern of relationships is all-important, and the persons only secondary. It is a direct statement of the narrative situation:

Erect above all for her was the sharp-edged fact of the relation of the whole group, individually and collectively, to herself—herself so speciously eliminated for the hour, but presumably more present to the attention of each than the next card to be played.   (II, 238)

The dramatic scene of the card game seems almost consciously symbolic for the participants, as Maggie feels. A vivid sense of significance beyond the actual, naturalistic scene, creates a climax. The link between 'propriety' and actuality is tenuous, so that Maggie feels 'that if she were but different—oh, ever so different! —all this high decorum would hang by a hair' (II, 239).

It is this 'vertiginous' sensation which forms the basis of the confrontation with Charlotte. The layers of appearance and reality are definite and clear to Maggie, and nothing but 'common solemnity' seems to prevent a 'lurid' revelation. There is a peculiarly graphic sense of the abstract, merging with the transparencies of the actual scene, in a fusion of metaphor and reality recalling the Princess's metaphorical door and the apt entrance of Amerigo at the beginning of the volume:

Her father and her husband, Mrs. Assingham and Charlotte, had done nothing but meet her eyes; yet the difference in these demonstrations made each a separate passage—which was all the more wonderful since, with the secret behind every face, they had alike tried to look at her *through* it and in denial of it.   (II, 240)

The urgency is 'an appeal, a positive confidence . . . that was deeper than any negation, and that seemed to speak, on the part of each, of some relation to be contrived by her, a relation with herself, which would spare the individual the danger, the actual present strain, of the relation with the others'. In Maggie's conception at least, everything depends on her: 'the scapegoat of old'. It is this positive 'idea' which occupies Maggie's thoughts, not a spirit of vengeance:

This idea of her simplifying, and of their combined struggle, dim as

yet but steadily growing, toward the perception of her adopting it
from them, clung to her . . . (II, 241)

The powerful symbol of the scapegoat is opposed to the extremity
of the violence 'of opportunity which had assaulted her, within,
on her sofa, as a beast might have leaped at her throat' (II, 241).
The proliferation of metaphor and symbol takes the scene beyond
naturalism, by locating it at the imaginative pitch of Maggie's
consciousness:

Spacious and splendid, like a stage again awaiting a drama, it was the
scene she might people, by the press of her spring, either with sereni-
ties and dignities and decencies, or with terrors and shames and ruins,
things as ugly as those formless fragments of her golden bowl she was
trying so hard to pick up. (II, 242)

Selecting one image after another, Maggie argues by metaphor, in
a question of feeling which could not be determined by logic and
should not be dealt with 'in any of the immediate, inevitable,
assuaging ways, the ways usually open . . .'.

When Charlotte follows Maggie on to the terrace, however,
this poise is threatened. If Charlotte acted as a 'splendid shining
supple creature', then Maggie would be at risk, and so would her
idea. The 'agitating image' suggests that Maggie may have to
satisfy Charlotte 'as to the reference, in her mocking spirit, of so
much of the unuttered and unutterable, of the constantly and
unmistakably implied'. Maggie feels trapped, at a disadvantage
imaged with extraordinary violence, 'of having been thrown over
on her back, with her neck, from the first, half broken and her
helpless face staring up'. But the whole scene being portrayed
through Maggie, the way these extremes all tell against her is
seen by the reader as intentional. Maggie creates an exaggerated
picture of herself, but does not distort her conception of Charlotte
in the same way: in her she notes 'a kind of portentous intelligent
stillness', and 'Charlotte's dignity'. This imbalance distorts both
tone and reason, so that the reader can only make sense of the
situation by accepting Maggie's viewpoint and her idiosyncratic
interpretation.

The dialogue between Maggie and Charlotte is brief and unimportant, but when they stand before the smoking-room window,
Maggie sees 'the full significance' of what it is. This 'picture'
means different things to 'a different interpreter', or in a different

situation. She might have shown it to Charlotte, but instead Charlotte is showing it to her, and 'as Charlotte showed it, so she must at present submissively seem to take it'. Despite all her efforts through melodramatic imaginings, exotic symbols, extreme self-abnegation and a deep respect for her rival, no expression of Maggie's alone can overcome the irreducible otherness of Charlotte. Both can look at the same object, and that is as near as they can get. Though Maggie's awareness of the fact demonstrates her understanding of the nature of communication, even this does not give her entry into Charlotte's consciousness, or lay her own mind open to the other woman. They, as much as those they are looking at, are 'absorbed and unconscious'.

This is an image of communication which makes no enormous claims, and Maggie, as the narrative consciousness, is freed by this of all suspicion of bombastic pretension. When Charlotte takes her by the hand and utters 'a few straight words', Maggie's helplessness is conveyed by an image which works on the narrative level, with psychological consistency, as she clutches her shawl and draws it 'round her as if huddling in it for shelter, covering herself with it for humility' (II, 254). It is Charlotte who sets the tone of their confrontation: Maggie has only to respond. Because Charlotte has presented the challenge, Maggie can lie with impunity: 'I accuse you—I accuse you of nothing' (II, 257). It is 'in tune with the right', in tune with the note Charlotte herself has given, for Maggie to 'humbug': to maintain consistency, 'It was only a question of not, by a hair's breadth, deflecting into the truth' (II, 258). Thus Maggie's 'honour' is set by the tone within the scene. She can drop her shawl, and achieve the stance Charlotte has challenged her to adopt, by swearing, 'Upon my honour'; and in the light of her awareness, her conscious adoption of a certain preferred tone, the lie becomes like Desdemona's 'sublime' lie, rather than echoing the ambiguous and shameful bargain between Kate and Densher in *The Wings of the Dove*.

The 'prodigious kiss' of the two women at the end of this scene is dangerous, but conscious: entirely fitted to its 'high publicity'. It is Charlotte's gesture: one to which Maggie 'couldn't say yes, but she didn't say no'. For the reader, it constitutes one term in a series. The conscious falsehood of this kiss contrasts on the one hand with the delusion of the Prince and Charlotte in their 'pledge', and on the other with the wordless understanding of the embrace between Maggie and her father, immediately after this interview on the terrace, and following Adam's 'threat' to take Charlotte off to America. It is thus Charlotte's 'tone' which has made the tableau of concord upon which Adam can base the fiction that the move to America would be a deprivation, rather than a relief, for Maggie.

The following chapter, XXXVIII, begins with a lengthy appreciation of the convolutions of this development, and includes the kind of summaries which draw together the reader's impressions. Significance, not action, develops; and the narrative method becomes more and more transparent. Though Maggie's consciousness is the vehicle of appreciation, it is the authorial effort we are to appreciate, through hers:

> to the degree that the whole evening hung together, to her aftersense, as a thing appointed by some occult power that had dealt with her, that had for instance animated the four with just the right restlessness too, had decreed and directed and exactly timed it in them . . . (II, 286)

Maggie's 'inner sense' works with a combination of speculative abstraction and imaginative proliferation which requires enormous concentration from the reader. Playing back over what the narrative has shown, and off in hypothetical suppositions, her thoughts are continually in movement, from which her image-making provides temporary relief. A momentary relaxation allows the reader to luxuriate in these similes, so that they achieve an effect heightened by stillness. The image of Maggie as 'clinging with her winged concentration to some deep cell of her heart, she stored away her hived tenderness as if she had gathered it all from flowers' (II, 289), is an unavowed emotional counterpart to the intellectual activity we watch her demonstrate. The Prince's helplessness is in unspoken contrast to this: 'walking ostensibly beside her, but in fact given over, without a break, to the grey medium in which he helplessly groped' (II, 289). Charlotte's movements and Maggie's mental steps are matched by a narrative method which places both in relation, without overbalancing into an identity which would obscure the sense of pattern. The feeling of separateness is conveyed through the sense of process:

> Marvellous the manner in which, under such imaginations, Maggie thus circled and lingered—quite as if she were, materially, following

her unseen, counting every step she helplessly wasted, noting every
hindrance that brought her to a pause.   (II, 291)

Maggie's penetration of Charlotte's point of view has not
prevented her being charged with coldness; but this can only be
done in defiance of authorial direction. Not only are we explicitly
told that 'Maggie's provision of irony . . . had never been so
scant as now' (II, 292), but this bald assertion is substantiated in
the tender images with which Maggie conceives of Charlotte's
anxieties:

things, these, that she carried about with her done up in the napkin
of her lover's accepted rebuke, while she vainly hunted for some corner
where she might put them safely down.

The transition from the care of the folded napkin to the anxiety
of the hunt, and from this to the appalling image of Charlotte's
relation to her husband, 'holding in one of his pocketed hands
the end of a long silken halter looped round her beautiful neck'
(II, 295), is uncannily sweet. The 'little meditative man in the
straw hat', when seen through Charlotte's eyes, has a kind of
'indescribable' magic power which has nothing to do with his
relation to Maggie; but from Maggie's intimations of Charlotte's
attitude, to her intimations of his, is an apparently easy progression, and what begins as a projected hypothesis becomes a
personal interpretation. The silence and gentleness of this
torture seem more dreadful than the violence of Maggie's earlier
fancies: 'a wordless, wordless smile, but the smile was the soft
shake of the twisted rope' (II, 296).

Maggie is by no means unaware of the 'sacrifice' entailed in
setting the situation to rights. But the dreadful 'shriek of a soul
in pain', which rouses her to protest to her father, prompts him
to turn to her with what she sees as a 'sharp identity of emotion'.
His understanding absolves him of malice, but not of responsibility; his implied acceptance of this is humble:

as, held thus together they had still another strained minute, the shame,
the pity, the better knowledge, the smothered protest, the divine
anguish even, so overcame him that, blushing to his eyes, he turned
short away.   (II, 301)

The narrative is honest, even to the point of acknowledging the
possibility of embarrassment at its own excesses:

There was, honestly, an awful mixture in things, and it was not closed to her aftersense of such passages . . . that the deepest depth of all, in a perceived penalty, was that you couldn't be sure some of your compunctions and contortions wouldn't show for ridiculous.

But this speculation is brought back into the narrative as the possible motive for Amerigo's leaving Fawns. Maggie's thoughts follow him as they have done Charlotte, and in such passages hers becomes the narrative imagination.

The second in the series of interviews with Charlotte is explicitly announced as part of a pattern: 'The relation, to-day, had turned itself round' (II, 305). A sense of seriousness is built up as the narrative is taken back before this encounter. A passage on Charlotte's supposed motives for retreat, followed by a conversation with Fanny Assingham, who tells Maggie, 'You've done it', and a glimpse of Adam Verver, immobile in the house, all precede Maggie's 'sallying forth' to Charlotte. This is no hasty or vindictive pursuit, but a measured climax, almost an anticlimax. It is stressed that 'It was a repetition more than ever of the evening on the terrace' (II, 319).

Leo Bersani's view of 'reality' in *The Golden Bowl* as 'the novelistic arrangements of the first half', with the second half giving 'the correction, the unashamed, radical revision which Maggie then makes of her own work' ('The Jamesian Lie', p. 73), prompts a recognition of a peculiarly witty narrative image here, as Maggie takes out to Charlotte the first volume of her romance, setting the story straight from the start: '*This* is the beginning; you've got the wrong volume, and I've brought you out the right' (II, 321).

The passage between the two women is related in terms of the images of buried treasure corresponding to Maggie's 'stage pirates', of burning ships recalling those of Adam's proposal, of veils and mantles related to Charlotte's tissue of decorum and to Maggie's protective shawl, of stage and scene, depths, and a 'shore' which corresponds in some sense to the edge of a continent, whether Britain or America. The novel's techniques of dialogue are also recapitulated here: the broken conversation, its sense taken up by one speaker after another; the word isolated by inverted commas, a dash, a question mark; the pronoun whose reference must be selected on a basis of common understanding; the ambiguous preposition; the recurrent thematic words. Charlotte claims,

'I've an idea . . . It has come over me that we're wrong. Our real
life isn't here.'

Maggie held her breath. '"Ours"—?'

'My husband's and mine. I'm not speaking for you.'

'Oh!' said Maggie, only praying not to be, not even to appear,
stupid.

'I'm speaking for ourselves. I'm speaking,' Charlotte brought out,
'for *him*.'   (II, 324)

Every word of this last sentence has an accumulated significance;
and there is a real achievement of understanding behind Maggie's
simply naming the name: 'I see. For my father.'

The situation is not simply an inversion of the last interview
between these women, but a variation on Maggie's earlier talks
with her father. Charlotte's words are those Maggie has used:
'Let me admit it—I *am* selfish. I place my husband first' (II, 325).
The situation Maggie has prompted Adam to propose is now
adopted by Charlotte as her own. It is Charlotte who can voice
the heroine's rationale. But her words remain ambiguous: 'I
want . . . to *keep* the man I've married. And to do so, I see, I
must act.' The mechanism of the declaration, Maggie's control
and Charlotte's inverted response, are finally thrown off at a
tangent from the real situation, and the mock showdown reaches
success with Charlotte's demand: 'You recognise then that
you've failed?' (II, 328). Maggie, 'ready to lie again', succeeds by
responding to this misplaced attack; for the real confrontation
has been elided by this demonstrative encounter, and she has
worked the truth indirectly into acceptance.

A scene with Fanny Assingham allows for the voicing of these
implications, the affirmation of Maggie's continuing pity for
Charlotte, and the expression of the two uncertainties that remain:
the fact that Maggie is not quite sure enough of her husband to
know whether he will be able, like her, to rise above Charlotte
by pitying her, and the fact that she does not know, and never
will, how many 'things her father knew that even yet she didn't!'
(II, 339). The question of Amerigo is explored in the penultimate
chapter, through the image we have already examined of 'some
famous poetic line in a dead language', and resolved in the delayed
embrace. The 'rhyme' between this and the final embrace of the
last chapter 'contains' the last scene in an ongoing yet secure
movement. The last embrace, in which Maggie buries her eyes and

the Prince 'sees' 'nothing but *you*' (II, 377), also 'answers' that at the opening of Volume II in which the Prince 'didn't see' (II, 17). With the relations between the Prince and Princess assured of fulfilment, there is long enough for a last look at those with Charlotte and Adam Verver, but only as a parenthesis, a subordinate consideration.

In this scene it is the passage between Maggie and her father which contains the moment of still appreciation and of unsatisfied questioning, both of which, as John Bayley puts it, 'are not settled and disposed of by the action but continue freely to inhabit the mind of the reader' (*The Characters of Love,* p. 210). The pair share a moment of perfect communication in looking at the 'Florentine sacred subject, that he had given her on her marriage' (II, 367). But their agreement that 'It's all right, eh?' (II, 368), it seems, 'symbolised another truth'. Looking round 'at everything else', their catalogue takes in not only all the furniture but the other 'noble persons'. Whether this is degradation or exaltation of their marriage partners is a challenge thrown out, not answered, by the novel, and to resolve it easily would falsify James's work. The Keatsian allusions in *The Golden Bowl* suggest one counterpart for an aesthetic dilemma which '[doth] tease us out of thought/ As doth eternity'; but James's tone is restrained, if his address is rhetorical, while Verver balances a revealing fluency in French with colloquial American understatement:

There was much indeed in the tone in which Adam Verver spoke again, and who shall say where his thought stopped? '*Le compte y est.* You've got some good things.'   (II, 369)

The 'note' of this scene is a poised withdrawal from expression; not a denial, but declining to assert, a challenge beyond the narrative. The ambiguity of the word 'relation' for the links between the persons or the narrative itself makes this the ultimate gesture of affiliation between author and protagonist:

the note of that strange accepted finality of relation . . . which almost escaped an awkwardness only by not attempting a gloss.   (II, 369)

This is the taciturnity where modesty and pride are indistinguishable, which corresponds to Maggie's impulse, 'for pity and dread', to bury her eyes at last in her husband's embrace. Having given Charlotte the correct first volume, Maggie withdraws in the end from the process of representation: the 'uttered word' and the light of understanding alike.

'The Princess' volume of *The Golden Bowl* is radically different in process from the 'The Prince', for the narrative follows only Maggie's consciousness. Apart from one scene between the Assinghams, showing that Adam Verver is a mystery in himself, not merely to Maggie, every perception and reaction is reached through the heroine, either directly or in her projections of the other characters.

Some perspective on Maggie, and a certain continuity of approach with the first volume, is preserved through the third-person narration, but the closeness of the narrative point of view to the heroine's raises many of the questions of authority associated with first-person narration. Maggie's words are frequently hysterical, but her tone rarely so: to distinguish her degree of control is one difficulty for the reader. Another, more disturbing problem, is in accounting for the words and images whose tone is laconic, but which strike the reader as shocking. The silken halter around Charlotte's neck, the comment that 'we got her' for a purpose, and Adam's approving 'You've got some good things' at the end, are more difficult to explain away as technical ingenuities of tact than, for example, Maggie's image of Charlotte as the music hall's 'bird in a gilded cage': an image she has earlier used of herself. The reader must accept these expressions of indifference as deliberately laconic, rather than unwittingly cruel treatments of issues whose seriousness is not unrecognized, but unspoken. The alternative is to find in them a condemnation of the Ververs: but Maggie, at least, we must trust, if we are to follow the novel at all.

The narrative structure of dramatic scenes demonstrating the evolution of Maggie's relationships, interspersed with elaborate reflections upon the problems and patterns, heightens our sense of Maggie's consciousness at the same time as showing how close this draws to the reader's own. Her authority is based upon this: that the process is analogous for heroine and reader.

Another supportive structure is that of character itself. Maggie is shown as knowing more than the Prince and Charlotte, saying more than Adam Verver, and understanding more than the Assinghams. They all learn to respect rather than to protect her.

Meanwhile her 'selfish' power is qualified by her concern for her father. Since, however, this concern is the reader's chief guarantee of his stature and probity, the argument is a circular one. Everything comes back to our reliance on Maggie.

The first volume has prepared for this reliance, by undermining the authority of other characters, who are ignorant or misguided, yet revealing that authority derived from sources other than the individual, such as social or linguistic forms, is inadequate to the complexities of human relations. What is needed is knowledge, as far as knowledge goes, and beyond this, a kind of trust which can only derive from individual integrity. Maggie has the active curiosity of a storyteller herself: 'Knowledge, knowledge was a fascination as well as a fear' (II, 145). She has also a quality we are not accustomed to regard as a virtue: the quality Milly Theale does not have, and which makes Maggie human and of this world in a way the dying benefactress never could be. Adam Verver tells her, 'I guess you're proud, Mag . . . I mean proud *enough*' (I, 189). This sense of the self, however, is poised against, neither dominated by nor subordinate to, a recognition of the limits of the self, and the existence of all that is outside it. This both confirms and limits individual responsibility. If Maggie can look out for herself, and must, so can, and must, everybody else:

> Once she was conscious . . . that she was something for *their* queer experience, just as they were something for hers—there was no limit to her conceived design of not letting them escape.

The Golden Bowl builds up a pattern of characters, of situations, of images and dramatic scenes, none of which is sufficient in itself to allow the reader to subsume under it all the others. They are not played off against each other directly, imagery against dramatic reality, personality against social form; but in their oblique relations, a great deal is done by negative definitions, silence, and withheld knowledge. Maggie's figure of the bath of luxury shows the self immersed; but her goldfish bowl image can only be seen from the outside. It is logically impossible to be both inside and out; but in taking this imaginative double posture, Maggie is doing what both author and readers attempt. The relation between the two states, of immersion and exclusion, or what, in *The Wings of the Dove* was called, 'being and . . . seeing', is essentially a problem of perception; but it is analogous to the problem of communication between people: between characters, between author and reader.

James draws attention to this difficulty throughout *The Golden Bowl,* through the interest of the characters in the essence of their situation: a pattern of forces which is repeatedly described and analysed in quasi-structuralist, abstract terms. In the second volume, Maggie's curiosity makes her 'a compositional resource . . . as well as a value intrinsic' (*The Art of the Novel,* p. 329). Her 'creative hand' both makes and is the interest of the book: it is with a process, rather than with fixed forms, that we have to do. Silence in the novel shows that forms are inadequate; yet paradoxically it shows their importance too. Silence is a state, rather than a process: like Maggie's 'eternity', it is essentially unmoving. The importance of silence in the plot is compounded by that in the view of character. After the silence of complicity comes Maggie's silence of integrity: one threatens the precise equilibrium of social and personal relations which the other restores. In contrast with Charlotte's 'active' silence of deception comes Adam Verver's silence of passivity, absorbing wrong into himself, and refusing to complain. Maggie, modulating between them, is both active and passive: the playwright and the scapegoat. Having manipulated silence as a means of expression, together with all legitimate and illegitimate fixed forms, from hyperbole to lies, Maggie sinks at the end into a silence larger than herself, as expression ceases and communication is perfect.

Adrian Poole writes of 'the intimate, ineffaceable spaces across which words and gestures are forced to leap to their fragile credibilities. James presses us towards feeling that those spaces, like the cracks in the golden bowl, are not merely inevitable but precious'. The conclusion of *The Golden Bowl* shows us Maggie renouncing the means by which it was created, much as Prospero at the end of *The Tempest* drowns his book. Yet Prospero, as one vision draws to a close, promises 'a chronicle of day by day'; Maggie gives Charlotte volume one of her romance, to start again. There is no easy, no absolute negation, any more than a final conclusion of the problems of 'process and effect' raised in and through *The Golden Bowl.* The crack, like the bowl, is precious, and inevitable.

VI

'Let us Go and Make our Visit':
The Last Works

THE WORKS before *The Golden Bowl* seem in retrospect a development towards that consummation of freedom within complexity: those after it a winding-down, if not a falling off, from that peak. Maxwell Geismar calls this period 'a postscript, an epilogue' (*Henry James and His Cult*, p. 335), and veils his scorn in a thin echo of Pope:

the final 'secrets' of this singular artist emerged more clearly and positively; the true values, motives, prejudices . . . transfixed by age, as it were . . . all pure and translucently displayed . . . for us to marvel at and ponder over in sheer incredulity.

Though it is easy enough to invert Geismar's irony and see translucency as a marvel indeed, those who admire James's last works prefer to leave that quality to *The Golden Bowl* and stress something different in the autobiographical and unfinished works, as well as the last short stories: James's continuing efforts to develop his form and its scope. Peter Buitenhuis speaks of James's 'vitality in the face of adversity . . . his ability to respond to new forms of perception and to embody these in changing forms and styles'.[1] D. W. Jefferson reminds us of James's debt to the American tradition of the tall story.[2] Others, such as J. A. Ward stress the modernity of the late James's treatment of the 'plight of the man of sensibilities in a naked world, institutionally and culturally bankrupt', and suggest that James was concerned with 'the possibilities of spiritual expansion outside a social context'.[3] This challenge is confronted with James's usual enquiring interest, however: no evasive fantasy. As Quentin Anderson remarks, the last stories reveal not what 'would have

---

[1] *The Grasping Imagination: the American Writings of Henry James* (1970), p. 267.
[2] *Henry James and the Modern Reader* (1964), p. 163.
[3] *The Imagination of Disaster: Evil in the Fiction of Henry James* (1961), pp. 158, 157.

been', but what 'has been', and he makes an important link between several key episodes here and one James records from his own youth in *A Small Boy and Others*. There James recounts 'the most appalling yet most admirable nightmare of my life' (*Autobiography*, 196). In the impressive setting of the Galerie d'Apollon at the Louvre, he confronts a strange presence, and terrifies what frightens him. Rather than yielding to a vision of evil, as both Henry James Sr. and William James had done in their experience of the supernatural, the younger brother outfaced his pursuer; but the experience remained with him, and constitutes the germ of some of his most powerful stories.

We can find many such links between the ostensibly historical and overtly fictional works of James's last period. James's note in *The American Scene* of the disappearance of Washington Place in New York, or the vanishing of 'the Ashburton Place that I anciently knew' between successive visits to Boston, suggest Spencer Brydon's converting a house into a skyscraper, and his reluctance to do the same with his own old home. The non-fictional works, however, are more than source-books of anecdotes for the late stories. The links are thematic, at the deepest level of felt experience. Thus James's autobiographical recognition that 'the effect of detachment [in America] was the fact of the experience of Europe' (*Autobiography*, 277), is transmuted into the sense of separateness which permits Graham Fielder poised appreciation of the 'American way' (*The Ivory Tower*, p. 74), arriving at 'the high pitch' (p. 248) of sensibility; but it is also behind the loneliness of Mark Monteith in the crowds of New York (in 'A Round of Visits'), developing into a sense of isolation just the opposite of Milly Theale's understanding that 'her only company must be the human race at large' (*The Wings of the Dove*, p. 205). Again, the underlying assumptions of the fictional world are made explicit in an echo of the autobiography when Mr. Betterman explains to Gray, like Henry James Sr. to his sons, 'Do? The question isn't of your doing, but simply of your being' (*The Ivory Tower*, p. 112). With the *naïveté* of a young James, but the penetration of maturity, 'Gray cast about. "But don't they come to the same thing?" '

Such interconnections could provide material for exhaustive analyses based on cross-reference. But this would involve a critical approach different from that applied to James's earlier works, where we found each novel establishing the conditions for its own reading through 'the process and the effect of representation'. We have seen how, building up and breaking down both familiar and sophisticated narrative patterns, James endowed the reader with that 'experience' which has 'the power to guess the unseen from the seen, to trace the implications of things', without forfeiting the resilience which resists reductive formulation. The 'interest' lies in the tension between these attributes: what James called 'the high price of the novel . . . form'. It is only to the novels, of course, that these criteria can be critically applied. *The American Scene,* the *Autobiography,* and the *Tales* cannot be assessed in terms they do not claim to meet. Nevertheless, we cannot ignore these works, close as they are to the unfinished novels, unless we find the novels themselves, like those of the major phase, coherent and self-sufficient.

The very fact that neither *The Ivory Tower* nor *The Sense of the Past* is complete belies that claim to sufficiency. Their existence implies that James did not recognize *The Golden Bowl* as his last novel; their incompleteness means that it was so in fact. The critical problem remains to determine whether the reasons for this were accidental, or a recognizable literary necessity. The incompleteness of the works precludes their claim to equal consideration with James's great novels; but would they, could they have been as important, or not?

Oscar Cargill, in *The Novels of Henry James*, gives a helpful account of the compositional histories of the unfinished works (pp. 462 ff., 482 ff.): enough circumstantial information to explain why neither novel was completed. What remains uncertain is why James abandoned *The Ivory Tower* on the outbreak of the Great War, and turned to the historical novel. What is the connection between biography and genre in the late James? Can such enquiries be extended to individual aspects of style: characterization, setting and theme? John Carlos Rowe traces a close connection between the biography of James, his 'reconstruction of . . . experience' and a 'sense of the mystery of style', through 'a burgeoning historical sense that is style itself'. This perception is derived from James's autobiographical accounts of his experience in Paris, but extended confidently over *The American Scene*, where 'the real story is that of the analyst'. Rowe suggests that 'the style and the narrative method of *The American Scene* reflect the structural complexities of the novels of the Major Phase'.[1] Buitenhuis makes a different claim: that the style helps establish the image of the narrator in *The American Scene,* but the link with James's other work is in theme, rather than technique: 'In a country in which values so rapidly changed, James saw that the very nature of identity was thrown into question. . . . All the protagonists of [James's] late American stories confront the self in some form, and investigate the values by which it lives . . .' (*The Grasping Imagination,* p. 210). If the distinctive quality of the late James is that his personal experience is brought nearer to explicit analysis, how does this relate to Edmund Wilson's comment that in James's works 'people, so far as "psychologising" goes, are not intimate even with themselves'?[2] Is there a real distinction in the last works, brought about perhaps by the visit James made, after a space of twenty years, to his native, but now strange, country?

All these approaches to the late works select some aspect of style or form and relate it to a 'deeper' level of meaning or theme. But Georg Lukacs warns against a misapprehension of the novel form:

> Every art form is defined by the metaphysical dissonance of life which it accepts and organises . . . The dissonance special to the novel . . . produces a problem of form whose formal nature is much less obvious than in other kinds of art . . . it looks like a problem of content . . .
> (*The Theory of the Novel,* p. 71)

James himself described the power of the novel 'to appear more true to its character in proportion as it strains, or tends to burst, with a latent extravagance, its mould' (*The Art of the Novel,* p. 46). It is only in the context of form that what James called 'imaged creative Expression' can be placed, as it is in a 'style handed over to its last disciplined passion of curiosity': that passion which James linked with 'our highest experience of luxury'.

Incompleteness prevents our attempting this as rigorously with *The Ivory Tower* and *The Sense of the Past* as in the finished novels: an obvious fact, but one rarely stressed enough by critics approaching the last works with ready appreciation. No conjectural ending, and nothing found in James's remarkably full

---

[1] John Carlos Rowe, *Henry Adams and Henry James* (1976), pp. 139, 164, 148.

[2] Edmund Wilson, *The Triple Thinkers* (1952), p. 123.

Notes to the last works can have the critical status of the texts themselves. It is reasonable to qualify a judgement of the existing works with the acknowledgement that James might well have altered them in revision: he did not publish what we read. But it is misleading to withhold all adverse criticism on these grounds, or to confine our consideration to broad questions of structure and theme without that attention to details of expression which we find so important in reading the finished works.

The Ivory Tower is particularly difficult to assess fairly, for a promise of extraordinary subtlety in the relations between characters, both in what we have of the novel and in the Notes, is not fully substantiated in the text as it stands. The story of Graham Fielder's recall from Europe to inherit the fortune he once avoided promises a vehicle for James to explore 'interest' through financial chicanery, personal manipulation, and the gamut of 'relations' between loyalty and treachery, with the added twist of an inverted 'American theme', in which the Europeanized hero is the 'innocent' protagonist. Buitenhuis sees the depth of complexity in the *donnée*, and points out that

James was not content merely to delineate his characters; he also arranged their associations antecedent to the action of the novel.

(Op. cit. 243)

There is a rich suggestion of intrigue rooted in the past, and of a developing connection between character and action: a hint of that charged sensibility between determinism and freedom which heightens the moral fineness of Kate Croy's 'case', and refines our view of Charlotte Stant. This historical depth also serves a formal function, as Buitenhuis notes:

this was a means by which James could avoid unnecessary exposition and clear the ground for . . . immediate intimacy . . . More important, it was one of the ways in which he could heighten the tension and moral ambiguity of his action.   (Ibid. 243–4)

Buitenhuis feels that *The Ivory Tower* 'would almost certainly' have been James's best 'essay of American life' (ibid. 260). He notes the element of fable in the subject, the dramatic skill with which the deathbed scene is set up; above all, the 'organic symbol' of the ivory tower itself: not even mentioned in the Notes, but central to the novel.

The tower, however, marks the point of our attack. Buitenhuis suggests that such a symbol 'opens up a work and mediates between writer and reader in a variety of ways' (ibid. 246), acting more flexibly than a 'literary schema' which 'tends to set limits'. Rowe links the tower with James's earlier symbols:

The golden bowl, the wings of the dove, and the ivory tower are the incarnations of the meanings for social relations in the novels.

(Op. cit. 198)

The link is just, but the interpretation curious. Rowe continues, more comprehensibly,

They are wrought by a curious and lost art, whose intricate process demands successive interpretations in order to be unlayered.

The bowl offers a parallel to the tower, in that it exists within the novel not only as a symbol, providing the title, perhaps the key, to the work, but also as a physical object, and the centre of certain scenes. These scenes, in *The Golden Bowl*, are important to the plot; they are set-piece displays, but their non-naturalistic, even melodramatic, mode obtrudes from the texture of the novel. The effect is one of deliberate overstatement. John Bayley (in *The Characters of Love*) compares the bowl with Othello's handkerchief. It marks those *'rigidities'* which it is the triumph of the work to overcome. The bowl is broken, but the concepts suggested by the bowl, its value, beauty, hidden flaw, live on, freed of the obtrusive fact of the bowl itself. The bowl merges into the interlocking structures of imagery and plot, demanding not fixed appreciation but a process of understanding.

This sense of a process is what *The Ivory Tower* fails fully to achieve. The elements are there, but the movement falters. The elaborate tower itself, 'a wonder of wasted ingenuity' (*The Ivory Tower*, p. 144), provides a symbol of the stylistic complications which carry situations beyond the characters through whom they are dramatized. We accede to this power of suggestion at the end of *The Golden Bowl*, in 'that strange accepted finality of relation . . . which almost escaped an awkwardness only by not attempting a gloss' (II, 369), for it has evolved gradually, withstanding the various challenges of action from Charlotte, question from the Assinghams, and statements made in private, besides 'public' lies from Maggie. But in *The Ivory Tower*, a preternatural sensitivity

seems to pervade the novel from the first. In the presentation of
scene and character, the insertion of significant history, the use
of setting and positively baroque imagery, James creates a sense
of the momentous which is not really sustained in the human
encounters, the very words and gestures, of the story. The tone
is too unmitigatedly exalted in reflection, too surprisingly deflated
in dramatic action, to enlist and guide our sympathies.

While the perceptions of *The Ivory Tower* fascinate us, a certain
exaggeration of language distances the intellectual from the
imaginative apprehension. At the same time, the interest in
language itself, the process of expression, which grew through
The Wings of the Dove, with its disconcerting variety of modes,
and *The Golden Bowl*, with its investigation of the very concepts
of form, of words, names, symbols, borders on static display in
The Ivory Tower. The recurrent 'question' is no longer a real
enquiry, but an elaborate mystery, portentously referred to
through the reflections of the characters, in the author's technical
and abstract terms of 'curiosity', 'interest', 'story', 'signs', 'type',
'facts', 'forms' and the 'hard-rimmed circle'. Though the characters are depicted with a larger-than-life solidity, and the recurrent
mythical connections (reminiscent of a Jacobean masque)
endow them and their story with the baroque trimmings of 'a
delightful violence', as Gray senses when he lands in America,
this Pilgrim's Progress is too heavily peopled with figures and
forms. Attempting to select an example, we are bemused by the
variety of choice: Rosanna, like a ship, her father, like a hawk,
Davey, Cissy, Gussy, the very nurse to Mr. Betterman: each is
endowed with a surprisingly solid physical presence, and all
but the last with a complication of interest, curiosity, and motive
that makes their musings hard to distinguish. What these gro-
tesques lack, in fact, is a voice. After Rosanna's impressive
entrance, bearing her 'vast pale-green parasol, a portable pavilion
from which there fluttered fringes, frills and ribbons that made
it resemble the roof of some Burmese palanquin or perhaps even
a Pagoda' (p. 1) (can this Pagoda, like Maggie Verver's, be intended as a narrative image of the predicament of consciousness,
we wonder?); after her peculiarly Jamesian appraisal of her father,
'which would have told his story, all his story, every inch of it
and with the last intensity, she felt, to a spectator capable of
being struck with him as one might after all happen to be struck'

(3–4); after her eyes have shown us this 'ruffled hawk', consumed in a calculation of Jonsonian, vulturine malignity: after thus presenting her narrative credentials, how does Rosanna open the dialogue with that monstrous parent?

'Don't you get tired,' she put to him, 'of just sitting round here?'
(*The Ivory Tower*, 12)

Not only do these words fail to enhance or justify the expectations aroused: they threaten a boredom all too likely to envelop us too. James had proved in *The Awkward Age* that he could manipulate into meaning the interstices of cliché in social small-talk. He had developed the technique: witty in *The Ambassadors,* disturbing in *The Wings of the Dove,* mysterious in *The Golden Bowl.* But in *The Ivory Tower,* the gap between speech and inner mono-logue is pushed too far for credibility. Confronted with Gussy, Rosanna's inner and her spoken words are perhaps equally involved; but their remove from each other is at a late-Jamesian stretch of the imagination, and of verbal energy. If *The Golden Bowl* tempts us to think of *The Tempest,* this is more reminiscent of *Cymbeline,* almost overbalancing into self-parody:

'Take her as an advertisement of all the latest knowledges of how to "treat" every inch of the human surface and where to "get" every scrap of the personal envelope, so far as she *is* enveloped, and she does achieve an effect sublime in itself and thereby absolute in a waver-ing world'—with so much even as that was Miss Gaw aware of helping to fill for her own use the interval before she spoke. 'No,' she said, 'I know nothing of what any of you may suppose yourselves to know.'
(*The Ivory Tower*, p. 49)

To Rosanna as she muses on Dave's proposal, James attributes a judgement all too appropriate to his own achievement in this novel:

It was his truth that had fallen short, not his error; the soundness, as it were, of his claim—so far as his fine intelligence, matching her own, that is, could make it sound—had had nothing to do with its propriety.
(p. 55)

Nor is Rosanna the only James in the cast. In Haughty's words to Gray, the fiction of conversation barely covers an authorial direction as to character which seems to flout the conventions of realism: what is the effect of this process?

'That you're mortally afraid of people is, I confess,' Haughty answered, 'news to me. I seem to remember you, on the contrary, as so remarkably and—what was it we used to call it?—so critico-analytically interested in 'em.'　　　　　　　　　　　　　　　　　　　　　　　　　(p. 183)

The dramatization is stilted, again, when Gray recalls the occasion on which his friend saved his life. The impression is of a technical need for the two to share some bond, rather than a sense of relation itself. Similarly, in the dealings between Rosanna Gaw and Haughty, or Rosanna and Cissy, their dramatic situation is conveyed as it were at one remove. As a development of Catherine Sloper from *Washington Square,* or a descendant of Strether's compatriot in *The Ambassadors,* who 'would be fat, too fat, at thirty; but she would always be the person who, at the present sharp hour, had been disinterestedly tender' (*The Ambassadors,* p. 328), Rosanna is a massive creation. But her 'inexplicable, her almost ridiculous type' (*The Ivory Tower,* p. 9) is qualified, beyond incongruity, to the point of attenuation, by the refinement of her sensibility. Though she is introduced as 'a person essentially unobservant of forms' (p. 2), Rosanna recognizes the minute social signals which betray motive, and she pursues implications with sensitivity and insight. She acknowledges them in the novelist's own terms, and her awareness merges with his metaphorical exuberance in a way reminiscent of the highest stretches of Maggie Verver. Yet what begins so confidently, presupposing more 'experience' on the part of the reader than this novel has cultivated, can lapse into a syntactical complexity and verbal particularity which is obscure rather than inspired. Gussy's gossip forms

a stream by which our friend's consciousness was flooded. 'Clues' these connections might well be called when every touch could now set up a vibration. It hummed away at once like a pressed button—if she had been really and in the least meanly afraid of complications she might now have sat staring at one that would do for oddity, for the oddity of that relation of her own with Cissy's source of anecdote which could so have come and gone and yet thrown no light for her on anything but itself; little enough by what she had tried to make of it at the time, though that might have been.　　　　　　　　　(p. 53)

It is important, and difficult, to respond accurately to such an extract. Its mingling of simple vocabulary, easily understood and unpretentious metaphor, even dead metaphor and cliché, with length, parenthesis, and qualification, all complicating factors, could be dismissed as disjointed. On the other hand we could discover here a remarkable account of the process of thinking, an opening out and definition of implications, caught between character and author. Without the finished work, particularly the tenth book, projected as balancing the first as 'Rosanna's affair' (*Ivory Tower*, Notes, p. 341), it is impossible to determine how far Rosanna is realized, and how far she is used. In the Notes, James enthuses,

It isn't *centrally* a drama of fools or vulgarians; it's only circumferentially and surroundedly so—these being enormously implied and with the effect of their hovering and pressing upon the whole business from without, but seen and felt by us only with that rich indirectness.

(Ibid. 331)

In the novel the tendency is perhaps too much the other way, towards a sense of consciousness suspended in an alien environment: held not by psychologically consistent forces, but a purely intellectual apprehension.

It is in the Notes that we find this epitomized with capital-lettered excitement, and the triumphant rhetoric of alliteration and repetition:

A Joint here, a Joint of the Joint, for perfect flexible working, is Horton's vision of his vision, and Horton's exhibited mental, moral audacity of certainty as to what that may mean for himself. (Ibid. 305)

But this approach could be matched from the novel itself, with the rhetoric of controlled unhappiness replacing that of triumph, yet equally subordinated, in effect if not in intention, to the display rather than the achievement of the process of representation. Rosanna's interview with Haughty is richly set in the history of his rejected proposal: so it is implied. But the richness is lost in an overwhelming refinement of analysis: a process attributed to Rosanna, but having little of the urgency of living or the distaste of dead passion, which we might expect. An intimate encounter is seen rather as a choreographed possibility, and Rosanna's language is that of analysis rather than of musing detachment:

His acceptance of his check she could but call inscrutably splendid— inscrutably perhaps because she couldn't quite feel that it had left nothing between them. Something there was, something there had to be, if only the marvel, so to say, of her present, her permanent, backward vision of the force with which they had touched and separated.

(p. 56)

The multiple negatives are portentous, yet Rosanna seems quite unimpassioned. Her language is both surprisingly fresh and curiously uninvolved:

It stuck to her somehow that they had touched still more than if they had loved, held each other still closer than if they had embraced: to such and so strange a tune had they been briefly intimate. Would any man ever look at her so for passion as Mr. Vint had looked for reason? and should her own eyes ever again so visit a man's depths and gaze about in them unashamed to a tune to match that adventure? (p. 56)

The questions are added to, rather than growing from, the situation. The tableau we see is simpler than the weight of exposition seems to claim:

Literally what they had said was comparatively unimportant—once he had made his errand clear; whereby the rest might all have been but his silent exhibition of his personality, so to name it, his honour, his assumption, his situation, his life, and that failure on her own part to yield an inch which had but the more let him see how straight these things broke upon her.

(p. 56)

Though such sentences as are examined here could probably be matched from James's completed novels, if extracts were quoted out of context, the verbal texture in those works supports individual examples of extravagant, abstract, melodramatic, or highly complex expression. It is that contextual support which is lacking in *The Ivory Tower*. The effect is summed up in an unfortunate example of very late James which sounds almost like a self-parody, when Rosanna asks Gussy,

'But do you really consider that you *know* him so much as that?'—she let Gussy have it straight, even if at the disadvantage that there were now as ever plenty of people to react, to the last hilarity, at the idea that acquaintance enjoyed on either side was needfully imputable to these participations. (p. 59)

It is this sense of the incidental importance of 'acquaintance', mingling occasionally with the relish of appreciation, that creates the 'American' tone of *The Ivory Tower*, which is recognizably close to that of *The American Scene* and the New York sections of *A Small Boy and Others*. A whimsical echo of the autobiography comes in Graham's words to Mrs. Mumby:

'Oh, I *understand* you, which appears to be so much more than you do me!... but am I really committed to everything because I'm committed, in the degree you see me, oh yes, to waffles and maple syrup, followed, and on such a scale, by melons and ice-cream?' (p. 80)

The naïve energy here is almost primitive by comparison with another statement of the same circumstance of character, when Gray, 'clean and in condition', sits by his dying uncle:

That such an hour had its meaning, and that the meaning might be great for him, this of course surged softly in, more and more, from every point of the circle that held him; but with the consciousness making also more at each moment for an uplifting, a fantastic freedom, a sort of sublime simplification, in which nothing seemed to depend on him or to have at any time so depended. (p. 106)

Another factor in the 'American' tone is the vigorous imagery. Picture after picture is added with relish, whether it be melons and ice cream,

nests or bags of other facts, bristling or bulging thus with every intensity of the positive and leaving no room in their interstices for mere appreciation to so much as turn round ... (p. 237)

a 'continuous block' like a skyscraper,

suggestive of dimensional squareness, with mechanical perforations and other aids to use subsequently introduced ... (p. 237)

a passage hovering 'to memory's eye like a votive object in the rich gloom of a chapel', now 'disconnected, attached to its hook once for all, its whole meaning converted with such small delay into working, playing force and multiplied tasteable fruit' (p. 243), or the ivory tower itself. In the Notes, James foresees 'the tight packing *and* the beautifully audible cracking; the most magnificent masterly little vivid economy, with a beauty of its own equal to the beauty of the *donnée* itself, that ever was' (*The Ivory Tower*, Notes, pp. 270–1). The cracking is certainly audible, but the control is less apparent. Indeed, America, like Haughty, seems to live 'in an air of jokes, and yet an air in which bad ones fell flat' (*The Ivory Tower*, p. 155). From bad jokes to bad taste, we find

Gray, in mourning, described by Haughty with gauche sensibility as 'a sort of "happy Hamlet"' (185). To Gray himself, on the same occasion, Haughty offers a jocular solution to the problem for a sensitive man of extravagant wealth, which again smacks of Jacobean grave humour:

'Of course you may dig the biggest hole in the ground that ever was dug—spade work comes high, but you'll have the means—and get down into it and sit at the very bottom. Only your hole will become then the feature of the scene, and we shall crowd a thousand deep all round the edge of it.'   (201–2)

The challenge of America is clear, but not the footing of the challenger. Buitenhuis has pointed out that a 'great reversal . . . took place in this novel. America is no longer the source of moral innocence . . . Its place is taken by Europe, which sends its innocent . . . over to face the corruption of the new world' (*The Grasping Imagination,* p. 260). America is no longer an Eden; but the corruption there lacks form, and James misses the opportunities for foreshortening offered by European civilization. Nor is there a simple reversal: Gray is not European, but an American expatriate, and neither his innocence nor his guilt can be taken for granted. The ambiguities are multiplied, but the formal perspectives which delineate such intangible situations in James's greatest works are not correspondingly sophisticated. The Notes show that James knew what he wanted to convey, but the novel lacks processes adequate for such an ambitious project:

The state of mind and vision and feeling, the state of dazzlement with reserves and reflections, the play of reserves and reflections with dazzlement (which is my convenient word covering here all that I intend and prefigure) is a part of the very essence of my subject—which in fine I perfectly possess.   (*The Ivory Tower,* Notes, p. 304)

Had James finished *The Ivory Tower,* it would undoubtedly have been a great novel; but the complexity of the problems it presents is indicated by his failure to do so. The advance required in technique would have necessitated an uncanny, even an incredible, development of character before this novel could have equalled *The Golden Bowl* in the balance between personal ambitions, understanding, and responsibility in a social context which acts as a counterpart within the novel to the relations between literary form, sympathies, and imaginative involvement of the whole novel process. It is hard to see how James could have overcome the tendency in the existing text for the sense of isolation marking the fine consciousness of the characters, the precondition of their imaginative freedom, to overstrain the process of representation through excessive stress on local effect.

The turn from *The Ivory Tower* to *The Sense of the Past*, an attempt to finish a work begun years before, involves too many considerations either to confirm or refute this view of James's difficulty. *The Sense of the Past* is, however, an easier work than *The Ivory Tower*. James re-uses many successful devices from earlier work, as indeed much of the existing text had been; if the date were not known one would probably place the work in the late 1890s, the period of *The Turn of the Screw*. The triumph of the novel is less in the sense of uncertainty, a crisis of identity located in the perspective of history and between continents, than in the ingenuity with which the transition to the early nineteenth century is plausibly executed. The portrait with the turned back, looking 'off into the dark backward that at once so challenged and so escaped his successor' (*The Sense of the Past*, p. 76), seems simply to be ushering us into the past. Ralph's interview with the Ambassador offers a civilized, diplomatic issue to the dilemma between 'the profound policy—of silence' and the 'pressing need to communicate' without which the tale could scarcely be related to the other 'third party': the reader. In this novel, there is a suspicion of sensationalism about an image successfully played down, domesticated, with Maggie Verver: Ralph

wondered that a knowledge of anything less than murder could be able to constitute in one's soul such a closed back room . . .   (p. 88)

Only in a late-Jamesian abstraction, a distance of language and style, is a sense of the strangeness of the situation communicated, when Ralph tells the Ambassador,

'Our duality is so far from diminished that it's only the greater—by our formulation, each to the other, of the so marked difference in our interest.'   (p. 103)

It is in this encounter of the protagonist's consciousness with his situation, rather than in the mechanics of suspense and the riddle of relationships miscalculated rather than misunderstood, that the strength of the idea lies. Much of the apparatus of the novel is superfluous to this, and the effect is to disperse the reader's interest rather than substantiate it.

J. A. Ward judges that James's main preoccupation in *The Sense of the Past* was with the mechanics of the situation; but he admits that 'if [it] were to have a meaning beyond its fantastic plot, it might have been a reworking of the theme of isolation and self-discovery' (Op. cit. 164). This forms a thematic link between the novel and one of James's most successful short stories: 'The Jolly Corner' (first published *English Review*, Dec. 1908). A similar analogy can be drawn between *The Ivory Tower* and 'A Round of Visits' (*English Review*, April-May 1910). If *The American Scene* and James's *Autobiography*, with their 'restless analyst' minutely observing the forms of a culture and reconstructing from his 'recoveries and reflections' (*Autobiography*, p. 454) 'the personal history . . . of an imagination', form one pole of comparison for our judgement of the last novels, the last *Tales* make the other. The 'historical' works gave James space, he saw,

in a word to draw [the man of imagination] forth from within rather than meet him in the world before me, the more convenient sphere of the objective, and to make him objective, in short . . . to turn nothing less than myself inside out.   (*Autobiography*, 455)

The tales, significantly, demonstrate the opposite procedure, but to the same end. Spencer Brydon's ghostly 'double', the man he might have been, and Alice Staverton could have loved, had he stayed in New York, appears in a dramatic encounter in the old New York house. The questions of what might have been and what has been are more absorbing than the mechanics of a tale which evokes them with superb economy. In 'A Round of Visits', the experience of returning to America is equally effectively concentrated, as the psychological environment for a crisis of conscience over responsibility and guilt in a financial fraud between friends.

Any account of the tales briefer than the works themselves is liable to do them less than justice; but some idea of their 'imaged creative Expression' supports the claim that it is here, rather than in the unfinished novels, that James communicates the 'joy of sovereign *science*'. 'The Jolly Corner' has been widely apprecia-

ted, but 'A Round of Visits' less so: Vaid merely mentions it to
introduce the other tale. 'A Round of Visits', however, comes
nearer our purpose, in combining the sense of geographical
detachment and cultural alienation which pervade *The American
Scene* and *The Ivory Tower* with the moral involvement hinted both
there and in the *Autobiography*, besides something of the whimsical curiosity of *The Sense of the Past*. The thematic links are
strong, the process markedly different, and what has been
described in terms of content can now be seen as a problem of
appropriate form.

The tale opens in New York on Tuesday. Wednesday, Wednesday evening, and Thursday, are noted, without our knowing
why. Details of setting and sensation are given with extraordinary
precision, and baldly juxtaposed without any explaining. Their
force is symbolic, and rather than 'solidity of specification', they
create a sense of heightened, alien awareness, set in a strange
environment, which is nevertheless in some unexplained way
bound up with the protagonist's situation. His illness merges
with New York, the weather, and his hotel, to generate anxiety,
which pervades his being and the surrounding world, to the
very days of the week:

> He had woken up on Thursday morning, so far as he had slept at all,
> with the sense, together, of a blinding New York blizzard and of a
> deep inward ache. The great white savage storm would have kept him
> at the best within doors, but his stricken state was by itself quite
> reason enough.   (*Tales*, 12, p. 427)

The obscure 'hurt' is fleetingly isolated, 'little by little detach-
ing and projecting itself, settling there face to face with him' (p.
427). This image is left in suspension until the encounter with
Newton Winch at the end of the tale recalls both this and its more
complex development: 'he might have been in charge of some
horrid alien thing, some violent, scared, unhappy creature . . .'
Phil Bloodgood's photograph marks a further connection:

> The image seemed to sit there, at an immemorial window, like some
> long effective and only at last exposed 'decoy' of fate.   (p. 429)

Vaid suggests that both Winch and Bloodgood are alter egos of
Mark Monteith, the protagonist. It is the use of multiple parallels,
and the omission of explicit connections which suggests such

possibilities. Narrative economy becomes the condition for imaginative potential, as the reader is required both to reconstruct the situation and project its implications.

Just as the image, the photograph and the dramatic encounter offer different but related views of character in ways which also contribute to the 'solidity of specification' of the tale, so the setting functions at a symbolic as well as a naturalistic level. Mark's hotel is a microcosm of the New York world, and a type of the city. The physical setting for a psychic loneliness, more monstrous than Kate and Densher's London or Venice, more anomalously public than Fawns for Maggie, colder and more alien than Graham Fielder's Newport, it looks forward to T. S. Eliot's Sweeney poems, and Virginia Woolf's lighthouse:

> The great gaudy hotèl . . . made all about him, beside, behind, below, above, in blocks and tiers and superpositions, a sufficient defensive hugeness; so that, between the massive labyrinth and the New York weather, life in a lighthouse during a gale would scarce have kept him more apart.   (p. 428)

The fellow guests make this great block a jungle, and Mark himself is not exempt from the primitive wariness of man in the city:

> he couldn't resign himself to bed and broth and dimness, but only circled and prowled the more within his cage.   (p. 428)

Fusing the various aspects of situation, setting and character through Mark's feverish imagination, James avoids delineating the elements of the tale too precisely. Each contributes to the whole effect and in turn absorbs the whole into itself: a process parallel to that which heightens Mark's 'case' without detracting from its typicality, and which is conveyed in social terms through Mark himself:

> There was nothing like a crowd, this unfortunate knew, for making one feel lonely . . .   (p. 434)

The sequence of encounters makes a similar point in dramatic terms, again with the economy of symbolic force, but none of the stiffness of allegory. James finds room to characterize the women who exploit Mark's sympathy as a listener. Mrs. Folliot, in particular, has the striking particularity of a grotesque, unnervingly at home in her environment. She is one of many

> vociferous, bright-eyed, and feathered creatures, of every variety of size and hue . . . half smothered between undergrowths of velvet and tapestry and ramifications of marble and bronze.   (p. 431)

The impressions are caught as they strike Monteith: wailing sounds alternating with bird-like, fluttering movements, while the hint of predatory proclivities comes through the imagery; meanwhile Mark's reflections sound intermittently, weaving into the texture of meaning as they do into the music of the sentence:

> She bewailed her wretched money to excess—she who, he was sure, had quantities more; she pawed and tossed her bare bone, with her little extraordinarily gemmed and manicured hands, till it acted on his nerves; she rang all the changes on the story, the dire fatality, of her having wavered and muddled, thought of this and but done that, of her stupid failure to have pounced, when she had first meant to, in season.   (p. 433)

Another sentence demonstrates the versatility of James's style by exemplifying a very different 'process of representation'. A sense of contingent immediacy despite the feeling of isolation is achieved through the juxtaposition of disparate elements of reflection and description, with an apt extended metaphor: instead of accretion on several levels at once, there is a sequence:

> That exquisite last flush of her fadedness could only remain with him; yet while he presently stopped at a street-corner in a district redeemed from desolation but by a passage just then of a choked trolley-car that howled, as he paused for it, beneath the weight of its human accretions, he seemed to know the inward 'sinking' that has been determined in a hungry man by some extravagant sight of the preparation of somebody else's dinner.   (p. 442)

Age, suffering, dead weight, hunger and the unsatisfied craving for comfort pervade the scene, but centre in the solitary being. The indirection of 'a district redeemed from desolation' offers an appropriate vocabulary for this modern hell, without limiting the suggestive force of the passage through explicit analogy.

The parable continues when Mark visits Newton Winch. Religious and psychological terminology offer alternative accounts of an experience more fundamental than any specific dogma:

Providence had, on some obscure system, chosen this very ridiculous hour to save him from cultivation of the sin of selfishness, the obsession of egotism, and was breaking him to its will by constantly directing his attention to the claims of others.   (p. 443)

The form and the fact are inseparable in 'the process and the effect of representation'; Newton Winch is linked with Mark Monteith through a parallel and an inversion of his 'case': he has practised fraud, like Phil Bloodgood, and Mark has shown him what it is to feel responsible for suffering. Newton, like Mark, has had 'flu: an illness which borders on the psychic in this tale. His is the third of Mark's visits, and an extension of the social round. The effectiveness of this patterning is demonstrated in the description of Newton's hands, so different from Mrs. Folliot's; he is refined by age, unlike Mrs. Ash:

There was a charm in his wide 'drawn', convalescent smile, in the way his fingers—had he anything like fine fingers of old—played, and just fidgeted, over the prompt and perhaps a trifle incoherent offer of cigars, cordials, ash-trays, over the question of his visitor's hat, stick, fur coat, general best accommodation and ease . . .   (pp. 444–5)

The sense of technical control approaches reckless gaiety towards the end in a series of puns which foretell the conclusion. It is 'the joy of sovereign *science*' which fuses the sense of an ending with the relish of the telling:

'I'd go like a shot. . . . And it's probably what—when we've turned round—I shall do' . . .   (p. 451)

'You save my life', Newton renewedly grinned . . .   (p. 453)

Winch knew by this time quite easily enough that he was hanging fire; which meant that they were suddenly facing each other across the wide space with a new consciousness.   (p. 454)

F. O. Matthiessen writes that the ending of 'A Round of Visits' 'breaks the situation to pieces rather than resolves it' (*The Major Phase,* p. 117), but allows that James achieved the opposite of 'the ethical tenuosities and withdrawals of *The Special Type.* He had penetrated into a world so corrupted by money that the only escape seemed to be by violence.' Though money is the currency of the tale, however, it is not the main interest. What we see in a series of cases reflecting on Mark Monteith's is a variation on the patterns of selfishness and irresponsibility to which money is incidental. When Winch shoots himself, there is no question as to his financial intrigues. Nor is there any doubt that Mark was in some way responsible for his death. The violent end does not dispose of the question whether Mark should have tried to prevent it, however, or whether his complicity was the only amends he could make for an earlier abnegation of responsibility which permitted his friend to become involved in fraud.

'A Round of Visits' raises many of the issues of *The Ivory Tower*, with an economic power lacking in the longer work. This drives through the tale towards the question of complicity consummated rather than disintegrating at the end. What lies beyond the short story, however, is the sense of a process behind the very formulation of the question: it is presented, to be confronted or evaded, but there is no doubt as to its nature. Nor is the process of representation itself either disturbed or disturbing: the power of the tale depends upon a strict sense of form. For this reason, the achievement of the tale, though greater than that of the unfinished works, cadnot be compared with that of the previous novels, where the scope of the subject is not restricted but grows with the challenge of form.

VII

Conclusion

APPROACHING JAMES with two questions—how do we read him, and why—we find him engaged with the same issues: at first stimulating, educating, but finally declining to dictate our response. Starting with one prerequisite for the novel—'that it be interesting'—James leads us through, round, and back, to rediscover as our reward what we had taken to be our method of proceeding. James's admiration and delight in 'the joy of sovereign *science*', which he found in the Shakespeare of *The Tempest*, was not proposed, but can be seen by us as a hint of his own 'irrepressible ideal'. 'Interest' *becomes* 'science', through the knot intrinsicate which binds together 'the process and the effect of representation'. Because they are mediated through the text, it is through this link too that author, reader, and protagonist are connected: perception involving expression, which in turn invites understanding. The novel form, in its elasticity, offers the greatest possible free play for these links. Yet, paradoxically, 'the high price of the novel form' also inverts this effect: it is most true to its character 'in proportion as it strains, or tends to burst, with a latent extravagance, its mould'. Through an ironical economy which James's novels discover, explore and finally (though perhaps despairingly) exploit, constriction comes precisely from the definition achieved by 'working' the apparently boundless potential of the novel form.

The culminating work of James's early career, *The Portrait of a Lady*, and the 'dramatic' novels, *What Maisie Knew* and *The Awkward Age*, followed in the transition to the major phase by *The Sacred Fount*, show the development of a novel 'language' which grows from a technique of expression towards a means of establishing boundaries for the form. Silence is one element of that language: at first a narrative resource, though also a symbol of moral isolation, it becomes a precise means of 'not saying' things; yet together with this linguistic use of silence as a kind of lie grows another, 'inner silence' of individual integrity. Where the unspeakable and the unsayable are not presumed to match, James's manipulation of the novel language renders the fluidity of the moral and social codes with paradoxical decorum. Further than this, it locates the 'interest' of the case, whether on the level of character, action or theme, through and in the process of representation itself: for to this process, silence is, paradoxically, indispensable, though alien.

In the three late novels, this crux is increasingly exactly conceived in terms of the novel form. James uses more and more codes of expression, from the social to the dramatic, pictorial to financial, appealing to a great range of patterned responses in the reader, only to show through sudden shifts of style the limitations of each mode, each preconceived reaction. The conventions are not worthless: Strether must 'place' his Parisian experience correctly before he can go beyond it; and so must Milly Theale in her world, and Maggie Verver, who knows 'that if she could only get the facts of appearance straight . . . the reasons behind them . . . wouldn't perhaps be able to help showing' (II, 54). The damage caused by inadequate categorization of experience is clear in the miscarrying of the various plots of *The Wings of the Dove*, and of the good intentions of all the characters in the first volume of *The Golden Bowl*. Through his manipulative technique, however, James shows that it is the process of 'naming' itself, the attempt to render the values of silence explicit, that is at fault.

In *The Wings of the Dove*, James refines the analogy between his own process of representation and the operations of a society where 'the worker in one connexion was the worked in another'. A fine consciousness is 'formed at once for being and for seeing', yet the two qualities seem unreconcilable, since the active and passive roles are opposed in any formal process, whether social or literary. In *The Wings of the Dove* this dilemma is avoided by the setting of the process in time. Milly, the only character perfectly capable of 'seeing', since she recognizes what she cannot see, is removed from 'being' in time, just as she has been emotionally and morally isolated: a process caught mimetically in the structure of the novel. Only after death does Milly actively influence those who have exploited her: and then only by bequeathing an opportunity for them to decide their own destiny. The novel changes during the 'double-time' period in Venice from an onward-moving story where one 'waited impatiently' to an elegiac appreciation of the lost opportunity which Milly might have presented.

The Golden Bowl turns upon the very problem which *The Wings of the Dove*, through the structural elision of Milly at the moment of 'being and seeing', avoids. Maggie must live through the whole process of being and seeing; and through her confrontation with a situation in which neither passivity nor activity can be guiltless, James's novel itself comes to terms with the problem of responsibility for 'working' others, even through one's own consciousness. This is the morality of the creative imagination, exercised by the individual in the process of perception, but also common to both author and reader in 'the process and the effect of representation' which is the essence of the novel form.

James's achievement in *The Golden Bowl* goes beyond the command of style necessary to remove preconceptions which could obscure perception and representation; though, as Jefferson says, this novel is linked with its predecessors in 'the questions which it succeeds in making irrelevant'. The 'Princess' volume proceeds to formulate and confront the questions which are relevant. Despite James's pertinacity, however, the problem of what William James called 'absolute insulation' between the perceiver and what is perceived, the teller and the listener, the self and the other, remains. Though Maggie can see the truth from her own point of view, and can imagine it from those of her husband and his mistress, she knows that her father's mind is beyond her, and, finally, so are all minds but her own. James's full realization of all the main characters, and the radical ambiguity which remains in our assessment of them, makes this point for the reader as for Maggie. When she ventures to the extremes of silence and hyperbolic exaggeration, and even to downright lying in support of her truth, we suspend narrow condemnation in the interests of a larger propriety. Though expression may violate the unsayable, much may be done through indirection. The novel is written. But it ends in silence, though one in which 'whatever next took place . . . was foredoomed to remarkable salience' (*The Golden Bowl*, II, 375).

The unfinished novels testify to James's continuing interest in the problem of form so daringly constituted, and thus confronted, in *The Golden Bowl*. *The Ivory Tower* approaches the question of manipulation through extreme sensitivity to character and situation, while *The Sense of the Past* turns on the element of time in the exploration of identity. Both works have a felicity which it is tempting to link with James's own experience, both as a young boy introduced to Europe and as an elderly man exposed to his native land after a long absence. The link appears in the echo of details from James's autobiographical works and *The American Scene*. Despite this intimacy, however, the last works are not on a level with those of the major phase, for neither achieves the precise balance of 'the process and the effect of representation' which in James's greatest novel reveals an analogy between the problems of form and theme, thus drawing together the 'interest' of author and reader with that of the characters within the novel. By using character as the pivot of both moral and ontological enquiry in *The Golden Bowl*, James sustains the question of interest as a question, without forfeiting the sense of life, for he presses an analogy between the vital processes and those of the novel form, in a work which both demonstrates and celebrates 'the joy of sovereign *science*'. Yet to read the unfinished novels, or the works of James's successors, suggests that the 'high price' of *The Golden Bowl* was a definition of the novel form constricting in proportion to its achievement.

Select Bibliography

WORKS BY HENRY JAMES

Autobiography, ed. with introduction by F. W. Dupee. Includes *A Small Boy and Others, Notes of a Son and Brother, The Middle Years*, first published 1913, 1914, 1917. London: W. H. Allen, 1956.

Hawthorne. English Men of Letters Series. New York: Harper, 1880.

Letters: Volume I 1843–1875, ed. Leon Edel. London: Macmillan, 1974.

Selected Literary Criticism, ed. Morris Shapira. London: Heinemann, 1963; rpt. Penguin, 1968.

The Ambassadors. London: Methuen, 1903.

The American Scene. 1907; rpt. New York: Horizon Press, 1967.

The Art of the Novel: Critical Prefaces, with introduction by R. P. Blackmur. 1934; rpt. New York: Scribner, 1962.

The Awkward Age. London: William Heinemann, 1899.

The Complete Tales of Henry James, ed. Leon Edel. London: Hart-Davis, 1964. 12 vols.

The Golden Bowl. New York: Scribner's; London: Methuen, 1904. 2 vols.

The Ivory Tower, London: Collins, 1917.

The Letters of Henry James, ed. Percy Lubbock. New York: Charles Scribner's Sons, 1920. 2 vols.

The Notebooks of Henry James, ed. F. O. Matthiessen and Kenneth B. Murdock. New York: Oxford University Press, 1961.

The Novels and Tales of Henry James, 'New York Edition'. New York: Charles Scribner's Sons, 1907–9. Rpt. 1962–5. 26 vols.

The Portrait of a Lady. London: Macmillan, 1881. 3 vols.

The Sacred Fount. 1901; rpt. with introduction by Leon Edel. London: Hart-Davis, 1959.

The Sense of the Past. London: Collins, 1917.

The Wings of the Dove. Westminster: Archibald Constable & Co., 1902.

Two Lectures. 'The Question of Our Speech' and 'The Lesson of Balzac'. Boston and New York: Houghton Mifflin, 1905.

Washington Square. London, 1881. 2 vols.

What Maisie Knew. London: William Heinemann, 1897.

BIBLIOGRAPHIES OF JAMES

BEEBE, MAURICE T., and STAFFORD, WILLIAM T., 'Criticism of Henry James: A Selected Checklist', *Modern Fiction Studies* 12, i (1966), pp. 117–77.

EDEL, LEON, and LAURENCE, DAN H., *A Bibliography of Henry James*, 2nd rev. ed. London: Hart-Davis, 1961.

RICKS, BEATRICE, comp., *Henry James: A Bibliography of Secondary Works*. New Jersey: Scarecrow Press, 1975.

OTHER WORKS ON JAMES AND ON THE NOVEL

ANDERSON, QUENTIN, *The American Henry James*. London: John Calder, 1958.

APPIGNANESI, LISA, *Femininity and the Creative Imagination: A Study of Henry James, Robert Musil and Marcel Proust*. London: Vision Press, 1973.

ARNHEIM, RUDOLPH, *Art and Visual Perception: A Psychology of the Creative Eye*. Los Angeles: University of California Press, 1971.

AUCHINCLOSS, LOUIS, *Reading Henry James*. Minneapolis University Press, 1975.

BARTHES, ROLAND, 'Style and its Image', *Literary Style: A Symposium*, ed. Seymour Chatman, Oxford University Press, 1971, pp. 3–16.

BARZUN, JACQUES, 'James the Melodramatist', *Kenyon Review* 5 (1943), pp. 508–21.

BAYLEY, JOHN, *The Characters of Love: A Study of the Literature of Personality*. London: Constable, 1968.

—— *The Uses of Division: Unity and Disharmony in Literature*. London: Chatto and Windus, 1976.

BEACH, JOSEPH WARREN, *The Method of Henry James*, revised ed. Philadelphia: Albert Sailer, 1954.

BEEBE, MAURICE, *Ivory Towers and Sacred Founts: The Artist as Hero in Fiction from Goethe to Joyce*. New York University Press, 1964.

BELL, MILLICENT, 'Style as Subject: *Washington Square*'. *Sewanee Review* 83 (Winter 1975), pp. 19–38.

BERSANI, LEO, 'The Jamesian Lie', *Partisan Review* 36 (1969), pp. 53–79.

BEWLEY, MARIUS, *The Complex Fate*. London, 1952.

BOOTH, WAYNE C., *The Rhetoric of Fiction*. Chicago University Press, 1962; rpt. 1969.

BOWDEN, ERNEST T., *The Themes of Henry James: A System of Observation through the Visual Arts*. New Haven: Yale University Press, 1956.

BRIDGMAN, RICHARD, *The Colloquial Style in America*. New York: Oxford University Press, 1966.

BUITENHUIS, PETER, *The Grasping Imagination: The American Writings of Henry James*. Toronto University Press, 1970.

—— (ed.), *James: The Portrait of a Lady: A Collection of Critical Essays*. Twentieth Century Interpretations. New Jersey: Prentice Hall, 1968.

CARGILL, OSCAR, *The Novels of Henry James*. 1961, Macmillan; rpt. New York: Hafner, 1971.

CHAMBERLAIN, VIVIEN, 'Techniques and Effects of Realism in the Late Novels of Henry James'. Unpublished thesis. Oxford, 1975. D. Phil. c. 1735.

CHATMAN, SEYMOUR BENJAMIN, *The Later Style of Henry James*. Oxford: Blackwell, 1972.

CONRAD, JOSEPH, 'Henry James: An Appreciation'. *North American Review* clxxx (Jan. 1905), pp. 102–8; rpt. in *The Question of Henry James*, ed. F. W. Dupee, 1945, pp. 44–7.

—— *Nostromo*. London: J. M. Dent, 1904.

—— *Youth, Heart of Darkness, The End of the Tether*. 1902; collected ed. 1946; rpt. London: J. M. Dent, 1967.

CREWS, FREDERICK C., *The Tragedy of Manners: Moral Drama in the Later Novels of Henry James*. New Haven: Yale University Press, 1957.

CULLER, JONATHAN, *Structuralist Poetics: Structuralism. Linguistics, and the Study of Literature*. London: Routledge & Kegan Paul, 1975.

DAVIDSON, A. E., 'James's Dramatic Method in *The Awkward Age*'. *Nineteenth Century Fiction* 29 (1974), pp. 320–35.

DUPEE, F. W., *Henry James*. American Men of Letters. New York: William Sloane Associates, 1951.

—— (ed.), *The Question of Henry James: A Collection of Critical Essays*. New York: Holt & Co., 1945.

EDEL, LEON, *A Biography of Henry James*. Philadelphia: Lippincott, 1953–72. 5 vols.

—— (ed.), *Henry James: A Collection of Critical Essays*. Englewood Cliffs, N. J.: Prentice. 1963.

ELIOT, T. S., 'On Henry James', 1918; rpt. in *The Question of Henry James*, ed. F. W. Dupee, 1945, pp. 108–19.

FORSTER, E. M., *Aspects of the Novel*. 1927; rpt. London, 1970.

GALE, ROBERT L., *The Caught Image: Figurative Language in the Fiction of Henry James*. Chapel Hill: University of North Carolina Press, 1964.

GARD, ROGER (comp.), *Henry James: The Critical Heritage*. London: Routledge & Kegan Paul, 1968.

GARDNER, HOWARD, *The Quest for Mind: Piaget, Levi-Strauss, and the Structuralist Movement*. New York: Knopf, 1973.

GARGANO, JAMES W., '*What Maisie Knew*: The Evolution of a Moral Sense', in *Henry James, Modern Judgements*, ed. T. Tanner. London, 1968. pp. 222–35.

GEISMAR, MAXWELL, *Henry James and his Cult*. London: Chatto and Windus, 1964.

GIFFORD, HENRY, 'Henry James: The Drama of Discrimination'. *The Modern Age,* ed. Boris Ford. Pelican Guide to English Literature, vol. 7. London: Penguin, 1961, rev. 1964.

GIRLING, H. K., 'The Function of Slang in the Dramatic Poetry of *The Golden Bowl*', in *Henry James's Major Novels,* ed. L. Powers, pp. 361–76.

—— ' "Wonder" and "Beauty" in *The Awkward Age*'. *Essays in Criticism,* VIII (Oct. 1958), pp. 370–80.

GOODE, JOHN (ed.), *The Air of Reality: New Essays on Henry James.* London: Methuen, 1972

GRAHAM, KENNETH, *Henry James: The Drama of Fulfilment: An Approach to the Novels.* Oxford: Clarendon Press, 1975.

GREENE, MILDRED S., '*Les Liaisons Dangereuses* and *The Golden Bowl*: Maggie's "Loving Reason" '. *Modern Fiction Studies* 19 (1973–4), pp. 531–40.

GROVER, PHILIP, *Henry James and the French Novel: A Study in Inspiration.* London: Paul Elek, 1973.

HALL, WILLIAM F., 'Caricature in Dickens and James'. *University of Toronto Quarterly* XXXIX (April 1970), pp. 242–57.

HARDY, BARBARA, *The Appropriate Form: An Essay on the Novel.* University of London, 1964.

HARTSOCK, MILDRED E., 'Time for Comedy: The Late Novels of Henry James', *English Studies* 56:2 (April 1975), pp. 114–28.

—— 'Unintentional Fallacy Critics and *The Golden Bowl*'. *Modern Language Quarterly* 35 (1974), pp. 272–88.

HEWITT, DOUGLAS, *The Approach to Fiction: Good and Bad Readings of Novels.* Longman, 1972.

HOCKS, RICHARD A., *Henry James and Pragmatistic Thought: A Study of the Relationship between the Philosophy of William James and the Literary Art of Henry James.* Chapel Hill: University of North Carolina Press, 1974.

HOLLAND, LAURENCE B., *The Expense of Vision: Essays on the Craft of Henry James.* Princeton University Press, 1964.

ISLE, WALTER, *Experiments in Form: Henry James's Novels, 1896–1901.* Harvard University Press, 1968.

JAMES, WILLIAM, *Pragmatism: A New Name for Some Old Ways of Thinking.* New York, 1909.

—— *The Principles of Psychology.* London: Macmillan, 1890.

JEFFERSON, D. W., *Henry James and the Modern Reader.* London: Oliver & Boyd, 1964.

JONES, GRANVILLE H., *Henry James's Psychology of Experience.* The Hague: Mouton, 1975.

KEATS, JOHN, *Letters of John Keats,* ed. Gittings. Oxford University Press, 1970.

KERMODE, FRANK, *The Sense of an Ending: Studies in the Theory of Fiction.* Oxford University Press, 1966; rpt. 1973.

KNIGHTS, L. C., 'Henry James and Human Liberty'. *Sewanee Review* 83 (Winter 1975), pp. 1–18.

KOCH, STEPHEN, 'Transcendence in *The Wings of the Dove*'. *Modern Fiction Studies* 12 i (Spring 1966), pp. 93–102.

KROOK, DOROTHEA, *The Ordeal of Consciousness in Henry James.* Cambridge University Press, 1962.

LEAVIS, F. R., *The Great Tradition: George Eliot, Henry James, Joseph Conrad,* new ed. London: Chatto & Windus, 1960.

—— '*What Maisie Knew*: A Disagreement by F. R. Leavis', in Bewley, *The Complex Fate,* pp. 114–32.

LEE, VERNON, *The Handling of Words and Other Studies in Literary Psychology.* London: Bodley Head, 1923.

LEYBURN, ELLEN DOUGLAS, *Strange Alloy: The Relation of Comedy to Tragedy in the Fiction of Henry James.* Chapel Hill: University of North Carolina Press, 1968.

LODGE, DAVID, 'Strether by the River', in *Language of Fiction.* London: Routledge & Kegan Paul, 1966, pp. 189–213.

LUKACS, GEORG, *The Theory of the Novel: A Historico-Philosophical Essay on the Forms of Great Epic Literature.* Berlin, 1920; trans. Anna Bostock, London: Merlin Press, 1971.

MACKENZIE, MANFRED, *Communities of Honor and Love in Henry James.* Harvard University Press, 1976.

MARKS, ROBERT, *James's Later Novels: An Interpretation.* New York: William-Frederick Press, 1960.

MATTHIESSEN, F. O., *Henry James: The Major Phase.* London: Oxford University Press, 1944; rpt. with appendix, 1963.

MILTON, JOHN, *Complete Poetry and Selected Prose,* ed. E. H. Visiak. London: Nonesuch Library, 1938; fifth impression, 1969.

MITCHELL, JULIET, '*What Maisie Knew*: Portrait of the Artist as a Young Girl', in *The Air of Reality,* ed. John Goode, London: Methuen, 1972, pp. 169–89.

MOONEY, STEPHEN L., 'James, Keats, and the Religion of Consciousness'. *Modern Language Quarterly* XXII (1961), pp. 399–401.

NOWELL-SMITH, SIMON, *The Legend of the Master.* London: Constable, 1947.

OATES, JOYCE CAROL, *New Heaven, New Earth: the Visionary Experience in Literature.* London: Victor Gollancz, 1976.

O'NEILL, JOHN P., *Workable Design: Action and Situation in the Fiction of Henry James*. National University Publications, Kennikut Press, 1973.

PEARSON, GABRIEL, 'The Novel to End All Novels: *The Golden Bowl*', in *The Air of Reality*, ed. John Goode, London: Methuen, 1972, pp. 301–61.

POIRIER, RICHARD, *A World Elsewhere: The Place of Style in American Literature*. New York: Oxford University Press, 1966.

—— *The Comic Sense of Henry James: A Study of the Early Novels*. London: Chatto & Windus, 1960.

POOLE, ADRIAN, 'Transactions Across the Abyss'. *Times Literary Supplement* No. 3, 891 (8 Oct. 1976), p. 1272.

POWERS, LYALL H., *Henry James's Major Novels: Essays in Criticism*. East Lansing: Michigan State University Press, 1973.

RAHV, PHILIP, *Image and Idea: Twenty Essays on Literary Themes*. New Directions Book; rev. enlarged ed., 1957.

RALEIGH, JOHN HENRY, 'Henry James: The Poetics of Empiricism'. *P.M.L.A.* LXVI (Mar. 1951), pp. 107–23.

RICHARDS, BERNARD, 'Henry James's Use of the Visual Arts'. Unpublished thesis, Oxford. B. Litt. 1965. Ms. B. Litt. d. 1089.

RICHMOND, P. G., *An Introduction to Piaget*. London: Routledge & Kegan Paul, 1970.

ROBEY, DAVID (ed.), *Structuralism: An Introduction*. Wolfson College Lectures, 1972. Oxford: Clarendon Press, 1973.

ROSE, ALAN, 'The Spatial Form of *The Golden Bowl*'. *Modern Fiction Studies* XII i (Spring 1966), pp. 103–16.

ROWE, JOHN CARLOS, *Henry Adams and Henry James: The Emergence of a Modern Consciousness*. Cornell University Press, 1976.

SAMUELS, CHARLES THOMAS, *The Ambiguity of Henry James*. Urbana: University of Illinois Press, 1971.

SAUSSURE, FERDINAND DE *Course in General Linguistics,* trans. Wade Buskin. London: Peter Owen, 1964.

SCHNEIDER, DANIEL J., *Symbolism: The Manichean Vision: A Study in the Art of James, Conrad, Woolf, and Stevens*. Lincoln: University of Nebraska Press, 1975.

SEARS, SALLIE, *The Negative Imagination: Form and Perspective in the Novels of Henry James*. Ithaca: Cornell University Press, 1968.

SEGAL, ORA, *The Lucid Reflector: The Observer in Henry James' Fiction*. New Haven: Yale University Press, 1969.

SHARP, SISTER M. CORONA, *The Confidante in Henry James: Evolution and Moral Value of a Fictive Character*. South Bend: University of Notre Dame Press, 1963.

SHORT, R. W., 'Henry James's World of Images', *P.M.L.A.* LXVIII (1953), pp. 943–60

SPENDER, STEPHEN, *The Destructive Element*. London: Jonathan Cape, 1938.

STANG, RICHARD, *The Theory of the Novel in England 1850–1870*. London: Routledge & Kegan Paul, 1959.

STEWART, J. I. M., 'James', in *Eight Modern Writers*. The Oxford History of English Literature, vol. XII. Oxford: Clarendon Press, 1963, pp. 71–122.

SWINDEN, PATRICK, 'Registration: Henry James', in *Unofficial Selves: Character in the Novel from Dickens to the Present Day*. London: Macmillan, 1973, pp. 100–20.

TANNER, TONY (ed.), *Henry James, Modern Judgements*. London: Macmillan, 1968.

THACKERAY, WILLIAM, *Vanity Fair*. 1848; Penguin, 1968.

THOMAS, WILLIAM B., 'The Author's Voice in *The Ambassadors*', *Journal of Narrative Technique* I ii (1971), pp. 108–21.

THOREAU, HENRY DAVID, *Walden*. Boston: 1854; Houghton Mifflin, 1899.

TILFORD JR., JOHN E., 'James the Old Intruder', *Modern Fiction Studies* IV (Summer 1958), pp. 157–64.

TODOROV, TZVETAN, 'La Lecture comme construction', *Poétique: Revue de Théorie et d'Analyse Littéraires* 24 (1975), pp. 417–25.

—— 'The Structural Analysis of Literature: Henry James', *Structuralism: An Introduction*, Oxford, 1973, pp. 73–101.

VAID, KRISHNA BALDEV, *Technique in the Tales of Henry James*. Harvard University Press, 1964.

VAN GHENT, DOROTHY, *The English Novel: Form and Function*. New York: Holt, Rinehart & Winston, 1953.

VEEDER, WILLIAM, *Henry James: The Lessons of the Master. Popular Fiction and Personal Style in the Nineteenth Century*. University of Chicago Press, 1975.

VITOUX, PIERRE, 'Le Récit dans *The Ambassadors*'. *Poétique* 24 (1975) pp. 460–79.

WARD, J. A., *The Imagination of Disaster: Evil in the Fiction of Henry James*. Lincoln: University of Nebraska Press, 1961.

—— *The Search for Form: Studies in the Structure of James's Fiction*. Chapel Hill: University of North Carolina Press, 1967.

WARREN, AUSTIN, 'Myth and Dialectic in the Later Novels'. *Kenyon Review* 5 (1943), pp. 551–68.

—— 'The New England Conscience: Henry James and Ambassador Strether', in *Henry James's Major Novels*, ed. Powers, pp. 346–57.

WATT, IAN, 'The First Paragraph of *The Ambassadors:* An Explication'. *Essays in Criticism* X (1960), pp. 250–74.

WELLS, H. G., 'Of Art, Of Literature, Of Mr. Henry James', in *Boon*, London, 1915, pp. 102–10; rpt. in *The Modern Tradition*, ed. Richard Ellmann and Charles Feidelson Jr. New York: Oxford University Press, 1965, pp. 317–28.

WILDE, OSCAR, *The Picture of Dorian Gray*. 1891; rpt. with introduction by Isobel Murray, Oxford University Press, 1974.

WILSON, EDMUND, *The Triple Thinkers*. London: John Lehmann, 1952.

WINNER, VIOLA HOPKINS, *Henry James and the Visual Arts*. Charlottesville: University Press of Virginia, 1970.

WINTERS, YVOR, 'Maule's Curse: Seven Studies in the History of American Obscurantism', in *In Defence of Reason*. London: Routledge & Kegan Paul, 1960, pp. 151–357.

WOOLF, VIRGINIA, 'A Sketch of the Past'. *Moments of Being: Unpublished Autobiographical Writings*, ed. Jeanne Schulkind. Sussex University Press, 1976.

YEAZELL, RUTH BERNARD, *Language and Knowledge in the late Novels of Henry James*. Chicago University Press, 1976.